# Anna Maria Island
# and more:
## the Best of Two Worlds

To Julie and Don Lind,
Two of our
"extra special" friends.

Phil de Montmollin
December 2013

ALSO BY PHIL DE MONTMOLLIN

*Recipes from the Florida Keys*

*How to Gain Thirty Pounds in Six Years:* A Restaurant Guide
and Cookbook from the Mountains of North Carolina

# Anna Maria Island and more:
## the Best of Two Worlds

Phil de Montmollin

College State of Mind
Publisher

FIRST U.S. EDITION 2013
ISBN-13: 978-1492846383
ISNB-10:1492846384

Library of Congress Cataloging-in-Publication is available
Published in the United States by College State of Mind, LLC

10 9 8 7 6 5 4 3 2 1
PRINTED IN THE UNITED STATES

# Contents

# Introduction

# God Has Saved the Best (Two) for Last

As a retired newspaperman and husband of an Episcopal priest, my wife and I have lived in some very diverse parts of our great country: Miami, Florida; Macon, Georgia; Lexington, Kentucky; Ft. Wayne, Indiana; the Florida Keys; New Haven, Connecticut; Rutherfordton, North Carolina and now Anna Maria Island, Florida. And we have traveled extensively, both throughout our own country and across the seas.

There is no place where we've lived, and few places that we've visited, that we have not enjoyed. There are good things to be found in almost every place in our world. We still have dear friends in every town and city where we have lived.

However it would appear that our moving has ended and that God has saved the best (two) for last.

Three years ago my wife, Dee, accepted a call to become the rector of *The Episcopal Church of the Annunciation* at Holmes Beach on Anna Maria Island, Florida. For the seven years prior to moving to Anna Maria Island, Dee had been rector of *St. Francis Episcopal Church* in Rutherfordton, NC. When we moved to Anna Maria Island, we kept our home in North Carolina and visit it as frequently as we can. One day, when or if my wife retires, we will probably spend half of the year there and half of the year on Anna Maria Island.

Either of these two places, Anna Maria Island or Western North Carolina, would be wonderful "last stops," but to have them both available to us is a true blessing.

**Thomas Traherne**, a seventeenth century English poet, mystic and a priest of The Church of England, was one of the most radiantly and infectiously happy mortals this world has ever known.

Historical records of his life indicate that he never had the opportunity to visit either Anna Maria Island or the North Carolina Mountains, but after reading the following passages from his *Centuries of Meditation* I wonder about that.

*When I came into the country and saw that I had all time in my own hands, having devoted it wholly to the study of Felicity, I knew not where to begin or end; nor what objects to choose, upon which most profitably I might fix my contemplation. I saw myself like some traveler, that has destined his life to journeys, and was resolved to spend his days in visiting strange places: who might wander in vain, unless his undertakings were guided by some certain rule; and that innumerable millions of objects were presented before me, unto any of which I might take my journey. Fain would I have visited them all, but that was impossible. What then should I do?*

*For which cause I made it my prayer to God Almighty that He, whose eyes are open upon all things, would guide me to the fairest and divinest.*

Traherne also wrote:

*Your enjoyment of the world is never right, till every morning you awake in Heaven; see yourself in your Father's Palace; and look upon the skies, the earth, and the air, as Celestial Joys: having such a reverend esteem of all, as if you were among the Angels. The bride of a monarch, in her husband's chamber, hath no causes of delight as you.*

*You never enjoy the world aright, till the Sea floweth in your veins, till you are clothed with the heavens, and crowned with the stars; and perceive yourself to be the sole heir of the whole world, and more than so, because men are in it who are every one sole heirs as well as you. Till you can sing and rejoice and delight in God, as misers do gold, and Kings in scepters, you never enjoy the world.*

*Till your spirit filleth the whole world, and the stars are your jewels; till you are as familiar with the ways of God in all Ages as with your walk and table; till you are intimately acquainted with that shady nothing out of which the world was made; till you love men so as to desire their happiness, with a thirst equal to the zeal of your own; till you delight in God for being good to all; you never enjoy the world.*

I believe that we have not *"wandered in vain"* and that God has guided us *"to the fairest and the divinest." The "sea floweth in our veins"* and we are *"crowned with the stars."* My wife and I are *"enjoying the world aright"* here on Anna Maria Island and in the North Carolina Mountains.

Come experience the wonders; join us!

# How the Book is Organized

Shortly before moving to Anna Maria Island I published a book titled *How to Gain Thirty Pounds in Six Years: A Restaurant Guide and Cookbook from the Mountains of North Carolina.* The book was originally designed to introduce readers to some of the small towns, attractions, activities and eating places that make the North Carolina Mountains such a special place. It ended up being that but also a collection of some of the recipes that contributed to my gaining thirty pounds while we lived there. Finally I included in the book several food-related essays and a few personal stories.

It was another book, *The Craft Heritage Trails of Western North Carolina,* that indirectly led me to writing my book. That book is a guide to more than 500 studios, galleries, heritage sites, and inns throughout western North Carolina. But it is more than a simple guide-book to craft. It is an invitation to discover a new world and the people in it.

The back cover of the book reads: *"Tuck this book under your arm and head for the mountains. Along the way, you'll happen upon some truly remarkable finds – often around the bend, deep in the narrow of a mountain cover, across a stream, or in a storefront along a postcard street."*

It was through this book and the encouragement of *Jeannette Smith*, the delightful woman who gave us a copy, that led us to explore some of the back roads and small mountain towns that we might otherwise never have visited, to recipes we might never have found, dining experiences we might never have enjoyed, and people we may have never met.

Through this book I hope to share with others some of the "truly remarkable finds" we have made during the past three years living in the paradise that is Anna Maria Island *and* some of the equally remarkable finds we have made these past ten years in our travels throughout the mountains of North Carolina.

The following pages will provide you with what my wife and I consider to be the "*best*" of these two very different, but very wonderful worlds. While I will include some of the general information that is widely available through guide-books and the web, I will focus on those lesser-known areas and activities and pleasures that await visitors and new residents alike: places and things that we feel make these two areas "extra special."

One of the joys of being retired is that you usually have time to "wander around." I don't mean wandering around because you are lost, I mean wandering around to experience the fun and excitement of discovering new and unexpected places and things.

The uncovering of many of the special places and things in this book are the result of our wandering around Anna Maria Island and the North Carolina mountains.

I've tried to lay out the book in a way that will provide you with the opportunity to wander through the pages, discovering new and unexpected things, while at the same time providing some structure for those of you who do not particularly enjoy wandering and want to get directly to the heart of things.

The first part of the book is divided into two sections. After these and the previous introductory remarks, follows an extensive section on Anna Maria Island and then a similar section on the North Carolina Mountains.

Included in these two sections will be historical in-formation as well as what to do, where to go and how to get there. Also included will be information on the types of accommodations available and how to find them and suggestions on what to eat and where to eat it. Mixed in among those pages will be an occasional personal story or short essay that relates in some way to the area.

Good food is an important part of a good life. Included in the book are not only reviews and listings of some of our favorite eating places, but also a number of recipes of dishes that are more-or-less indigenous to each area. I've also included a couple of recipes from my first book, *Recipes from the Florida Keys*.

The back section of the book will be devoted to these regional recipes from both the island and the mountains and some short food-related essays.

People make a difference. In addition to what to do and where to eat and stay, scattered through the book I will briefly introduce you to some of the "extra special" people in each area.

Finally, at the back of the book is a detailed Index that will allow those Type-A folks who absolutely do not like wandering around to quickly find those pages of immediate interest.

None of the lists: people, places, things, will be all-inclusive; it is impossible to discover all the good things in any location. But what I have included are what we consider the crème de le crème, the best of the best of what we have discovered.

And, by the end, I will have either regaled you or bored you with some stories that do not necessarily tie to either area, but are stories I enjoy telling. Those of you who have read me before know that some might say I have a somewhat weird sense of humor. Part of that weirdness is that I think some stories are so good they are worth telling over and over again. So, some of the stories may be familiar to you. Either enjoy them again or skip over them; I won't be offended.

Sales of my original North Carolina book were not as spectacular as the waterfalls of North Carolina, but it did garner enough attention for me to be interviewed by *Our State* magazine.

Unfortunately the book was out-of-print for a while, although I see you can now again order a copy. Since it was out-of-print, I updated some of the pages from that book and included them in this one.

When word gets out that I am writing a book promoting the attributes of both places there will likely be a few folks in each area who will say to me, *"Shush! Stop! Don't give away all our secrets. We don't want any more people coming here."* I can understand how some people might feel that way, but that is not our nature. We live an abundant life and want to share it with all . . . that is with all who will love it and appreciate it and care for it as we do.

I hope you enjoy reading this book at least half as much as I have enjoyed writing it. But more importantly, I hope the book will motivate you to visit Anna Maria Island or the North Carolina Mountains or both. They truly are wonderful but very different places.

Now sit back and let me tell you about Anna Maria Island and more: the Best of Two Worlds.

# Anna Maria Island

# A Personal View
# of Anna Maria Island

Dee and I were both born in north Florida, as were each of our parents. Both families moved to Miami when each of us was about a year old. We both grew up and went to school in Miami, but on opposite sides of town. Neither of us lived anywhere else until I, in my late twenties and Dee in her early twenties married and a few years later moved to Georgia.

The point being, we know Florida. We've lived in Florida, off and on, for most of our lives. Our careers have taken us away from Florida four times and four times we have returned. And while for most of our years in Florida we lived in various parts of Miami/Dade County, we have both traveled extensively throughout the state. We've visited beaches on the east coast from Key West to Jacksonville and most everywhere in between. We've been to the panhandle, we've vacationed in Naples and Sanibel Island and Longboat Key on the west coast.

We've known and experienced Florida from back in the *"good old days."* I stood on the beach at Cape Canaveral with Jack O'Connor, a high school chum, and my two younger brothers and watched Alan Shepard and John Glenn take off on the first sub-orbital and the first orbital flights. Dee and I were aboard a small boat on the Intercostal Waterway, so close to the launch pad that we could see the Saturn rocket as it lifted off to take the crew of Apollo 11 to the first moon landing. I grew up fishing in Biscayne Bay and the Everglades, the Florida Keys and the Gulfstream.

We've experienced Florida in more recent times from a tourism perspective; in the 1990s and early 2000s we owned a 30-unit motel in the Florida Keys. Our two sons live in Florida, as does my daughter from a previous marriage. I have two brothers living in Gainesville. We are Floridians; we have the proverbial sand in our shoes. We love Florida.

Why am I telling you all of this? To give some credibility to the following statement: **Anna Maria Island is the best place in Florida I have ever lived or ever visited!**

The amazing thing is that until we moved here three years ago not only had I never visited the island, I had never even heard of it. It had been that big of a secret. Well, the secret is out and has been for several years, but the treasure is still there and will remain there. Part of that treasure is that Anna Maria Island is in many ways still like what much of the rest of Florida was like *"in the good old days."* But most of the rest of Florida changed, and not always for the better. Anna Maria Island in many ways has not changed and that definitely *is* for the better. Some say they feel like they've gone back in time when they are on the island. A visitor from New York wrote, *"This was a beach vacation with small-town charm. If it wasn't for real, one would think Anna Maria Island is a scene in a cartoon version of Old Florida."*

A staff writer for visitflorida.com explained it best when she wrote: *"The laid-back culture is both a natural by-product of the serene tropical environment as well as a deliberate effort by local government to preserve the natural and cultural richness of the island."*

For those of you who are as unfamiliar with Anna Maria Island as I was, it is located on the west coast of Florida just north of Sarasota and south of Tampa and St. Petersburg. A barrier island, it is just a little over seven miles long and very narrow, connected on the south by a bridge to Longboat Key and Sarasota. The main access is across one of two causeways leading from the town of Bradenton.

The island is made up of three separate little towns and each has its own style and feel and individual characteristics. But the informal, relaxed atmosphere pervasive throughout the entire island creates the sense of a single community but with different neighborhoods. Bradenton Beach is located at the southern third of the island, the town of Anna Maria is at the northern end, and the town of Homes Beach is in the middle. It is in Holmes Beach where my wife's church is located. On subsequent pages I'll describe each of the towns in more detail.

# f History
## ıa Maria Island

—a Maria Island Historical Society tells us that the
ıvn inhabitants of Anna Maria Island (to which I
ır usually refer to as "AMI" or just "the island")
s American Indian tribes including the Timucans
and the Caloosans.

Apparently the island and the waters surrounding it were prime fishing and hunting sites. There is still an abundance of birds and sea turtles that visit the island but they are protected. Most of the rest of the wildlife have left for safer and less-populated areas. But there are still plenty of fish in the sea and you *are* allowed to catch them.

Among the first European explorers to discover the island were the Spanish, led, among others, by Hernando De Soto who claimed the island and surrounding areas for the Spanish Crown. Later in the book you can read about the De Soto National Monument and Historical Site located off the east coast of the island in Bradenton.

In spite of Florida formally being ceded by Spain to the United States in 1821 and Florida becoming a state in 1845, it was not until 1892 that the first permanent resident arrived on AMI. George Emerson Bean, the first arrival, homesteaded much of what is now the Town of Anna Maria.

John Roser, the Fig Newton® king, arrived not too much later. The two of them, along with Bean's son Will, developed the area in the early 1900s by laying out streets and side-walks, building homes, and adding a water system. Roser built the island's first house of worship in honor of his mother. *Roser Memorial Community Church* still stands on its original site but has been expanded to meet the needs of a growing population.

The community continued to grow in spite of the fact that the only way to reach the island was by boat. It was not until 1921 that the first wooden bridge was built to connect the island to the mainland. The bridge extended westward from Cortez, a tiny fishing village on the mainland, over to the island. A fishing pier now exists at the base of the island-side of that old bridge. Aptly named Historic Bridge Street, the area has developed into one of the island's most popular dining and shopping destinations.

Over the years the island has continued to grow both as a vacation destination as well as a place of permanent residence. Throughout this development, however, the island remains a mixture of residential homes, vacation properties, and businesses working in harmony and in cooperation with the three local city governments to preserve and enhance the island's "Old Florida" heritage. And they have been very successful in doing that.

One of the island's true treasures is **Carolyn Norwood**, author, long-time island resident, and community historian. Copies of her books *The Early Days* and *Tales of Three Cities* can be purchased from the *AMI Historical Society*. The Society office, Museum, and Historical Park are located at 402 Pine Ave., Trolley Stop #42, Anna Maria. Open Tuesday-Saturday, 10 am- 4 pm, November – May; 10 am – 1 pm, May – October. Norwood's books can also be ordered online at http://amihs.org. Copies are also available as rentals from both island libraries.

# Anna Ma-REE-a
# or Anna Ma-EYE-a ?

Old timers from Miami (and I am one) usually pronounce the name of the city MI-am-uh, not MI-am-ee, as most folks do. I worked for a number of years for *The MI-am-uh Herald*.

A similar situation exists on Anna Maria Island. Some of the old timers pronounce the name Anna Mar-EYE-a, not Anna Ma-REE-a, as most people say today. But apparently the pronunciation of the name used by the early settlers was Anna Ma-RYE-a, using the German term for the wind, since it was named for the strong winds occurring at the time the island was first settled. You may remember the song *They Called the Wind Maria*, from the Lerner and Loewe musical *Paint Your Wagon*. In the movie version the song was sung by Harve Presnell.

But rather than connecting this beautiful place to *Paint Your Wagon*, I think AMI more nearly matches up with the lyrics of many of the Rogers and Hammerstein songs from their smash-hit musical *South Pacific*. Especially *Bali H'ai*, that wonderful song sung by Bloody Mary when she refers to *"my special island."*

Or, after spending *some enchanted evening* on Anna Maria Island I felt *younger than springtime* after *I washed that sand right out of my hair.*

And coming back from an afternoon at the beach I can tell you without a doubt, *there is nothing like a dame*! Oh, enough! Enough! I'm being as *corny as Kansas in August*.

Please don't stop reading. It gets worse.

# Physical Characteristics that make Anna Maria Island Special

Some of the physical characteristics that I feel make Anna Maria Island different and better than other beach communities in the state include:

~ It's a unique piece of geography. The west coast of the island is on the Gulf of Mexico, the northern end of the island faces Tampa Bay, and the east side of the island is on Anna Maria Sound and Sarasota Bay. And it is so narrow; we have a relative that owns a place that is just two blocks in one direction to the beach and two blocks in the other direction to the bay. And you can swim in water that is warm enough to swim in comfortably all twelve months of the year. Simply, it is a quiet, beautiful place in the sun that is easily accessible yet gives you the feel of being on a remote island.

A blogger commenting on he and his family's first AMI vacation said, *"When we were done with our stay we didn't click our heels together and say 'There's no place like home.' We got home, clicked our heels together and said, 'There's no place like Anna Maria Island.'"* We feel the same way and we're sure you will too.

~ It's cooler and less humid in the summer than in other parts of the state. July, August and September can be brutal on the east coast, in the Keys and in the center part of the state, with the afternoons so sweltering that most do not even want to go outdoors between 2 and 5 pm. Not so on AMI. It seems like there is always a gentle breeze blowing and with humidity lower than in most parts of the state it can be pleasant even when the temperatures hit the low nineties, which is about as high as it ever gets. Most summer days average in the mid-eighties. In the summer morning and evening temperatures are usually in the mid-seventies. Don't get me wrong; it does get hot in the summer, just not as hot as it gets in most of the rest of the state.

Winters, of course, are wonderful! Just ask any of the dozens of Canadians and the hundreds from the Northeast and Midwest who arrive beginning in November and stay until spring. But it is hard to understand why they would want to leave then. It's usually dry in the spring and daytime temperatures are in the seventies and cooler in the evening. Fall days are mostly sunny and comfortably warm. The National Weather Service reports that the average year-round temperature on AMI is 74.8 degrees F. There are not very many places in the country where you can say that the weather is almost perfect all year long. The weather on Anna Maria Island comes close.

~ The white sandy beach, with its low dunes and sea oats, is amazing. Used to the crushed-shell sand that makes up most of the beaches on the east coast, the soft, powdery sand that lines the seven miles of beaches on AMI is a pleasant change. I heard someone once comment that it was like walking on talcum powder. Another refers to it as "sugary." You just softly brush the sand off as you leave the beach area. I can remember having to practically scrub off the sticky shell-sand from the east coast beaches.

And the beaches are kept pristine, not spoiled, corrupted or polluted by uncaring visitors. Sometimes the garbage cans along the street are near overflowing, but that is because there is little that has been left on the beach, and what has been left gets quickly picked up. A visitor who has been vacationing on AMI every year for more than twenty- five years was recently quoted as saying, *"The beaches are superb and they have kept the quality the same for every year since we started coming here."*

~ There are no high-rises on AMI. Earlier, when there were no height restrictions, a developer built two seven-story condo buildings next to the beach. Whoa there! The residents were outraged. Never again! Height restriction legislation was quickly passed. Those are the only two buildings on the entire island that are more than three stories tall. And compared to the twenty and thirty and taller story hotels and condo and apartment buildings that line the beaches in most parts of the state those two little buildings are hardly offensive.

~ You can visit here, you can live here, and never need an automobile. It is never further than walking distance to the beach regardless of where you are staying or living on the island. You can own or rent a golf cart; you can ride a bicycle or rent a Segway; you can ride the free trolleys which make a full circle loop of the entire island. Even if you want to go to Longboat Key or Sarasota you can take the free trolley to the southern end of the island and connect with another trolley/bus that will take you there for a seventy-five cent fare. There is good public bus service going across the causeways to Bradenton.

And there is little need to ever leave the island if you don't want to. I can walk to the grocery store, the drug store and the hardware store; I can walk to the bank and the barber shop and the library. I seldom need to, but I can walk to my doctor's office. And I pass a number of good places to shop and eat regardless of in which direction I take off.

Automobile traffic can get a little heavy during peak season and on holiday weekends, but with all the alternative modes of transportation you don't have to let it bother you. And if you do get in your car, don't plan on driving any faster than 35 miles per hour. That's the maximum speed limit on any part of the island and it is 25 miles per hour in most of the areas.

(There is one short stretch at the south end of the island just before you get to the Longboat Key Bridge where you can push it up to 45 mph. But who wants to? There's no need to hurry.)

~ I guess the most important physical characteristic is its location: for those of you into these things, Anna Maria Island is at latitude 27.513N, longitude -82.719W. The following chart gives the mileage to Anna Maria Island from various cities around the US and the world:

| | |
|---|---|
| Atlanta, Georgia | 504 miles |
| Bangkok, Thailand | 9,593 miles |
| Chicago, Illinois | 1,220 miles |
| Dallas, Texas | 937 miles |
| London, England | 4,459 miles |
| New York City, New York | 1,186 miles |
| Paradise | 0 miles |
| Seattle, Washington | 2,560 miles |
| Toronto, Ontario | 1,385 miles |

Later in the book I will give you some suggestions as to how to easily get to the island by land, sea and air.

Mark Twain once said, *"Everybody talks about the weather, but nobody does anything about it."* On Anna Maria Island nobody needs to!

# The Gulf of Mexico

The "ocean" that hits the beaches of Anna Maria Island is the Gulf of Mexico, but is technically considered part of the Atlantic Ocean. It is the 9th largest body of water in the world. From east to west the waters extend 960 miles and from north to south 540 miles. This totals over 500,000 square miles of water. The Sigsbee Deep, located nearest to Florida in the southeast quadrant of the Gulf, is its deepest point, at somewhere around 16,000 feet.

The Gulfstream, entering from the Caribbean Sea and flowing out to the Atlantic via the Florida Straits, is the principal oceanic current moving waters into and out of the Gulf. This is one of the reasons that the Gulf of Mexico is one of the most fruitful fisheries in the world. The Gulf sustains over 200 varieties of salt water fish. Over 1 billion pounds of fish are harvested from these waters each year. Nearly 2 billion pounds of fish and shellfish combined are harvested from the five U.S. Gulf states.

Seventy-three percent of the nation's shrimp come from the Gulf and fifty-nine percent of the nation's oysters. About one-fourth of total U.S. commercial fishing income comes from the Gulf and is valued at some $900 million a year.

A description of the varieties of fish most-often caught in the Gulf and inland bays near Anna Maria Island will follow later in the book, along with tips on how best to catch them.

But the Gulf of Mexico is not only a good place to fish it is also a good place to swim. Descriptions of the AMI beaches that face the Gulf are coming on subsequent pages.

# Three Towns,
# One Community

When I grew up in Miami there were about a dozen separate municipalities in the county, individual communities with their own government and elected officials. More recognizable of these included the cities of Miami, Miami Beach, Coral Gables, Hialeah, and Miami Springs.

What I remember most was that until the voters passed new home rule legislation establishing a centralized metropolitan county government in 1957, these separate cities spent much of their time arguing with each other. Today there are 34 separate municipalities in Miami Dade County, providing such city-type services as police protection and zoning regulations. I think the arguing has slowed down, but probably because there are so many of them they don't know with whom to argue.

But things work differently on Anna Maria Island. There are three separate towns, the cities of Anna Maria, Holmes Beach, and Bradenton Beach, but they get along well, work together and in most everyway function as a true "community." They speak of each other as "sister cities" and "sharing the island" is a common reference.

The City of Anna Maria, at the north end of the island, is the more-residential of the three towns, although there are rental properties available. The City of Holmes Beach, the largest of the three, is located in the center of the island and is the commercial center of AMI. While there are a number of commercial accommodations, most of the town is made up of single family residential,  with many of the homes available for weekly, monthly and seasonal rental. The City of Bradenton Beach is at the south end of the island, ending at the bridge leading to Longboat Key and has more emphasis on tourism although there are many permanent residents in the city.

*The City of Anna Maria:* the estimated population of the city is 1,800, although many of the home owners are part-time residents. And, of course, the population swells during the seasons when tourists fill many of the homes that are available for rental. At the last count there were 1,696 residential units in the city.

The entire city is a bird sanctuary where you can see many species of shore and water birds. The aquatic life is remarkable as well. Bottlenose dolphin and manatees are in the surrounding waters and you can often see them from the beach shore or from one of the two fishing piers in the city. The fishing, for sport or for dinner, is excellent. Our friend *Duane Cowgill*, who lives on AMI half the year and in Michigan the other half, is fishing at the *Rod and Reel Pier* at daybreak almost every morning from November through April. Get up early and go out there and introduce yourself. He'll help you catch a fish and will also offer to cut your hair later at the barber shop in Holmes Beach.

The *Anna Maria City Pier* stretches 710 feet into the area where the waters of Tampa Bay meet the waters of Anna Maria Sound. The Rod and Reel Pier is a little shorter and is located further north. Even if you are not a fisherman, a walk out on the piers is an enjoyable experience and you can enjoy a nice meal at the restaurant located at the end of each pier.

Pine Avenue, which leads from Gulf Drive, the main north/south road on the island, to the City Pier, is an exciting and growing commercial area offering an array of unique shops, boutiques, art galleries and various service establish-ments. Most are housed in beautiful new buildings that have been tastefully designed to retain the quaint, old town feel of the island. There are a number of eating places also, offering both eat-in and take-out dining.

There are a number of other dining and shopping opportunities in the *City of Anna Maria* which will be listed and reviewed on other pages of the book.

***The City of Holmes Beach:*** Incorporated in 1950, currently has an estimated  population of around 3,800, *Holmes Beach* is the largest of the three cities and is located in the center of AMI. The Manatee Causeway (SR-64) ends at the main public beach, or as the promotions say, "*Where Manatee Avenue runs right into the Gulf of Mexico.*" Well, I guess that would be true if you didn't have to drive across *Manatee Public Beach* first. Manatee Beach is a great place to spend the day. When you get tired of just relaxing in the sun, get up and join the group that is almost always there playing volleyball. Or take the small children over to the playground and swings. You can wade out into the water and surf fish. Or join the kids learning to skim board. Or, go shelling; this beach is one of the best shelling areas on the island.

Getting hungry? Did you bring something to cook out on one of the grills? Or a picnic lunch you can eat at one of the shaded picnic tables? No? Don't worry, this is where the *AMI Beach Café* is located. One of the island's most popular eating and hanging out places, the café is a nice casual dining place where you can eat breakfast, lunch or dinner. You order at one of the outside windows and then find a seat inside or out. The servers will find you and deliver your order. One of the most popular menu items is the "all you can eat" pancakes and sausage served every day from 7:30 am until noon.  A more detailed description of the café and a listing of our favorite menu items will be included in the restaurant pages later in the book.

*Holmes Beach* offers perhaps the greatest variety of accommodations among the three towns, but, of course, it is the largest. Single and multiple-family homes, condo units, motel rooms, bed and breakfast units, and efficiency apartments are all available for rental.

Other than Manatee Beach described above, the Holmes Beach beaches do not provide life guards, concession stands or restroom facilities, but are some of the loveliest on the island. Parking is limited to the side streets that end at beach access points (at the ends of almost every side street in the town). But the beach is never more than a few blocks away from a free trolley stop.

About a dozen blocks north of the end of the causeway Gulf Drive takes a sharp left turn. You are now entering the main shopping and commercial area of the town. Banks, service station, several strip shopping areas, a hardware store, barber shop, real estate and rental services, bicycle rental and much, much more are all located within a three or four block area.

Several of the most popular restaurants on the island are located in this same area. Get off at the trolley stops on every side of the streets and spend an hour or two wandering through the shops and art galleries.

Or, in the late afternoon or early morning cross the street to the marina where most of the charter boats on the island are located and speak with one of the captains about a charter fishing trip. Some days they do not have full charters and have room for one or two additional fishermen. On other pages of the book are described the great variety of fish and types of fishing that are available in the Gulf and bay waters surrounding AMI. It is with the assistance of these captains and guides that you can make the most of the experience. You can also book a sunset cruise from this marina.

As with *Anna Maria* and *Bradenton Beach*, more detailed descriptions of some of the eating establishments located in *Holmes Beach* follow on separate pages, as do listing of some of the more interesting shops and art galleries.

**The City of Bradenton Beach:** The city's motto includes the following: "History, hospitality, and spirit are the hallmarks of our thriving waterfront . . . we are committed to maintaining our city's Old Florida charm and to respect its bountiful natural resources." And charm and natural resources they have! The city was incorporated in 1952 and at the last estimate has a permanent population of about 1,500.

In addition to the amazing Coquina Beach reviewed later in the book, two other significant areas are Cortez Beach and the Historic Old Town District. When the old original wooden bridge was replaced by a new span the island side of the old bridge was turned into a fishing pier which still stands today.

Of course, it has been completely renovated and the entire area was rejuvenated a number of years back. The street is now beautifully landscaped and lined with quaint and charming buildings which house unique shops, restaurants, bars, and accommodations. Parking in the Historic Old Town District can be a challenge at peak times of the year but the free trolley is always an option to take to visit the area. Or, just stay in Bradenton Beach and take the trolley to other areas of the island.

Cortez Beach is one of the nicest beaches on AMI, extending from 5th Street to 13th Street. This is a smaller, family-oriented beach with plenty of children who quickly learn how to use a skim board or fly a kite or build a sand castle. If you would prefer a beach with life guards and shower and restroom facilities you'll have to go down the road a piece to Coquina Beach.

As just one example of the sense of "community" that abounds in Bradenton Beach, the town has its own library; not a branch of the county library system, but its own independent, non-profit corporation-run library funded by generous donations and operated by friendly volunteers. No tax dollars are used and the library is open year-round.

As you can see, there are special things about each of the towns that make up Anna Maria Island. And with it being only seven miles from one end of the island to the other, it is possible to stay in any one of the towns and still be able to experience the island as a whole, the "community" of Anna Maria Island.

# In the Middle of Nowhere
# and in the
# Center of Everything

A friend of ours in North Carolina once referred to Rutherfordton as being "in the middle of nowhere and in the center of everything." In many ways I could say the same thing about Anna Maria Island.

Once you are here you do get the feeling of being in the middle of nowhere. The relaxed, laid-back atmosphere; the soft, white sandy beaches and warm breezes; the amazingly beautiful sunsets; the lounging around in casual island wear and a pair of sandals or flip flops; riding on a trolley; far, far away from the hustle and bustle of your regular busy life. A-a-a-ah, does it get any better than this? On an island, in the middle of nowhere.

Yet at the same time you are in the center of everything. If it's action you want it is just a few short bridges away. To downtown Bradenton is a 10-mile drive. *St. Armand's Circle* on Longboat Key is a half-hour away; you can be in downtown Sarasota in less than 45 minutes. Tampa and St. Petersburg are only an hour or so away, as is the *Hard Rock Hotel and Casino*. You can reach Orlando and *Disney World* in two hours.

In the middle of nowhere, in the center of everything.

But don't let me leave you with the thought that there is nothing to do on Anna Maria Island but relax. Not so.

Some of the following pages will highlight the great variety of activities that await you, if you so choose. I recall once hearing a local remark that, *"If you ever get bored on Anna Maria Island, you must be pretty boring yourself."*

But boring is not always bad. I remember one of my wife's sermons when she quoted a theologian who once said, *"Our language has wisely sensed the two sides of being alone. It has created the word "loneliness" to express the pain of being alone and it has created the word "solitude" to express the glory of being alone."*

Isn't that true? Haven't we all, at some time in our life, remarked at the difference between being lonely and being alone? And haven't we all, at some time, felt the need to be alone?

If that is what you need, or what you want, Anna Maria Island is a wonderful place to do it. Sitting on the beach, or under the shade of a palm tree, reading a book or just meditating or praying, you can be as alone and as boring as you want; you are in the middle of nowhere.

But, if you want to get up and go there are plenty of things to see and do; you are in the center of everything. Many suggested activities will be covered later in the book.

# In the Middle of Nowhere, but Easy to Get There

Another one of the great things about Anna Maria Island is that while off to itself, it is still easy to access, by land, air, and, of course, by sea.

If traveling by automobile it can't get any easier: take Exit 42 off of Interstate 1-75 coming from either the north or the south and head west. This is the exit for State Road 64 which takes you directly to the island and the beach. No turns, just stay straight on Hwy. 64, which is Manatee Avenue. Manatee Avenue ends at Gulf Drive at the middle of Holmes Beach. Turn left and you head toward Bradenton Beach; turn right and you head to the town of Anna Maria.

You have the choice of three international airports if arriving by air. All are within reasonable driving distance from the island and all three offer shuttle service and rental cars.

***Sarasota Bradenton International Airport*** (SRQ) is the closest, less than 40 minutes away. Flights are more limited than into and out of ***Tampa International Airport*** (TPA), but TPA is an hour and fifteen minutes away.

The Sarasota Airport is served by ***Jet Blue, Air Canada*** and ***Delta*** and ***US Air*** and their regional carriers, ***ExpressJet, PSA Airlines*** and ***Mesa Airlines***.

***Tampa International*** is a very major US airport that is served by all major US carriers and a number of inter- national carriers. It is also one of the easiest airports in the country to get around in and to park. I fly to Canada five or six times a year and hate to land and change planes at Chicago O'Hare. Landing and changing planes in Toronto or Minneapolis St. Paul, my other two choices to get to Winnipeg, is not much better. But it is almost enjoyable to fly out of and into Tampa. Almost.

Our preferred airport, however, is **St. Pete Clearwater International Airport** (PIE). It is an hour away, but is served by **Allegiant Air**, a great low-cost carrier. Allegiant only serves two large US cities out of PIE, Chicago and Detroit, but travels non-stop, direct to and from more than two dozen medium-size markets. It is especially easy for us to get to the mountains by flying either to Asheville, NC or Greenville/Spartanburg. SC. And we can visit friends in two of our other old stomping grounds, Lexington, KY and Ft. Wayne, IN. Our Canadian visitors can use Allegiant Air from Toronto by driving to the Buffalo, NY airport, or from Montreal by driving to the Plattsburg, NY airport, or by taking **AirTransit** from Halifax, NS. Allegiant does not fly to every one of these towns every day, but the lower cost fares make it an easy decision to juggle your schedules. And, if you land in St. Pete or in Tampa, you get to drive across the beautiful **Sunshine Skyway Bridge** which connects St. Petersburg to Bradenton.

Want to cruise in on your sailboat or yacht? There are lots of choices as to where to anchor or dock. Check your marine guides. You might want to first check Keyes Marina, Bradenton Beach Marina, and Mainsail Marina, all are quality full-service facilities. If you do not have a nautical chart of these waters the NOAA chart number is 1425, (Charlotte Harbor to Tampa Bay). If you are arriving by boat you will also want a copy of *Costal Pilot #5,* which covers the Gulf of Mexico from Key West to the Rio Grande. This NOAA publication contains important supplemental information that is difficult to portray on nautical charts.

# Where to Stay

The very best idea is buy a house or condo, move here and stay at your own place. If you are not yet ready for that, how about talking one of your relatives into buying a place down here and then you can stay with them.

If neither of those ideas will work don't worry about it; there are plenty of other alternatives. You can rent a house, a beach-side cottage, or a condo for a week or a month or a season. Or, you can stay at one of the several nice motel-type properties or at one of the historic bread-and-breakfasts that are scattered up and down the beach.

What you will not find are large, luxurious five-star resorts. This is just not that type of island. If that is what you are looking for there are a good number of options south and north of here either in Sarasota or St. Petersburg.

But you are most likely reading this book because you are looking for a more casual, relaxed stay. A place where you do not have to "dress" for dinner, where you can hang your wet beach towel from the balcony, where you can walk to the beach from where you are staying in your bathing suit with or without a cover up, where you can load up at the one super market on the island (*Publix*) and not worry about having to sneak the packages back to your room.

If so, this is the place for you. As with most things now days you can find a lot of options on your own using guide-books and the internet. But that can be time-consuming and sometimes as frustrating as having    to    "speak"    with    a computer    when you are trying to reach a customer service representative.

If you do want start on your own I suggest you begin by going to **www.VRBO.com**. This is the *Vacation Rentals by Owner* site. It has received many good reviews for its ease of use, its honest listings, and the quality of the listings.

But the easiest and usually most satisfactory way to find the perfect place for you and your family to stay is to use a professional service.

There are a number of good ones that advertise in our two island papers, but I will make two personal recommendations: if you are looking to rent a home, apartment or condo for a week, a month or a season, contact *John Donato* by emailing him at john@johnsellsfl.com.

I recently heard someone use the term *"staycation"*. My guess is that they were referring to a place where you go for vacation and enjoy it so much that you want to, or do, stay there. A perfect description of AMI. Most of the permanent residents discovered the island while on vacation and decided they wanted to live here full time, or at least during the winter months. If you are looking to stay and want buy a place on the island or in a near-by off-island development, contact *Sue Hookom* with *A Paradise Realty Co*, at 941-404-0525, or write her at Suehookom@hotmail.com. Sue says *"My client's goals are my goals."*

She's another of those "amazing AMI women" that I've mentioned in other places in the book. If you are "into" classic cars you'll want to speak with Sue. Before "retiring to Florida", Sue owned and operated the largest classic car showroom in Canada, selling and trading classic automobiles and vintage parts world-wide. She and her husband Don are special folks.

Both John and Sue are personal friends of ours and I know they will help you find just the right place. Just tell them that Phil asked you to call or write.

# Getting Around

I wrote earlier that one of the great things about Anna Maria Island is that you do not have to own an automobile if you do not want to.

One of the most popular modes of transportation is *walking*. Again, almost anywhere you live or stay on the island is within easy walking distance to the beach. The northern end of the island is a little wider than the middle and southern end, but most of the housing in that area is for permanent residents; most of the rental properties and commercial accommodations are on or within a few blocks of the beach. Many of the streets have sidewalks or walking and bicycle-designated lanes, including the main Manatee Causeway to the mainland.

Many of the permanent residents, and more than a few of the visitors, utilize *golf carts* to get around. They must be street legal and registered, which means you must have a driver's license and proof of insurance. Rental carts that seat 2, 4 or 6 passengers are available for hourly, daily or weekly rental. Various rental companies also advertise in our local papers.

*Scooters and mopeds* are available for rental, but for whatever reason they seem to be far less popular than at other beach and tourist areas. Since they are not all that safe that suits me just fine.

*Bicycles* are very popular. There are designated bicycle lanes on almost all parts of the major roadways, including on the causeway to the mainland. There are single, tandem, and three-wheel bikes available for rental. Crime is not a problem on the island but occasionally someone will pick up a bicycle that is not theirs. Do not tempt them; bring a lock.

I'm seeing more and more Segways tooling around these days. They look easy enough to ride but I have yet to try one. I think I'll put it on my "not-to" bucket list, along with sky diving, bungee jumping, rock climbing and alligator wrestling. There are several Segway tour packages offered for the young and young at heart (you must be able to walk and chew gum at the same time).

The *Free Trolley* is the best deal around for my money. (That's a little joke. "*Very little,*" my wife says.) Daily trolley service runs from 6 a.m. to 10:30 p.m. every 20 minutes from Anna Maria City Pier on the north end of the island to Coquina Beach at the south end. Trolley stops are every two to four blocks along the entire seven mile stretch of the island, or a run of a little more than fourteen miles for the entire circle route.

There are three stops, the pier, Manatee Public Beach in Holmes Beach, and at the end at Coquina Beach, where the trolley will wait at each location for approximately three minutes before continuing its route.

All trolley stops have a green sign with a trolley on it and most of them have a covered seating area while you wait. Trolleys offer air conditioned and open seating areas and even have a bike rack on the front of the trolley where you can load your bicycle.

The free trolley partners with *Sarasota County Area Transit* and for just 75 cents you can catch the *Longboat Key Trolley* from Coquina Beach to downtown Sarasota, with stops on Longboat Key and St. Armand's Circle. The service runs daily from 6 a.m. to 11 p.m., every 30 minutes.

The free trolley also connects with *MCAT,* the Manatee County *public bus line,* for service to Bradenton and the mainland.

You don't see *taxi cabs* driving around town waiting to

be hailed, but there is limited taxi service available. AMI Taxi offers on-call service on and to off the island. There are also several airport shuttle services available. Check with the airport of your choice.

If you absolutely insist in driving around in your *automobile* let me give you these notes of caution. Obey the speed limits, traffic signals, stop signs, parking and other traffic control devices. Take your time. You didn't come to the island to be rushed; you probably came to the island for exactly the opposite of being rushed. The three small towns that make up AMI are not speed traps, but if any of the city or county police officers see you breaking one of the laws you will be given a ticket. Nothing will put more of a damper on an otherwise enjoyable vacation than getting a traffic ticket.

If you visit the island at one of the peak seasons or holiday weekends know that the traffic on to the island in the morning and afternoon will be heavy and slow and the same will be true getting off of the island in the afternoon or early evening. There are hundreds of people who do not live or are not staying on the island that come across the causeway to get to the beach and they all want to travel at the same time. My wife was training for a 21-mile walk as part of the Big Sur Marathon and was taking every opportunity she was offered to get in some additional training miles. The traffic was backed up coming on the island and we were about two-and-one-half miles away from home. *"I'll just get out here and walk the rest of the way,"* she said as she hopped out of the car. She beat me home! That's why I mentioned that one of the nice things about living or staying on the island is that you do not have to have an automobile. The rest of the year the traffic is not bad. Just why drive if you don't have to.

Finally, you can take the AMI Water Shuttle. Monday through Friday it makes a different trip each day. For example, on Monday it make a loop to Longboat Key; on Wednesday it makes a Bradenton Day Trip. Every day they make drop-offs and pick-ups at Egmont Key and have nightly Sunset Cruises.

For the current schedule go to their web site: www.amiWaterShuttle.com. They also offer private charters.

# Sneak Previews
# and Movie Reviews

Some of you may be old enough to remember *sneak previews*. These were early showings of a movie that was opening usually the next day. You'd buy a ticket to see the regular movie that was showing and then stay in the theatre after it ended to see the sneak preview film for free. Lots of luck getting to see a free one now days.

And can you imagine, these were the days when there was only *one* screen. Yep, none of these 24-screen multiplexes. You'd go to a movie theatre and it had one screen. Choice of what movie to see? If you wanted to see a different movie you'd go down the street to the other one-screen theatre. Oh, occasionally the theatre would be showing a *double feature.* That's when they would show two movies, back-to-back, for the price of one. Also lots of luck getting a free one of these today either.

But, you can get a movie sneak preview of Anna Maria Island and some of the surrounding areas. A number of films have been shot on AMI and near-by locations over the years. Some are memorable (*Greatest Show on Earth*, winner of the Best Picture Oscar in 1952); some are not so memorable (*The Alley Cat* (1985), one reviewer said "It's so bad it is funny.").

The following is a partial list of other movies filmed in the area. Several show a good number of outside scenes which give you a flavor of the area. Each year there are decent films that fall under the critics' radar and don't get reviewed or undeservedly receive "bad" reviews. A couple of these fall into that category.

**On An Island with You** (1948). One of the best *Esther Williams* movies. Not as much water ballet as in her other movies but it is romantic and entertaining with some great dance and song numbers. It also stars *Peter Lawford, Ricardo Montalban, Cyd Charisse* and *Jimmy Durante.* You can purchase it from online DVD retailers.

**Palmetto** (1998). Starring *Elizabeth Shue* and *Woody Harrelson.* An entertaining neo noir film (that's a modern-day film noir production). (Palmetto is the small town across the river from downtown Bradenton.) Shue gives a classic femme fatale performance. Rent or buy it from online video streamers.

**Great Expectations** (1998). A loose modernization of the classic story by Charles Dickens of a man of modest means who falls in love with a rich girl. The film was shot around the fishing village of *Cortez* and at the *Ringling Muse*um in Sarasota. The sea gulls, the pelicans, the Cortez commercial fishing docks, the view of AMI on the distant shore, the water, the clouds and the fish, all scenes of great beauty, but matched by the unbelievable beauty of *Gwyneth Paltrow.* A great cast that also includes *Ethan Hawke, Anne Bancroft, Robert De Niro* and *Chris Cooper*, who gives a wonderful performance as Uncle Joe. Rent it from online video streamers.

**Out of Time** (2002). *Denzel Washington* plays a well-respected Police Chief on small Banyan Key, but allows his flawed personal life to get the best of him. He finds himself in a race to solve a double homicide before he himself falls under suspicion. This is another film with great femme fatale performances; this time by *Eva Mendes* and *Sanaa Lathan.* This film can also be rented or bought from online video streamers.

**House Hunters** (Season 69, Episode 6). Television series that shows a couple looking for a home on Anna Maria Island. With the help of a real estate agent they look at three properties on the island before deciding which one to buy. The hour-long show offers a good look at the beaches and residential neighborhoods on AMI. This can also be rented from online video streamers.

This has absolutely nothing to do with Anna Maria Island or the North Carolina Mountains, but since I have been writing about femme fatales let me tell you that the greatest femme fatale performance ever was by **Linda Fiorentino** in the movie *The Last Seduction (1994)*. Her performance would certainly have earned her a Best Actress nomination and probably the Oscar, but unfortunately the film was made for HBO. It showed on television before it was released to the theatres and therefore was ineligible for an Oscar. She was robbed! (Jessica Lange, another scary gal, won that year for *Blue Sky)*. If you are into tough, beautiful, cut-your-you know-whats-off women, don't miss *The Last Seduction*. It is available from the video streamers.

# Water Sports and Activities

As one would expect visiting or living on an island, there are a wide variety of water sports and activities available: swimming, snorkeling, scuba diving, shelling, boating, sailing, fishing, kayaking, wind surfing, paddle boarding, and more, even sand castle-building competitions.

On the following pages you will find separate descriptions of some of the major activities.

Activities covered will include those of interest to the experienced water sports enthusiast as well as those for the novice or less-experienced visitor. For example, certified divers will find dive boats to take you to explore numerous wrecks and reefs off shore, while those whose experience in the water is limited to snorkeling will find equally as-interesting underwater sights to see at lesser depths.

Those with limited fishing experience will find fishing from one of the three piers, or the bridges, or from one of the fishing party boats as exhilarating as the seasoned fisherman will catching his or her first tarpon or bonefish while fishing with one of the local guides.

I don't want to sound like an old father, or an old mother, but as someone who has to make frequent visits to the dermatologist, let me remind you to put on sunscreen before participating in any of these outdoor activities. I mentioned earlier in the book that a traffic ticket can put a dampener on an otherwise great vacation; so can a sunburn.

# Fishing

Fishing is a major sport and industry in Florida, along all the coasts, the keys, offshore, the Gulfstream, the Everglades, and the Gulf of Mexico. Even fresh water fishing in the lakes and streams throughout the state is a major activity. But some of the best fishing in the state, especially for certain species, is right here in the waters around Anna Maria Island. Offshore, nearshore, and inshore around the bridges and piers, are all abundant fishing grounds.

There are a variety of types of fishing available: boatless – fishing from the surf, or from one of the several fishing piers and bridges. From a boat – your own, a boat you have rented, or in a charter boat with a licensed captain or guide. Each has its advantages.

*Boatless*, fishing from a pier or bridge or from the surf, is the least expensive way to fish. All you need is a license, a rod and reel or throw line, and some bait. And you'll meet some of the friendliest people there, most of whom are happy to share stories, answer questions and give advice. There are three fishing piers on AMI and several bridges from which to fish on the two causeways. On the next few pages you will find a listing of the species most often-caught in these nearby waters. Anglers will be pleased to learn of the good number of species of fish that especially like to hang around and feed near bridges and piers. You stand a better chance of landing certain of these fish fishing from a pier than you would if you were in a boat.

I've mentioned this in another part of the book but it is worth mentioning again. If you fish from the *Rod 'n Reel Club Pier*, look for my friend *Duane Cowgill*. He is there almost every morning at daybreak from November through March. A nicer or better pier fisherman it will be hard to find. There are three types of boats from which to fish: your own boat, a boat that you have rented, and from a boat owned and operated by a licensed guide or charter captain. And depending upon the size of the boat, you can either fish inshore or nearshore waters or fish in deep offshore waters. This is a polite way of saying "Don't go offshore in a small boat or into waters of which you are not familiar."

Having fished much of my life in Florida waters I've tried them all and, as I said, each has its advantages, and disadvantages. But, if I wanted to *catch* some fish, and not just *fish* (the verb) and if I had only a few days in which to do it, I'd head immediately to the charter boat docks. Local captains know *what is biting*, and that varies depending upon the season and the weather; *where they are biting*, and fish do move around and do not just tread water in one spot waiting for someone to come along and offer them something to eat; and *what they are biting*, and that changes also. I've wasted more hours that I care to remember fishing in the wrong spots, with the wrong baits, for the wrong fish. And I have usually ended up eating pizza rather than fresh fish for dinner that night.

Charter boat fishing is not inexpensive: boats are expensive to buy and maintain, fuel costs are high, and insurance, licenses, and gear and bait that is provided all go into the costs. But, as with most things, you get what you pay for. In the long run, fishing with a charter captain can be one of the least expensive ways to catch fish and certainly one of the most productive. And you don't need a fishing license.

If not fishing from a boat with a licensed charter captain or guide, a recreational saltwater fishing license is required to take or attempt to take saltwater fish, lobster, crabs, or other saltwater organisms. And there are additional permits required to fish for snook, tarpon or lobster. A yearly license for a Florida resident is $17. Non-residents can purchase a 3-day license for $17, or a 7-day license for $30, or a yearly license for $47. There are numerous regulations regarding minimum and maximum size fish allowed to be kept and not released; certain dates that certain fish are not allowed to be fished for; and bag limits, or the number of fish you are allowed to catch per day. Charter captains and guides are all familiar with these regulations. But if you are fishing alone or in your own boat you need to be aware of them. The regulations are posted on the piers and are available when you purchase your license or you can download and print a set of the regulations from the internet by going to www.eregulations.com/florida/fishing/saltwater.

Our two island newspapers have multiple pages of fishing news each week, including tide tables and ads from guides, charter boats and rental boats and equipment.

Following is a list, in no particular order, of the most common varieties of fish caught in these waters, along with some tips on where to fish for them and what type of bait is likely to be most successful:

***Bonefish:*** A highly prized game fish that must be caught and released, unless fishing in a tournament and you have a tournament exemption permit. Found inshore inhabiting shallows often less than a foot deep, usually over grass flats or white sand. Live shrimp and small crabs are preferred baits. Average size 3 to 5 pounds. Pound for pound one of the hardest fighting fish in the sea. Also one of the hardest fish to catch. I had fished for years and never caught a bonefish. I fished with a guide in the Florida Keys and caught and released three before 8 am. Peak season October to March. Go fish alone and maybe you'll have better luck than I had. Go fishing with a bonefish guide and you'll stand a much better chance of catching one!

***Dolphin (Mahi-Mahi):*** A great fighting fish. Swims at speeds up to 50 knots. Caught offshore in warm water trolling with medium tackle and rigged ballyhoo or by casting with light tackle along Sargassum weed lines or floating debris with live or cut bait or artificial lures. I've had great luck casting weed lines with a silver *MirrOlure* plug or a spoon. Single fish common to 30 pounds; schooling fish in the 5 pound range. No minimum size in Gulf waters; daily bag limit 10 per person. Very good eating fish with flaky, dense meat that has a sweet and unique taste. My third most favorite eating fish.

***Black Drum:*** Largest member of the drum family. Primarily an inshore fish found in bays and lagoons. Bottom dweller often found near oyster beds. Feeds primarily on oysters, crabs and shrimp. Anglers usually use cut bait (mullet), shrimp and sand fleas. It is important to keep the bait on the bottom where the drum feed. Spinning tackle with 15 to 30 pound test line will suit most conditions. Common to 30 pounds. Size limits: not less than 14", not more than 24". Bag limit 5 per day with one fish greater than 24" allowed. Not one of my favorites, but basically a good eating fish.

***Spotted Sea Trout:*** Found nearshore or inshore over grass and sandy bottoms. Feed primarily on shrimp. I have caught my limit numerous times using a *Creek Chub* broken spotted yellow darter plug. Creek Chub no longer makes this plug but you can find one on E-bay. Average about 3-4 pounds in these waters. Size limits: not less than 15" or more than 20". Bag limit: 4 per day with one fish over 20" allowed. Excellent eating fish.

***Gulf Flounder:*** Bottom dweller caught inshore on sand or mud bottoms. Frequent catch from AMI piers. They feed mainly on crustaceans and small fish. Anglers usually use light spinning tackle  with live shrimp or cut bait or jigs. Live mud minnows are choice bait, if you can find them. Flounder can be caught at night with use of a lantern. Common to 2 pounds.

Minimum size: 12". Bag limit: 10 per day. Excellent eating: very light meat, extremely mild.

**Black Grouper**:  (see separate essay about grouper in general, pg. 67) are mainly found offshore although young may occasionally be caught inshore in shallow water. Usually found on rocky bottoms in waters over 60 feet deep. Medium to heavy gear fished near the bottom with live fish or dead cut or whole fish as bait. Blacks are excellent eating fish (my favorite). Common to 40 pounds; may exceed 100 pounds. A prize catch for the charter boats. Minimum size: 22". Daily bag limit: 4 per day.

**Red Grouper:** A shallow water grouper. Bottom dweller associated with hard bottoms. Young fish (1-6 years) found on nearshore reefs; older fish usually found offshore. Declared overfished in 2000, strict regulations have restored populations to target levels. They feed on a wide variety of fish, octopus, shrimp and lobsters. Size common to 15 pounds; can reach 50 pounds. Bag limit: 4 per day. Excellent eating fish. Sweeter and milder than Black Grouper and preferred by some. Meat is lean, white, moist and flaky. Bag limit: 4 per day.

**Gag Grouper:** Often misidentified as Black Grouper. Gag's tail and fins have white edges while Black's do not. This is important to know as regulations and limits differ between the two fish. Adults found offshore over reefs and rocks and prefer ledges and depressions. Younger fish can be found in sea grass beds inshore. Was once one of the most abundant groupers in the Gulf, it is now overfished and rebuilding plans have been implemented. Excellent eating fish; more similar to the Red than to the Black in terms of taste and texture. Common to 25 pounds. Minimum size: 22"; bag limit: 2 per day; open season July 1; season closes Dec 1.

**Sheepshead:** Hard *not* to catch one if you are fishing from one of the piers. Also found around oyster beds, seawalls, and tidal creeks. Best bait: fiddler crab or shrimp. Use light to medium spinning tackle. Keep a tight line as sheepshead are known nibblers. A popular saying on the piers is "to catch one you must jerk your line just *before* they bite." Common size: inshore 1-2 pounds, offshore to 8 pounds. Minimum size: 12". Bag limit: 15 per day. Very good eating fish.

*Spanish mackerel:* A schooling fish found inshore, nearshore and offshore, especially over grass beds and rocks. They are aggressive feeders and thus fairly easy to catch. Light spinning or bait-casting tackle with 10 to 15 pound monofilament line is adequate, but be sure and use a 40 to 60 pound leader as mackerel have razor sharp teeth. To find the fish follow the birds who are diving on schools of bait fish. Chances are a school of mackerel is below driving the bait fish to the top. I haven't fished for mackerel in a number of years, but a white or yellow bucktail was a favored lure, as was a silver spoon. Minimum length 12". Daily bag limit: 15 per day. Average size less than 2 pounds. Most often caught in winter months as fish migrate north in the spring. A popular eating fish.

*Florida Pompano:* a prized catch, especially of surf and pier fishermen. Tastes similar to flounder, but lots, lots better. Common in inshore and nearshore waters, especially along sandy beaches, along oyster beds, and over grass flats. But they also are caught in water as deep as a hundred feet or more. Best bait: sand fleas. Pompano is a good example of a fish whose location is influenced by tides and water temperatures. Size usually less than three pounds. Minimum size: 11". Daily bag limit: 6.

*Yellowtail Snapper:* Young fish found inshore on grass beds; adults found nearshore and offshore over sandy areas near reefs. Fun to catch using light tackle with artificial jigs or cut bait. Good fighters for their size. Average to three pounds. Minimum size: 12". Daily bag: 10 per day. An excellent eating fish. If you see it on a menu, order it.

**Snook:** Another prized game fish. Oh, did I love catching them when I was a young boy. Found inshore and nearshore in coastal and blackish waters, along mangrove shorelines, seawalls and bridges. The season for snook in Gulf  and Atlantic waters was closed in January 2010 due to the impact of severe cold weather that winter. Atlantic snook were less impacted and the ban was lifted for Atlantic snook in the fall of 2011. Finally the ban of snook fishing in Gulf waters was lifted effective September 2013. However, regulations are continued: the season is closed from December 1 through the end of February and from May 1 through August. Size limit not less than 28" or more than 33". Bag limit 1 per day. Most catches are in the 5 to 8 pound range. Snook permit required. A very good eating fish that may NOT be sold commercially.

**Tarpon:** The "silver king" is truly the king of the game fish. A challenge to catch on any type of tackle, the current rage is to fish for them with saltwater fly gear. Not edible. A catch and release fish. New regulations went into effect September 2013. Tarpon are powerful, explosive and acrobatic, making them one of the most exciting and challenging nearshore fish. Tarpon can be caught on a variety of baits: live and dead bait, jigs, streamers, floating and diving lures, and flies. The tackle to be used depends upon where you are fishing and what size fish you are targeting. *Captain Rick Gassett* says the big ones have recently been tearing up DOA Baitbuster plugs. Near bridges and cuts are most popular spots to fish. Best to use a guide. He will know the regulations as well as where the fish are currently located and what type of tackle and bait to use. Common in these waters at 40 to 50 pounds, but fish are regularly caught in the 100+ pound range. Summer months are best times to fish for tarpon.

**Amberjack:** Only so-so eating, but what a fight! Caught offshore near rocks, reefs, and wrecks, typically in 60 to 250 feet of water. They swim in schools and feed on bait fish, squid and crabs. Commonly used bait include: live blue runners, pin fish or grunts. Occasionally amberjack will get excited and come to the surface and explode on top-water plugs, jigs and spoons. They are extremely hard fighters with great endurance. Common to 40 pounds, but you'll think you've hooked something twice that size. My wife, Dee, caught a thirty-five pounder one time and it took her almost an hour to land it. The mate on the charter boat kept offering to assist her, but no way was she going to let go of that rod. Limit 1 per day. Season closed in June and July. If you're on a charter boat the mate or captain will take care of this, but if you are fishing by yourself make sure the drag is set light enough. Twice I've witnessed an amberjack (we think) pull the rod and reel right out of the hands of the fisherman. There went a couple of hundred bucks and we didn't even get the fish. Take a charter.

**Redfish:** Actually a red drum; also called a channel bass or just a "red". One of Florida's most popular sport fish. They inhabit nearshore and offshore waters. Most popular fishing method is floating a live shrimp under a popping cork, but good fisherman can be successful casting spoons, jigs and even top-water plugs. Size limits: minimum 18", maximum 27". Bag limit 2 per day. An excellent eating fish. Management of redfish is a success story. In the late 1980s, red drum was seriously overfished and conservation measures had to be put in place to reduce fishing pressure. Stock has rebounded and is currently meeting or exceeding the management goals. Regulations continue to change, however.

**Ladyfish:** I've saved the worst for last. I hate these things and only include them because if you fish these waters long enough you're going to catch one. Sort of fun to catch because they often leap out of the water when hooked. Trash fish; not good for anything, although the pelicans may feel otherwise. I don't even like to take them off the hook. Common to 2-3 lbs.

These are just a few of the fish that you are likely to catch when fishing in these waters; everything from a *grunt* (pan fry them and eat them with grits) to a *shark* (don't eat them) to a stingray (don't try and unhook; cut the line and re-rig.).

Just go ahead and wet a line; whether from a bridge or a pier or twenty miles offshore in a charter boat, you'll have fun either way.

*The worst day of fishing beats the best day at work.*

# Keep a-Goin'

Our friends *Julie and Don Lind* gave us a book of inspirational poetry as an anniversary gift this past year. Among the collection was a poem by *Frank L. Stanton* titled *Keep a-Goin'*.

I'm going to make a copy of the first verse, retitle it *Ode to an Angler,* laminate it and paste it inside my fishing tackle box. It goes like this:

> *Ef you strike a thorn or rose,*
> > *Keep a-goin'!*
> *Ef it hails or if it snows,*
> > *Keep a-goin'!*
> *'Taint no use to sit an' whine*
> *When the fish ain't on your line;*
> *Bait your hook an' keep a-tryin' –*
> > *Keep a-goin'!*

Good advice in any situation, I think.

**Note:** Frank L. Stanton was an American poet and lyricist born in Atlanta in 1857. He was the first poet laureate for the state of Georgia. You may recall hearing the lyrics of *Keep a-Goin'* once recited by actor Henry Gibson on the *Dick Van Dyke Show.* Gibson later turned it into a song for the Robert Altman film *Nashville.*

# Fish for a
# Florida Grand Slam

***The Grand Slam Club*** celebrates a variety of Florida sport fishes and the achievement of anglers catching a particular set of three species in a single day. There is a different slam inspired by fish caught in each of the state's four geographic regions and the redfish is included in three of them.

You do not have to be in the region listed to achieve that region's Grand Slam. For example, you can get an East Coast Grand Slam while fishing on the west coast, so long as you catch all three East Coast species of fish in a 24-hour period.

**Regional Grand Slam Fishes**:

*North Florida* – Redfish, spotted sea trout, cobia.

*West Coast* (includes AMI) – Redfish, snook, tarpon.

*East Coast* - Redfish, spotted sea trout, tarpon.

*South Florida* – Tarpon, bonefish, permit.

A tough challenge even with the assistance of a guide, but you'll stand a better chance of achieving a Slam with one. The Grand Slam Program is conducted in collaboration with the International Game Fish Association (IGFA) and requires anglers to fill out an application. Your guide can help you with that.

Once you've caught your slam fish, or any fish, let our friend *Liz Lang* rub it for you. See the following page.

# Fish Rubbing

Gyotaku (GEE-oh-TAH-koo) is the ancient Japanese art and technique of fish printing. Gyo is "fish"; Taku is "impression". It has developed into an art form that is practiced around the world.

But just because it is practiced around the world does not suggest that the skill of fish rubbing is a common one; it is very difficult and many a fish has been "wasted" by artists trying to master the technique.

Our friend, *Liz Lang*, of Holmes Beach, is one that has mastered it, however. And, not only does she rub the fish, she catches it! A master fisherwoman, she is a member of an all-female fishing group called the *Reel Darlins*.

The mission of the *Reel Darlins* is to unite women who are passionate about fishing and boating. They not only consider fishing a sport or a hobby, but a lifestyle. They are all about anything and everything that has to do with this lifestyle, from fishing competively as a team and as individuals, to giving fishing tips and boat and equipment reviews. To learn more about the organization, and meet some of the darlins, go to their web site: www.reeldarlins.com.

But, back to the fish rubbing. In Japan, fishermen would make gyotaku to preserve records of their catches. The oldest known gyotaku was found in Japan, dating back to 1862. Lord Sakai caught a very large red sea bream one night and commissioned a now-unidentified artist to preserve the memory.

There are several techniques of fish rubbing, but the most authentic and highest quality rubbing is done by the direct method. In the direct method ink or paint is applied directly on the fish and rice paper or canvas is placed on the fish and carefully rubbed by hand, transferring the ink to the paper.

The direct method allows the artist to capture all the details, even the fins and the scales of the fish, giving an exact replica of the fish as the print has been taken straight from the specimen.

Originally done in black ink, many of today's artists, including our friend Liz, make their rubbings in the natural colors of the fish. Dee and I own two of Liz's rubbings: one a medium-size Parrot fish with all its red brilliance; the other is a five-foot long bull dolphin (Mahi-Mahi to you land lubbers). One of Liz's sons caught the parrot fish; Liz caught the dolphin.

Liz also makes most of her own frames. The frame for our dolphin was a joint effort of Liz and *Chris Collins*, another local artist who is primarily a photographer and framer. Chris built the frame and then Liz finished it. I think she told us that it took thirteen coats of lacquer to achieve the almost porcelain-like finish.

Unfortunately Liz recently lost her entire studio to a fire and with it most of her prints. Hopefully she'll be back in production soon. Her talents are too wonderful not to be expressed and seen. It's sort of like Michelangelo taking a break and never getting around to carving *David*. Well, maybe that is a little of an overstatement, but she is a great talent! And one of our favorite persons on the island.

By the way, did I mention that she is a great cook and hostess? She catches the fish, paints them, rubs them, cleans them, cooks them, and then serves them. And the lucky ones of us get to eat them. An amazing woman!

To you single readers: Forget it. She's happily married to a wonderful fellow named Bob.

# Grouper Straight Talk

Grouper belong to the Sea Bass family, one of the largest fish families in the sea (over 300 species). Some grouper species range from as far north as New England, as far south as Brazil, and as far west as Texas and Central America.

Three of the most common varieties found in the Gulf waters off of and around Anna Maria Island are listed in the previous *"Fishing"* essay. Others include the Nassau, the Warsaw, and the Goliath, formerly and still locally called a Jewfish. These latter giants can live for 30 to 50 years and grow to as large as 800 pounds. The Florida record is 680 pounds. The goliath has been totally closed to harvest since 1990.

While the name *"group-er"* suggests that they tend to congregate together, they actually are a somewhat solitary fish, especially the large ones. Occasionally you will find a grouper that will chase a bait, but they prefer to wait in hiding until an easy meal swims by, or is dangled from a hook in front of them. Divers will often see grouper that have backed into a hole in a reef. Their coloration and the ability to change hues or shades allows them to ambush unsuspecting bait fish. They rush out, inhale their prey and quickly return to their lair.

Fishing for grouper is fairly easy. There are basically three methods used: straight bottom fishing, free-lining live bait, and slow trolling. My experiences fishing for grouper in the Keys and the Atlantic side of the state have been exclusively bottom fishing, although anglers in the Gulf seem to also have good success slow trolling.

First of all, don't expect to land one using light or even medium-weight spinning gear. That's a good way to lose a lot of line and even a rod. The fish are too large, live too deep, swim too hard, and make their home in places where there are lots of sharp edges on which to cut your line.

The ideal rig for fishing for grouper is a conventional reel in the 30- to 50-pound class paired with a medium-heavy boat rod. Fifty pound test monofilament line attached to a heavier mono leader of 5 to 6 feet in length can handle most grouper you will hook. (Wire leaders are too visible to the fish.)

The usual bait for bottom fishing for grouper is cut bait, either squid or small fish. Some captains prefer to use a small live bait.

The challenge is not so much how you hook a grouper as it is to how you land it. There is a popular saying "Grouper are easy to hook, but hard to catch." Once the fish has grabbed your bait it will immediately try to head back to its hole or hiding place. Your goal is to as quickly as possible reel in enough line as to prevent that. It is a battle between the fisherman and the fish and the fish usually wins.

If the fish gets back into its hole you have two choices: (1) break off the line and start over again, or (2) give the fish plenty of loose line and wait for the fish to relax and swim out from its hiding place. This may take a while, and may not work at all, but with today's prices for hooks, leader, and weights it's worth a try.

As I have mentioned earlier, fishing on your own can be successful and rewarding, but it can also be disappointing. If you are serious about catching these large and delicious-eating fish, take a charter. The captain fishes almost every day of the year and knows where these big boys are hanging out, what baits will most-likely entice them, and what rigs and techniques will be most successful in landing them.

# The Sex Life
# of a Grouper

Many of you may elect to just skip this page, but those of you who have an inquiring mind and an interest in totally useless information perhaps will want to read on. You never know, you might end up on *Jeopardy* one day.

First of all, groupers are mostly *monandric protogynous hermaphrodites*. For those of you who are not already well-versed in the sex life of fish, that means that female grouper have only one grouper husband at a time (mondandric), and while having been born a female, at some point in their life they will change their sex to male (protogynous). That must be a relatively easy thing to do since the grouper is born with both male and female reproductive organs (hermaphrodite).

If that didn't build your interest, how about this: groupers often *pair spawn*, which enables large males to competitively exclude smaller males from reproducing. If you do not know what pair spawning is all about, Ethan has a video on *YouTube* showing his wild imbellis pair spawning. (I skipped watching that and you might want to also. I'll also skip writing about grouper testes size.) But it may interest you to know that the largest male grouper often control harems containing 3 to 15 females.

How did I learn all this fascinating information? Mostly from reading a scientific paper titled: *A New Version of the Size-Advantage Hypothesis for Sex Change in Grouper, Incorporating Sperm Size-Fecundity Skew.* Can you believe there are actually people studying such things and that some-one or some organization is actually paying them to do it? But if all this helps produce more grouper to satisfy the anglers and the fish-eaters I suppose it's all right. However, my guess is that the grouper might do just fine on their own if they didn't have all these folks swimming around trying to measure the size of their testes and record how many times they group spawned (fish orgies, very popular back in the sixties), as opposed to pair spawned.

*A single grouper can produce over a million offspring. God knows how many the married ones can churn out.*

# Kayaking and Eco-tours

A kayak is ideal for fishing, exercise or just a day of fun in the sun. There are a number of places to rent a kayak on the island and I encourage you to check them all to find just the right match for your needs and skill level. But there is one company that seems to have covered it all.

***Almost Heaven Kayak Adventures*** is the largest kayaking and eco-touring company in the AMI, Bradenton/Sarasota area. They provide a wide range of kayak eco tours throughout the area, including AMI, Myakka River, Longboat Key, Egmont Key and others.

The various tours have varying requirements of kayaking skill levels. For example, the *Anna Maria Island tour* is limited to intermediate or higher skill levels due to the possibility of swift currents and rapidly changing weather conditions.

The eco tour that seems most ideal for families and all skill levels is the *Lido Mangrove Tunnels tour*. The 2½ hour tour is great for beginners as well as advanced kayakers. It launches from the north entrance to Lido Park on Lido Key, just a mile or so past St. Armand's Circle on Longboat Key, just south of AMI. The tour will take you through mangrove tunnels and Sarasota Bay, which is frequented by manatees and dolphins. No alligators on this tour, but you can see them on the *Myakka River tour*.

The Anna Maria Island tour is ideal for intermediate kayakers who are looking for an adventure in and around Anna Maria Island. You can explore shallow bayside tidal flats or the Gulf of Mexico. During the bayside tour you will travel by the two bayside piers, Rod-n-Reel and Anna Maria Island City Pier, with the backdrop of the Skyway Bridge and Egmont Key off to the north. On the Gulf of Mexico the tour travels along the calm Gulf waters while viewing the sandy white beaches of AMI. The launch point will be determined by which tour you choose at the time of making reservations. Each tour lasts 2 ½ hours.

The company also offer kayaks for one or three-day rentals. They also have weekly rates. They have kayaks of all shapes and sizes to fit all body types. And free pickup and delivery service is included.

For additional information or reservations call 941-504-6296. There is no better way to experience Florida's untouched beauty, exquisite landscapes and unspoiled waterways than by kayaking.

I asked our friend *Bill Wait*, who has kayaked these waters many a time, if I had only a limited time for a kayak tour of the waters around this area where would he suggest I go. His answer was to put in on the west end of the Manatee Causeway and paddle the bay side of Anna Maria Island. Lots of protected water and interesting things to see.

# Sailing and Cruising

If you are not into fishing or snorkeling or scuba diving, a great way to experience the waters around Anna Maria Island is to take a cruise or sailing charter. There are several different types of experiences on a variety of vessels leaving from the several marinas in the area. A couple that we especially like include:

*Kathleen D Sailing Charters:* Their three boats are USCG certified and inspected; their captains are fully licensed. Their two 41' catamarans take up to six passengers on a variety of sails. There is a twice daily dolphin-watch sail; a 5-hour trip to Egmont Key that includes sailing, shelling, snorkeling and exploring. All equipment and lunch is included. The cats also make nightly 2-hour sunset cruises. Both boats have bathrooms and galleys. One sails from the Keyes Marina and the other from the Mainsail Marina, both in Holmes Beach. They also have a 50' motor launch that carries up to 49 passengers. It also departs from the Mainsail Marina. Stop by one of the marinas for additional information and reservations or call 941-870-4349.

*Gnarley Mangrove Coastal Cruises:* USCG licensed Captain Don Meilner and his 23' Beachcat specializes in personalized small-group charters. It's like having you own boat and a personal captain and host to take you wherever you want. Set up an early morning cruise to go bird watching; go dolphin sighting and shelling on remote shores; take a sunset cruise and stop by your favorite waterfront restaurant. Go for a half-day or all day, or for just the two-hour minimum. Call Captain Don at 941-778-3875 to arrange your personal cruise.

*Fun and Sun Tours:* Relax and enjoy the typical narrated boat tour. The 90-minute tour will explore the Intracoastal Waterway and Sarasota and Palma Sola Bay. The boat is berthed in downtown Bradenton but will pick you up at the City Pier on Bridge Street in Bradenton Beach. Tours are available Tuesday thru Sunday and leave at 10 am, noon and 2 pm. On Friday and Saturday nights they offer a Sunset Cruise. Call 941-465-8624 for additional information and reservations.

# Scuba Diving

Artificial reefs and wrecks abound along the Gulf coast. Several coastal communities have enacted aggressive artificial reef programs, sinking everything from boxcars, to demolished bridge sections, decommissioned military vehicles and ships and barges of every size.

There are more than eighty artificial reef systems off of Manatee, Sarasota, Lee and Charlotte counties to the south and many more to the north off of St. Petersburg and Clearwater. In these locations you can make dives that range from shallow dives to deep dives of over 110 feet.

Unfortunately there is not a dive boat operating out of AMI that I feel comfortable at this time recommending. But, there are excellent operations both to the north and to the south of the island. And, of course, experienced divers can dive from their own or rental boats, which are available.

There are four excellent diving wrecks in Manatee County:

***Fin Barge:*** Latitude 2729.715, Longitude 8305.695. Located in 85 feet of water about 25 miles off Long Boat Pass (at the south end of AMI), the 300' wreck rests upside down. The bow section has an open door where divers can peek inside. Divers need to keep their eyes open for the large population of Goliath groupers (Jewfish) that inhabit the wreck. If you see one keep your distance; some of them are aggressive and large enough to suck you in right along with a mouthful of bait fish. (Just kidding, but be careful.)

***Doc's Barge:*** Latitude 2730.395, Longitude 8259.137. Resting upside down in 60 foot of water, 18 miles out from Long Boat Pass. The hull is broken in the middle and the structure forms great cover for large fish. A great place to fish, spearfish, or dive. Always loaded with bait fish, snapper, grouper and amberjack.

***Mexican Pride:*** Latitude 2731.375, Longitude 8237.6. A 200-foot bulk cargo ship that is broken in half and covered with marine life. Known for its huge amberjack, Goliath grouper and cobia.

***South Jack Wreck (Nohab):*** Latitude 2726.45, Longitude 8259.85. Originally a 142' X 23' steel-hulled luxury pleasure ship, its flattened remains are now scattered over a 150' X 50' area located 15 nautical miles off of Egmont Key. Its engines, boiler and twin shafts remain. A site popular for amberjack fishing, hence its nickname South Jack Wreck.

A dive operator that has received very high marks is ***Florida West Scuba and Charters***, in Venice, FL, just south of Sarasota and about an hour's drive from Anna Maria Island. They are a full service dive shop with sales, rentals, repairs, instructions and charters. Their vessel is a 31' diesel-powered Island Hopper certified by the Coast Guard to carry 12 divers or 18 passengers.

One of their more interesting dives, and one that you will not make anywhere else, is their *Shark Tooth Dive*. Venice is known as the "Shark Tooth Capital of the World". The waters off of Venice were prehistoric feeding grounds for the ancient giant shark, *Carcharocles Megalodon*. On one of their specialized dive charters you can find giant shark teeth, manatee bones, whale bones, prehistoric horse bones or other unique fossils. All fossil dives are in 25-35 foot depth range allowing for plenty of bottom time.

Located at 509 C. North Tamiami Trail, off US 41, in Venice. Call 941-483-3483 for a description of upcoming dives and additional information.

To the north of Anna Maria Island, in St. Petersburg, we've heard some good thing about ***Jim's Dive Shop***. Call and see what you think, 727-393-3483.

A little further away (1:15 drive from AMI), in Clearwater, is ***Tanks-A-Lot Dive Charter***. Two impressive credentials: 15 years in the same location and the only US Coast Guard inspected and certified dive boat in the Tampa Bay area.

Two of the more interesting dive spots to the north of Anna Maria Island are:

***USCGC Blackthorn:*** Latitude 2752.57, Longitude 8311.28. In 1980 the 935-ton cutter collided with a tanker at the mouth of Tampa Bay and sank when the tankers anchor crashed through the hull of the cutter. The wreck was subsequently raised and carried out into the Gulf and sunk in 80' of water. Now broken in two, it is covered with marine life with lots of fish.

***Sheridan:*** Latitude 2752.578, Longitude 8311.15. The rusting hulk of a 383-ton, 180-foot tug boat lies about 575 feet from the Blackthorn. Many consider this to be the finest wreck dive in the AMI area. It lies upright and fully intact in 75-80 feet of water. The top of the wreck can be reached at 40 feet. Home to several Goliath grouper and barracuda; amberjack, crevalle jack, snapper, trigger fish and an occasional shark visit the reef site. Experienced wreck divers will enjoy exploring the open compartments. A great site to take photographs of the large grouper. Just don't get too close.

# Snorkeling

With all the miles of shoreline you can always snorkel along the beach on AMI, but you will not see as much sea life as you would snorkeling above a reef or a wreck.

There is a wreck off of Bradenton Beach that is frequented by divers and snorkelers because of its easy shore access. The Regina (Latitude 2728.135, Longitude 8242.14), a barge carrying sugar, sunk during a storm in 1940. Located in about twenty-feet of water and about 200 feet off of Cortez Beach, near 7th Street, the site is marked with a buoy. Best time to snorkel or dive the wreck would be on a sunny day following several days of calm water and at a slack tide.

The best snorkeling in the area is off Egmont Key, but you will need a boat to get there. The key is a Florida State Park (pg. 111) and is located just a few miles north of Anna Maria Island at the mouth of Tampa Bay.

You will see lots of marine life snorkeling over the sunken ruins of Old Fort Dade. The ruins are an artificial habitat for trout, grouper, sheepshead and other fish as well as sea horses, sand dollars and starfish.

There are two recommended snorkel boat trips to visit Egmont: one leaves from the Keyes Marina in downtown Holmes Beach; the other involves a drive to St. Petersburg Beach. Each is unique and offers a different experience.

***Kasay Gunter*** is a young, hands-on captain that offers small personalized dolphin, snorkeling and sightseeing excursions in his new 22-foot fast and sturdy Boston Whaler docked at Keyes Marina.

Kasay is a USCG captain certified in CPR and first aid. You'll need to bring a towel and sunscreen, but that's it. Capt.

Kasay provides the snorkel gear for adults and children as well as snacks and water. You are welcome to bring other drinks.

Your choice of experiences includes a 1½-hour dolphin sightseeing tour, a 2-hour dolphin and snorkeling tour, and a 3-hour trip to Egmont Key. All of the tours leave at 9 am. Call Captain Kasay at 941-201-8429 or 941-778-1977 for more information and reservations.

The second option is aboard the brand new *Calypso Cat,* a 45-foot catamaran operating out of Magnuson Marina Cove Resort in St. Petersburg. It will involve an hour's drive to get there, but you will have the opportunity to drive across the magnificent Sunshine Skyway Bridge (pg. 123) which connects Bradenton to St. Petersburg. Or you can ask folks at the Calypso Cat if you are eligible for their free shuttle service.

The Calypso Cat offers half-day fun excursions to Egmont Key. The first stop will be to snorkel at the sunken ruins of the old fort. Then the catamaran will beach itself on the island and you will have an hour to explore the island, including the nature trails, the old Spanish-American War forts, the old soldier's cemetery and the lighthouse. You will have time to do some more snorkeling as well as some shelling and looking for shark's teeth.

On the way to the key and back to the dock you will be on the lookout for bottlenose dolphin that often swim alongside the boat.

The goal is to provide a fun, affordable and memorable vacation experience that the entire family will enjoy. The captain and the boat are USCG certified and there bathrooms on board. Fins, masks and snorkels will be provided. You'll want to pack your own lunch and beverages, however. Contact **Island Boat Adventures** at 727-871-2628.

# Shelling

The beaches on Anna Maria Island are perfect for shelling and beachcombing in general. Our friends *MJ* and *Ron Bopp* are master shellers (I'm not sure there is such a thing, but if there is, they are one). Ron has won so many awards for his shell displays that they've had to close in their garage to hold them all. The heck with the cars; let's protect those shells!

And protect those shells they do, and encourage others to do the same. In this case by *protecting the shells* they are referring to the live ones. There are State regulations regarding the harvesting of live sea life. Salt water fishing licenses are required to take, or attempt to take, fish, lobsters, crabs and other saltwater organisms. Basically the "rule" is, unless it is a live species that you do not have in your collection, pick it up, look at and examine it, and then carefully deposit it back where you found it. If you do collect a live shell, make sure you only collect one. There are plenty of shells without organisms in them to collect.

From my limited research there is a difference of opinion as to the "best" time to go shelling. Some say right after a high tide; others say just before a low tide. I trust MJ who says the best time is before a low, low tide or immediately after a storm when there have been waves crashing on shore.

Where on Anna Maria Island is the best place to shell? Again a difference of opinion. Some say along the north shore of the island, others say at the south end of the island at Coquina Beach. MJ tells me she and Ron prefer to shell the beach just south of the Manatee Beach area where the *AMI Beach Café* is located. With that many different opinions my guess is that shelling is good everywhere on the island.

Shelling on the bay side of the island is where you will find the most live shells, but again, these are for looking at not collecting. Egmont Key also has loads of shells.

Dozens of varieties of shells will be found on the island beaches but the most abundant are lightening whelk, common olives, moon snails, apples murex and cockles.

This area of the state is also an exceptional area in which to collect fossil shells. I guess you could say that Ron is also a "master fossiler." His fossil shell collections and displays have won numerous awards as well. He presented Dee with a beautiful shadowbox display of nineteen different varieties of fossil shells he found on the island. (The fossil shells were originally dug from a pit is Sarasota County and were being used as paving on the island.) He has dated them as being 1.8 to 5 million years old. More than half of the shells in the collection are of species that are now extinct, including our favorite, a murex shell (chicoreus florianus). The collection proudly hangs on our living room wall. It probably should be displayed in a museum.

Shelling is an adventure that the entire family can enjoy, especially young children and grandmothers. And it's even more fun when they do it together! And it's free.

*No cowboy was ever faster on the draw than a grandmother pulling grand baby pictures up on a smart phone!*

# Other Outdoor Activities

In addition to all of the water sports activities there are a number of other outdoor activities to enjoy while you are on the island.

***ParaSailing***: I guess you could call this a water sport because you do start off from a boat and then end up on a boat, but most of the time you are 500 feet high in the air. You are being towed behind a boat while attached to a parasail wing which is similar to a parachute, soaring above the blue-green waters of the Gulf of Mexico while enjoying a breathtaking bird's eye view of Anna Maria Island and Longboat Key. It is easy, fun, and an experience that few will ever forget. Whee-e-e-e! You can sail alone or with one or two other persons, all seated side-by-side. There are no age restrictions. Some operators offer sunset sails and one even can arrange to have you married while in air. There are several parasailing operators in the AMI area. See the ads in the *AMI Islander* and *The Sun*.

***Horseback Riding in the Surf***: This also could qualify as a water sport, but it is the horse that is in the water, not you. You are on the horse's back. This is something you usually just see in the movies, but you can do it in the bay waters along the Manatee Causeway leading to the island. Imagine the thrill of riding a horse on a beach and then into Palma Sola Bay. You will actually be riding a horse that is swimming. Each ride lasts approximately one hour. You can also signup for lessons on how to *HorseSurf* and *HorseSki*. Usually rides are available twice a day, at low tide to give you the widest possible area on which to ride. Call 941-907-7272 for additional information and reservations. T'aint cheap.

*Golf:* I'm not sure I would come to AMI if I was looking for a golfing vacation, but if you do want to get in a round while the kids are at the beach you will have that opportunity. There is not an 18-hole course on the island and the Key Royale 9-hole course is private, although monthly summer memberships are available. Off-island, however, this is a golfers' Paradise. There are almost fifty courses between the Manatee and Sarasota counties. Everything from interesting par threes to challenging championship eighteen-hole courses. But even more significant is the world-famous IMG Golf Academy located in Bradenton. Professional golfers, like Paula Creamer, as well as future superstars, have trained at the Academy. Half-day, full-day, and three and five-day training programs are available. Call 1-800-872-6425 for more information.

**Tennis:** You can play tennis on the island and many of the local residents play year-round. There are three public courts on 62 Street in Holmes Beach, across from the marina and behind the police station. They are generally available on a first-come, first-served basis. And you can play at night. There is a light switch on the post as you enter the courts. In addition, many of the vacation housing accommodations have their own private courts, as do a number of the condo units that are available for rental. The famous *Nick Bollettieri Tennis and Sports Academy* is located in nearby Bradenton. Many of the international tennis superstars, including *Maria Sharapova*, train there. Call 1-800-872-6425 for information about adult and youth programs.

**Miniature Golf:** Putt-putt-type golf is available on the island for the young and the young at heart. *The Fish Hole Miniature Golf* is located at 115 Bridge Street in Bradenton Beach. It is open 9 to 9 seven days a week. Dad, take the kids for a round. They'll love playing and love being with you as well. It may also be a welcome hour or two break for mom, or she might enjoy playing also.

*Bicycling:* This is one of the most popular forms of transportation and entertainment on the island. There are lots of bike lanes along the major roads and the slow automobile speed limits make traveling on the side streets very safe. And you can take your bike with you on the free trolley. They have bike racks on the front of the vehicle. Two-wheel, tandem, and three-wheel bikes are available for rent at a number of locations on the island.

*Horseshoes:* All are invited to participate in the free horseshoe games played every Wednesday and Saturday mornings at the Anna Maria City Hall horseshoe pits. Warm-ups begin at 8:45 am, followed by random team selection.

*Polo: The Sarasota Polo Club at Lakewood Ranch* is one of the largest clubs in the country, with nine outdoor polo fields. During the season over 600 horses are stabled in and around the club. Matches are open to the public every Sunday between mid-December and early April. Matches begin at 1 pm; gates open at 10 am. The Polo Grounds are located in the town of Lakewood Ranch, just west of I-75 in the southern part of the county. Go to: www.sarasotapolo.com.

*The Pittsburg Pirates and more:* The Pirates hold their spring training camp in Bradenton and the city has a minor league baseball team as well.

The *IMG Academy* in Bradenton is one of the best athletic training environments in the world. Go to: www.imgacademy.com.

There is a world-class *Rowing and Aquatic Sports Center* at Nathan Benderson Park that may be selected as the site for the U.S. Olympic Trails for the 2016 Olympics. Go to www.worldclassrowing.com.

# Beach Yoga

There are a number of good yoga classes on the island, but these four are special: they are actually on the beach and they're free (donations accepted). Forget about bringing a yoga mat; a bed sheet is best to use on the sand. No reservations are needed; just show up.

***Anna Maria Beach:*** Saturdays and Sundays on the beach just north of the *Sandbar Restaurant* (Spring Street). Phone instructor Erin for times: 570-497-7801.

***Manatee Public Beach:*** Tuesdays and Thursdays on the beach just south of the *AMI Beach Café*. Phone instructor Rachel W. for times: 941-405-3377.

***Bradenton Beach:*** Wednesdays, Saturdays and Sunday on the beach on the south side of the *BeachHouse Restaurant,* across from City Hall. For times phone instructor Judy: 941-779-3222; Saturday's instructor is Amy.

***Coquina Beach:*** Two classes on Mondays at 8 am and 9 am. Meet at the main entrance to the beach, near the café and the Long Boat Key Bridge. Rachael E. is the instructor. 941-580-4540.

# Big Cat Habitat and Gulf Coast Sanctuary

*Big Cat Habitat and Gulf Coast Sanctuary* is a non-profit safe haven for big cats, bears, and native and exotic wildlife. Founded by Kay Rosaire, she began rescuing big cats in 1987; she has more than 30-years of experience working with and caring for exotic animals.

She and her son Clayton provide educational training demonstrations using positive reinforcement techniques developed by Kay. Their unique style of gentle handling, praise and treats encourages the natural behaviors of big cats on cue and in a sequence of the trainer's choice. Clayton is one of the few men in the world who can put his head inside a lion's mouth.

There are three large indoor/outdoor housing complexes with adjoining exercise habitats. Each habitat has a swimming pool, toys and palm trees to provide emotional enrichment that maintains optimal mental and physical health of the animals.

The facility is open to the public Wednesday thru Sunday. Gates open at 4:30 pm and close at 7 pm. Educational demonstrations are held each day at 5:30 pm. Before the demonstrations browse and learn about their exotic and endangered Siberian Tigers, Royal Bengal Tigers, African Lions, and rare White Tigers.

During the demonstrations they gently encourage the cats to show off their magnificent natural behaviors. Guests will be enthralled and entertained by these majestic animals as they demonstrate their athletic abilities and unique individual personalities.

Entertaining and informative, every demonstration discusses the importance of habitat preservation in the hopes of saving these amazing creatures from extinction in the wild. Their commitment is for their lifetime, which is more than 20-years – double their normal life span in the wild.

This is a unique opportunity to see the animals in a close encounter of the exotic kind. Every demonstration is thrilling to watch.

Big Cat Habitat offers life-long sanctuary supported by income from the demonstrations and from donations. Donations are tax deductible. The sanctuary is located at 7101 Palmer Blvd, in Sarasota. For additional information and driving instructions phone 941-371-6377.

# Come Out and Play in the Dirt

Our friend *Chris Collins*, the photographer and framer mentioned earlier, recently had a birthday experience to end all birthday experiences: his wife, *Luanne*, told him she had arranged for him to go out and play in the dirt!

Have you ever driven past a construction site and seen the huge earthmoving equipment digging, dumping or pushing the dirt and thought, "*Gee, that looks like fun. I wonder what it would be like to operate one of those giant pieces of equipment?*"

Well, wonder no longer. Now you can drive a bulldozer or operate a giant excavator or test your skills on a skid steel loader. *People at Play* is the only construction playground in the Southeast United States. Located on an undeveloped 21-acre "job site," the Heavy Equipment Experience allows you the opportunity to learn how to operate construction equipment . . . purely for the fun and adrenaline rush!

There are several levels of activity depending on the amount of time and how many pieces of equipment you are interested in operating. The Heavy Equipment Experience operates by appointment only and is available seasonally on most weekends. Phone 941-756-0886 for more information.

"*What did you do on your vacation?*"

"*Well, I just drove a Caterpillar D3 Steel Track-type Bulldozer and operated a 20,000 pound CAT Track Excavator. What did you do on your vacation? Oh, you just played golf, huh.*"

*People at Play* office location: 6029 33ʳᵈ Street East, Bradenton. Open Monday – Friday from 9 am to 4:30 pm. Or email to allsa@comeplayinthedirt.com.

Job Site location: 2450 Tallevast Road, Sarasota.

# Coquina,
# The Beach

Coquina (ko-KEE-nah) Beach, on the extreme southern end of AMI, truly represents an old-style Florida beach. With the tall Australian pine trees lining the beach, it reminds me, in many ways, of Cape Florida, at the end of Key Biscayne, in Miami, before it was nearly blown off the map during Hurricane Andrew in 1992.

How many beaches have you visited recently where there was free parking, lifeguards, grills and picnic tables, restrooms and showers, water fountains, a concession stand, shade trees, and a children's playground to go along with a picturesque wide, white sandy beach? None? That doesn't surprise me. Oh, and I forgot about the boat launch, and the *Coquina BayWalk* at *Leffis Key*, and that you don't need a car to get there; you can ride the free trolley from anywhere else on the island.

Anna Maria Island has its own preserve at Leffis Key. Across the road is the BayWalk , a 0.8 mile series of trails and boardwalks that lead you through unspoiled tidal lagoons to a mangrove shoreline. The observation decks hidden away in the mangroves offer great views of Sarasota Bay. Or, climb to the top of the 26-foot high hill for a view of the bay and the gulf. Open from dawn to dusk, the shell paths and 1,500 feet of boardwalks are suitable for strollers and assisted wheelchairs. And there is no fee.

Coquina Beach, a slice of Paradise, is perfect for families.

# Coquina,
# The Rock

Who would think that a fort made of seashells would last for 27 days under cannon fire? Or, more amazing, would last for over 340 years in spite of repeated enemy attacks, hurricanes, and millions of tourists climbing over it? It's true. Coquina rock forms the walls of the *Castillo de San Marcos*. Built in 1672 by the Spanish, the fort is one of the main historical attractions in St. Augustine, Florida, the first permanent settlement in North America.

Coquina rock began to be formed during the Pleistocene Ice Age, approximately 1.8 million years ago. The end of the Pleistocene Era corresponds with the retreat of the last continental glacier. The Florida landmass was rising from the sea and coquina rock began forming along a portion of Florida's coast and Florida became as we know it today. Marine life flourished in the seas before the Ice Age and, after the receding ice, quickly recovered.

As the resident coquina clam died, the shells accumulated in layers, year after year, century after century, for thousands of years forming submerged deposits several feet thick. As the sea levels dropped, these shell layers were exposed to air and rain. Eventually, the shell became covered with soil, then trees and other vegetation.

Coquina rock is mainly composed of incompletely consolidated sedimentary rock. It is formed of billions of the small clam-like coquinas. Overall composition of most coquina rock is a mixture of coquina, crushed oyster shell, mollusk shell, fragmented coral and fossils, limestone and sand and a little clay.

Coquina rock is quarried or mined and has been used as a building stone for more than three hundred years. It was used in the construction of nearly every Florida plantation and sugar mill. The historic coquina masonry work of Florida is considered exceptional for the quality of its workmanship.

And the stone is still being quarried and sold for use in building today. When first quarried, coquina is fairly soft. This softness makes it very easy to remove from the quarry. In order to be used as a building material, the stone is left out to dry for approximately one to three years, which causes the stone to harden into a useable building material.

The stone has both architectural and structural uses. Large pieces of coquina of unusual shape are sometimes used as landscape decoration. The stone today is sold by truckloads and as individual pieces. A 15-cubic yard truck load sells for about $675., plus delivery. Small individual rocks, under 12 inches, sell for around $2. a piece. Large stones sell for about $50. for a three foot rock, and up to $250. for a five foot stone.

To learn more about this amazing stone or to purchase a truckload or a piece, go to www.coquinarock.com, web site for the *CoquinaRock Company*, with locations in both Ormond Beach and Daytona Beach, Florida.

# Coquina,
# the Seafood

Someone once stated that *"Ounce for ounce there is probably no more delicious seafood than coquina. The problem is getting an ounce of them."*

As a child I remember digging for these tiny clams that burrow into the sand as the tide washes ashore. Families could be seen collecting coquina during the summer months all along the Florida beaches. Back in those days we incorrectly called them periwinkles. Periwinkles are spiral-shaped edible marine snails; coquinas are tiny marine bivalves that are pastel-hued, usually pink, lavender, yellow and silvery white. Some people refer to them as cockles.

You may remember the words of a traditional Irish song:

> *In Dublin's fair city,*
> *Where the girls are so pretty*
> *I first set my eyes on Sweet Molly Malone*
>
> *She wheeled her wheelbarrow*
> *Through streets broad and narrow,*
> *Crying "Cockles and mussels alive, alive, oh."*

Actually, coquinas is a Donax (DOE-aks), which is a small, edible marine bivalve that is found throughout the world. In Florida the species is Donax varibili. The tiny coquina clams are about the size of the fingernail on your little finger, rarely longer than a half inch. That is why it is so difficult to acquire even an ounce of the meat.

The coquina live in colonies just below the surface of the sand  at  the edge of the surf  so  each incoming wave can bring them food. During the summer months they can still be found along the beaches of AMI, but you have to hunt for them.

To harvest coquina I suggest using two people with a small shovel or a large serving spoon, a colander and a bucket. It is easiest to find them just before and after low tide and at a flat area of the beach. You'll want to find an area where the waves gently wash ashore, not where heavy waves crash against the beach.

When a wave comes ashore and recedes you will likely see tiny bumps dotting the sand that then quickly disappear into the sand. The first person should move quickly and scoop up a shovelful of wet sand and place it in the colander. The second person then carefully rinses away the sand in the gulf waters and then dumps the remaining coquina in the bucket which is filled with the salt water. A shovelful of sand can contain dozens of the tiny shells. Those found lying on top of the sand should be left well alone as they are already dead.

*Donax* means "a thing of beauty"; the species name, *variabili* means "changeable", referring to coloration. *Coquina* is Spanish for "tiny shell".

I had planned to include a recipe for Coquina Soup in the last section of the book but have decided that collecting enough coquina to make a decent size pot of soup is not worth the effort. There are so many fun and interesting things to on AMI that spending hours (or days) digging for baby shells seems like a waste of valuable fun time. It will still be a fun activity for the kids, however.

# De Soto National Monument

This National Monument, administered by the US Department of the Interior and the National Park Service, is on the site where most historians agree that Spanish Explorer Hernando De Soto landed with his exposition in May 1539.

It's a great place to visit if you are interested in history; and it's a great place to visit even if you are not interested in history. First of all, admission is free. The visitor's center has a nice small artifact museum and a small theatre where they continuously show a 20-minute film on De Soto's Exposition.

De Soto was in search of gold and traveled through the southeast part of what is now the United States, and westward across the Mississippi River, ending up back at The Gulf of Mexico. But with no gold.

As much a park and a preserve as a Monument site, the park encompasses 26 acres, with 3,000 feet of shore line. Thirty percent of the acreage is mangrove swamp. There is a self-guided nature trail of about a ½ mile in length. You follow a printed map (also free) that leads you to a dozen or so markers where you learn about many of the native flora growing at the site.

If you are into plants you don't want to miss a visit to this place. The visitor's center lists 83 native plants and trees growing at the park and an additional 25 exotic plants and trees.

The richness of the vegetation also provides habitat for many bird species: bald eagles are occasionally seen fishing offshore in the Manatee River; brown pelicans may be viewed all during the year and in winter months are often joined by white pelicans and common loons. Occasionally the endangered wood stork may be seen feeding in the mangroves.

The marine habitat also attracts a variety of gulls, terns, and shorebirds whose species change with the seasons. Snowy, reddish, and great egrets are frequently found along the park's shoreline or feasting on invertebrates in the mangrove forest, as are great blue, little blue, and tri-colored herons. A complete bird list is available at the visitor's center.

There is a wooden walkway around the water (where the Manatee River meets Tampa Bay) and a small beach area where you can wade and cool your feet. If you have your saltwater license you can even fish from the shore or wade into the river and bay to fish. If you do, keep your eyes open for small sting rays that inhabit the area and don't step on one. They won't hurt you unless you do.

Want to experience the park in a different way? From May through late October on Saturdays and Sundays there are FREE ranger-led Kayak tours. They supply all the equipment; you just have to call ahead and make a reservation. 941-792-0458.

The Park grounds are open from dawn to dusk, but the Visitor's Center and parking lot are open from 9 to 5. The parking lot gates get locked at five o'clock. Open daily except on New Year's Day, Thanksgiving and Christmas.

Visiting a National Monument may on the surface not seem like something you'd want to do while on a vacation on an island. Don't be mistaken; a visit to the De Soto Monument and park will be an hour or an afternoon well-spent.

*Driving Instructions:* From AMI, take the Manatee Causeway (SR 64) to the first traffic signal on the mainland (75th Street W.) Turn left on 75th Street, traveling north, for approximately four miles until the road dead-ends at the entrance to the De Soto Park. Distance from AMI: 9 miles.

# Hernando De Soto, Patron Saint of Barbecue Restaurants

It is a little known fact, but Hernando De Soto is the state's Patron Saint of barbecue restaurants.

Yep, when De Soto landed on the shores of what is now the City of Bradenton in 1539, he brought the first herd of pigs to Florida to provide food for his exposition.

A number of the pigs escaped and flourished in the wild. Many of their descendants turned into wild boar and have caused havoc with yards, golf courses, and fields in many parts of the state ever since.

On the positive side is that the descendants from the better side of the pig family that escaped became domesticated and for many years have been providing hams, shoulders, ribs and other parts of their bodies to barbecue restaurants in every part of the state.

*"Thank you, Hernando."*
*"By the way, are you still in your hideaway?"*   Ole!*

*I hate having to explain some of these things, but many of you were probably not around in 1953, when Doris Day sang this hit song *Hernando's Hideaway* in the film *Pajama Game*.

# Visit the Region's Diverse Ecosystems

Manatee County's conservation properties include more than 30,000 acres of natural land which spans the region's diverse ecological community.

Visitors can explore more than ten different properties, viewing a spectrum of habitat that ranges from the salty marshes of the coast to the dry prairie and sandy scrubs of the east. Even better news is that six of the ten properties are within a short distance from Anna Maria Island.

*Robinson Preserve*, one of the larger preserves, has its own write-up but there are other properties worthy of your attention as well. Some of these include the following:

***Emerson Point Preserve:*** This preserve has a special location at the mouth of the Manatee River where it meets Lower Tampa Bay. It is a 365-acre preserve located at the tip of Snead Island in western Palmetto. Visitors can take in the beauty of Florida's wildlife and native plant life communities while exploring both prehistoric and historic sites and wandering the sandy trails through a tropical hammock.

Historical resources include the Portavant Temple Mound, southwest Florida's largest Native American Temple Mound. There are multi-use trails, boardwalks and an observation tower. There are two places to launch a canoe or kayak: one canoe trail meanders through mangrove tunnels until you reach Terra Ceia Bay. The other provides access to the mouth of the Manatee River. Basically open from 9 am until 4 pm although hours vary according to the season.

*Driving directions:* From AMI take the Manatee Caus-

Way into downtown Bradenton. Turn left and take U.S. 301 north over the De Soto Bridge. Turn left onto 10th Street West. Stay on this road, heading toward Snead Island. After crossing the bridge, take the immediate right (across from the Yacht Club). Turn left at the first stop sign and drive west to Emerson Point Preserve. Parking is available. Entrance is free to the public.

**Rye Preserve:** A little bit of a drive from AMI, but this is a wonderful opportunity to experience a slice of old Florida. Rye preserve is a 145 acre property located just northwest of the Lake Manatee Dam. The preserve features nature trails, horseback trails, picnic areas, a playground, and a canoe/kayak launch.

The preserve's trail system leads visitors through four distinctive ecosystems, including sand pine scrub, xeric oak scrub, oak hammocks, and the river community. A variety of interesting creatures can be seen in these areas including the rare gopher tortoise and Florida scrub-jay.

Rye Preserve is home to a piece of Manatee County's early pioneer history. Within the preserve visitors can view the Rye Family Cemetery, the last remaining reminder of the old Rye river community.

Camping is available on a first-come-first-served basis. Camping fees are $20 per night. Otherwise, admission to the preserve is free to visitors. Open sunrise to sunset.

*Driving directions:* From AMI take Manatee Causeway (SR-64) through town and past I-75 heading east. Turn left onto Rye Road and continue north. After crossing Rye Bridge, make an immediate right and drive to the preserve.

**Perico Preserve:** This 176-acre property was originally farmland and the extensive mangrove fringe is currently undergoing restoration. Recently a group of 49 adult  and student  Bay  Guardian  volunteers  with  the Sarasota Bay Estuary Program planted 3,500 Florida native plants at a shore line area of the preserve. The restoration plans include the construction of a lagoon to support seagrass growth and a bird rookery island. During construction, public access is only permitted through sneak peek tours hosted on weekends by Manatee County Natural Resources department. Work is nearing its end and hopefully the preserve will be open by the time you read this book. 11700 Manatee Avenue West (the Causeway). Close enough to AMI to bike there.

**Neal** and **Ungarelli Preserves:** These are two other preserves that are currently undergoing restoration and are expected to be reopened soon. The *Neal Preserve* is the closest to AMI at 12300 Manatee Causeway. *Ungarelli* is also nearby at 4000 Palma Sola Blvd. Both will be worth a visit.

**Jiggs Landing:** For many years Jiggs Landing was a fish camp and boat ramp. Once the county acquired the property they began improving it. Today it is still a perfect place to launch a boat to cruise the Braden River (the ramp is open 24-hours a day), but it has become much, much more. There are picnic areas, boardwalks, a food-drink-bait concession stand, wildlife viewing areas and a nature-themed playground for children.

A new handicap accessible canoe/kayak launch is located at the site. The launch gives paddlers access to the entire Braden River and its freshwater system. And fishermen, this is a perfect place to try your hand at freshwater fishing. Please note, however, that your saltwater license will not work in freshwater. You need a separate freshwater license.

*Driving instructions:* From AMI, take the Manatee Avenue Causeway to the first traffic light on the mainland (75th Street W.); turn right on 75th Street, heading south, and follow it through a number of traffic signals until you reach the roundabout. Take the roundabout to the left exit heading east. This is   SR-70 or 53rd Avenue. Go east to ward I-75. Take a right  on Caruso Road.  Continue  south on Caruso Road to the bend in the road; Jiggs Landing is located at the point where the road turns to the east. The preserve section, which includes the picnic pavilions and boardwalk, is open from sunrise to sunset. There is no cost to enter the preserve.

***Riverview Pointe Preserve:*** This is an 11-acre site located adjacent to the De Soto National Memorial. Although small in acreage, the preserve is home to a variety of wildlife uplands and coastal habitats including the rare scrub ecosystem, oak hammock, and mangrove forest. This location is also home to a thriving gopher tortoise colony.

Riverview Pointe has a rich cultural history. The area claims to be the approximate landing site of the 1539 Hernando De Soto expedition, although the exact location of the landing site is subject to discussion and controversy among historians. They do agree that the exact landing site is close and that's close enough for me.

Recreational activities include; hiking and nature trails, dog-walking, and wildlife viewing. Entrance is free. Open daily, but hours vary. Call 941-745-3727 for times.

***Duette Preserve:*** This is the largest preserve in the Manatee county preserve system. At over 21,000 acres, it is almost entirely contained within the north portion of the Lake Manatee Watershed. The site is located in the area of the county with the highest quality and most productive, deep groundwater Floridian Aquifer. This is the headwaters of the Manatee River. The river, and its chief tributary, the Braden River, serve as the principal sources of water supply for Manatee and Sarasota counties.

There are hiking trails, picnic areas, horseback riding trails, managed fishing and hunting, and picnic areas. The preserve is a long drive from Anna Maria Island, but it is a unique opportunity to see areas that are being restored to a native condition with regular applications of prescribed fire. Replicating historic and repetitive ground cover fire is an important tool used by staff to perpetuate native species, many of which depend on fire for survival and reproduction.

The preserve is open from 8 am until sunset to pedestrian, bicycle and equestrian traffic. Parking for access is available at two different locations: one is at Trail One off Duette Road, the other is at Bear Bay Road.

*Driving Instructions*: From AMI, take SR 64, Manatee Avenue Causeway east to I-75. Continue east on SR 64 until you reach Duette Road (approximately 25 miles). Turn left, heading north. Turn left onto Rawls Road (6 miles from SR 64) and you are at the preserve.

# Robinson Preserve

One of the great treasures of the area. Located just a short way off of the island, in northwest Bradenton, in the Palma Sola area, this almost 500-acre preserve has been transformed from disturbed farmland into amazing coastal and wetland habitats.

A joint-project of a number of state and local agencies, the land has been restored to its natural state. It is another example of where concerned citizens and government agencies have been able to "*turn back the clock*," restoring areas to the way they were "*in the good old days*", recognizing the unique and special values of the coastal lands and their environmental potential.

Originally opened to the public in 2008, over 300,000 visitors a year visit this popular spot. And now plans have been unveiled to add an additional 150 acres to the existing 487. The improvements will include a lake and education center, in addition to more trails and marshlands, including a "canopy walk" through old trees.

The education center will mimic the leafy grace of a treehouse and will include an indoor-outdoor classroom. The lake will incorporate shorebird nesting areas with an assortment of low-level marshes and emergent islands.

But enough about what is coming, let me tell you about the great things that are already here in the preserve:

The preserve is a diverse area of marshlands, open water and nature trails along the Manatee River and Palma Sola Bay. There are 10 acres of uplands with six nature trails.

Some of the trails allow biking and horseback riding. There is a 500- foot boardwalk and an observation tower.

There are picnic areas at various sites throughout the preserve on a first-come-first-served basis. Fishing is available throughout the preserve, subject to Florida Fish and Wildlife regulations.

There are three miles of internal kayaking and canoeing streams. A 5-mile roundtrip adventure would start at the launch and meander through the preserve to Palma Sola Bay and back.

A variety of birds and wildlife can be seen throughout the preserve in the restored ecosystems. There is even an area where you can bring your dog; just three simple rules: use a leash, scoop that poop, and stay on the trails.

*Driving Instructions:* There is a backdoor off of the Manatee Causeway, but the best way to experience the preserve is to come through the front door, where the visitor's center is located. From the island use the Manatee Causeway and once you reach the mainland turn left at the first traffic light (75th Street West). Go north on 75th Street and drive to 17th Avenue Northwest. Turn left and continue to the end of the street. Robinson Preserve is located on the corner of 17th Avenue Northwest and 99th Street West. Usually open daily from 9 am until 4 pm, but additional times vary according to the season.

# Egmont Key
# State Park

Accessible only by private boat, Egmont Key is an island located just a few miles north of Anna Maria Island at the mouth of Tampa Bay. Although the park is primarily a National Wildlife Preserve, it is unique in many ways.

One is its cultural history: during the 19th century, the island served as an internment site for captured Seminoles on their way to reservations in the Midwest at the end of the Third Seminole War. The island was later occupied by troops from both sides during the Civil War and was a quarantine site for troops returning from Cuba during the Spanish American War. The fortifications on the island were built as coastal defense during that war. Fort Dade was built on the island and remained active until 1923. The fort, now offshore and underwater, is a favorite snorkeling site.

The lighthouse that stands on the island was built in 1858 and is still maintained by the Coast Guard as an aid to navigation for ships and recreational boaters.

The island offers a wide variety of animals from loggerhead sea turtles and gopher tortoises to numerous nesting shore birds and migratory birds. The southern end of the island is a bird sanctuary, the site for twice-a-year Audubon migratory bird counts.

After touring the historic sites and trails, visitors can enjoy swimming, fishing, wildlife viewing, shelling and picnicking. The island is about a mile and a half long and less than a half-mile wide.  If you arrive in your own boat or one that you have rented, you can simply anchor at the edge of the beach and wade ashore. In addition to the snorkeling tours to Egmont Key that are described in other pages of the book, several of the other  more popular ways to get to the key are included in the essay on *Sailing and Cruising*.

Be sure and note, however, that there is no food, water or restrooms on the island. Unless you arrive by a boat that includes food and drink you will need to bring your own and use the restroom before you arrive. No alcoholic beverages are allowed in any state or county park.

# Felts Audubon Preserve

Of all the wonderful places to see and things to do on and around Anna Maria Island, a visit to the Felts Audubon Preserve is near the top of the list. A work in progress, the preserve is maintained and operated by the *Manatee County Audubon Society*.

In 2002, Otis and Anita Felts left this 27-acre parcel to the Society when they passed away. Their dream was to keep the land natural and to support the wildlife, especially birds in their habitat. Their dream has been fulfilled and expanded to including using the property as an environmental educational center for people of all ages.

While through a variety of innovative ways to educate the public on environmental issues, the land is mainly being used by an abundance of different animals including many migratory birds. To-date the Society had documented 160 avian species and 33 butterfly species at the preserve. A complete bird list is available at the preserve or may be downloaded from the web site (www.ManateeAudubon.org).

There is no charge to enter the preserve, but donations are encouraged and greatly appreciated. Improvements made at Felts Audubon Preserve by donations to the Manatee County Audubon Society have included: new trails and park benches; an elevated walkway; a bird blind for comfortable wildlife observation and excellent bird, butterfly and wildlife photography; a butterfly garden; wildflower meadows to attract a wider variety of wildlife, especially migratory and nesting birds and colorful butterflies; and more.

Felts Audubon Preserve is open to the public daily from dawn until dusk. On the first Saturday of the month from November through April there are free Guided Nature Walks. The walks last about 90 minutes. Your visit to the preserve will be most enjoyable if you bring binoculars, a camera, field guides, hat, water, insect repellant and sunscreen.

To reach the preserve, which is located at 4600 24th Avenue East, in Palmetto, take US 41 from downtown Bradenton across the De Soto Bridge and through downtown Palmetto. Turn right on Experimental Farm Road (49th St. East). Drive 1.1 mile, turn right onto 24th Avenue East and drive 0.2 miles to the preserve. Park on the street and use the walk-in entrance next to the main gate.

If you enjoy the preserve you can show your appreciation by making a contribution to the Manatee County Audubon Society or by becoming a member of the Society. Annual membership is only $20 per year per household. Or, consider making a donation in memory of loved ones or to honor someone for a special occasion.

# Bradenton Riverwalk

Earlier in the book I wrote of AMI being "in the middle of nowhere and the center of everything." With so much to enjoy and do without ever leaving the island, except maybe on a boat, I hesitate to include too much about the "center of everything". But there are a couple of things off-island that are just too interesting or too enjoyable to not mention.

One is the *Bradenton Riverwalk*. Opened in October 2012, this 1.5 mile area along the Manatee River offers something for all ages. Whether in a stroller or in a walker or wheel chair, or anything in between, there is something to interest you, soothe you, energize or excite you. It's in downtown Bradenton and an easy drive from the island.

And you can visit by boat. There is a 350-foot dock at the west end of the park where boaters can tie-up for the day while they enjoy the park. No overnights, however.

If you are into that "being boring" that I wrote about earlier, there is a *Great Lawn* on which to do it, a spacious grass area where you can hang out and unwind, read a book or just gaze at the river. This is also a great area for picnicking, or tossing a Frisbee or participating in a scheduled exercise class.

The *Botanical Walk* showcases the area's plants and flowers and has a *Butterfly Garden*. About a dozen adults from Community Haven for Adults and Children with Disabilities, Inc. helped grow and plant native plants at the garden.

The 400-seat *Mosaic Amphitheatre* is a venue for live entertainment such as plays, concerts, school performances, and other community events.

With its colorful splash fountain and playgrounds the *Family Fun Zone* is one of the most popular areas in the park.

There are two playgrounds, one for children up to the age of five and one for children ages 6-12. And there is a nice adjoining area where parents can relax and still be able to keep their eyes on their children. The *Splash Pad* is an interactive water fountain for children and the young at heart to cool off on hot summer days.

If you've caught your limit at the three piers on AMI, try your luck on the 300-foot long *Fishing Pier*. This area of the Manatee River, which empties into Tampa Bay, is a haven for redfish, trout and snook.

How about enjoying an *Outdoor Living Room*. These peaceful shaded areas are where visitors can sit back and relax and enjoy the river view in comfortable lounge chairs and benches.

The *Flex Lawn* is designed for wellness classes such as yoga and tai chi, and for just relaxing with friends and family. It is a perfect spot to "cool off" after a run across the De Soto Bridge and back.

The *Tidal Discovery Zone* offers close-up observation of the ecosystem along the river's edge. And the discovery marsh changes between low and high tide. Programs are held in this area to explore the ever-changing interaction between land, water, plants, animals and people.

*Regatta Plaza* is the perfect spot for drum circles, kite flying and special events. Visitors can view boat races and other water-based events that are an exciting part of downtown festivities.

A *Kayak and Canoe Launch* is available for those who want to start or end an exploration of the Manatee River.

There are two *Beach Volleyball Courts*. Kick off your shoes and join a pick-up game or sign up for a tournament.

*Skateboard Park*. Already an award winner, the course overlooks the Manatee River and is below the De Soto Bridge. Named one of the very best and most-challenging skateboard courses in the area, the designers of Riverwalk thoughtfully located the course near the entrance to the Emergency Room of Manatee Memorial Hospital. Enough said about skateboarding.

There are two memorials in Riverwalk: a *Veterans Memorial* to honor the men and women who have served our country, and a *First Responders Memorial* honoring the Manatee County men and women who have died in the line of duty.

Riverwalk runs from the Green Bridge (9th Street E./US-Business 41) past and under the De Soto Bridge (US 41-301) to the Manatee Memorial Hospital area on the east. Admission is free. There is ample public parking. The park abuts Old Main Street in downtown Bradenton with its interesting shops and restaurants. The park is also close to the cultural history museum, planetarium, manatee aquarium, and performing arts center.

# Mixon Fruit Farms and Wildlife Refuge

An enjoyable and different way to spend a morning or an afternoon is to visit the *Mixon Fruit Farms*. But it is so, so much more than just a fruit farm.

The Mixon family has been growing citrus in Manatee County for more than 75 years. It started in 1939 with 20 acres and a mom and pop roadside stand. Today the company has grown to more than 350 acres of citrus groves with a 14,000 square foot processing plant and gift shop. Throughout all these years and all this growth the business has remained true to its family roots. Co-owner Janet Mixon says, *"We're not just a fruit stand anymore, but we're still a family business."*

Not just a fruit stand indeed! The 350 acres sit on what used to be a sugarcane plantation in the 1800s. A visit to Mixon's is an opportunity to learn about Florida's history and cultural heritage, citrus origins, growth and industry. You will see old and new farm equipment in a working citrus grove. In season (November through early May), they'll treat you to a free cup of fresh squeezed orange or grapefruit juice and you can sample the many varieties of seasonal citrus. If you visit during the week, you can also take a self-guided tour of the packinghouse and juice processing facility and see employees processing fruit, sorting for quality control and sending fruit to be juiced.

A highlight of your visit will be the *Orange Blossom Express Tram Tour.* It is an experience the entire family will enjoy. The tram will travel past the Children's Magical Maze, Wedding Pavilion, Gazebo, and Wetlands Pond with a stop at the Wildlife Rescue.

The Mixons share a portion of their citrus grove with *Wildlife Inc.* for a **Florida Wildlife Care and Education Center**. They provide much needed land and shelter for orphaned and injured birds, animals, and reptiles. Their mission is to rehabilitate Florida wildlife for release back into the wild, and to promote education, appreciation, and respect for wildlife. The animals kept on the Mixon property often have been injured or were found living in inappropriate circumstances.

Cages are built in the grove next to the orange trees. Tram visitors are invited to come and visit and meet the animals up close. Bring your camera to preserve these special moments. You're sure to leave inspired by the beauty of these creatures.

The animals and birds come and go as they are treated and rehabilitated, but on any given day you may see raccoons, a feral pig, white-tailed deer, a Burmese python, iguanas, great horned and screech owls, tortoises, and more.

At its animal hospital on Anna Maria Island, Wildlife, Inc. treats about 6,000 cases of injured animals a year.

The tram tours leave at 11 am and 1 pm, Monday through Saturday, weather permitting, and last for about one hour. Tours are $10 for adults and $5 for children 3-10. Children under 3 are free.

Before or after the tour you will want to visit the Gazebo and Koi Pond. Koi, the amazing ornamental fish, are members of the carp family. Koi varieties are distinguished by coloration and patterning. Some of the major colors are red, white, black, blue, yellow and cream. Carp were first bred for color mutations in China more than a thousand years ago. You will have the opportunity to feed the Koi while you are at the pond.

Finally you will not want to miss a stop at the large gift shop and café. *FloridaCulture* magazine described the gift shop best when they wrote: *It is reminiscent of* Cracker Barrel *meets Amish country meets a roadside fruit stand.*

You'll discover some of Florida's finest treats, such as homemade jellies, marmalades and salad dressings all made using fruit from their groves. You are also invited to sample a selection of Florida wines, some of which are made from Mixon oranges. You'll also find gifts for every occasion.

To complete your visit you might want to stay for lunch at the Groveside Café where a variety of sandwiches, soups and salads are offered at reasonable prices.

The Groveside Market and Gift Shop is open from 10 am to 3 pm; the café is open from 8:30 am to 3 pm; the Tram Tours and Wildlife Preserve are at 11 am and 1 pm. All facilities are open Monday through Saturday. Everything is closed on Sunday.

# Sunshine Skyway Bridge

If you traveled to Anna Maria Island by first flying into either the Tampa or the St. Pete/Clearwater airport then after leaving you drove across Tampa Bay on the Sunshine Skyway Bridge. This cable-stayed main span has a total length of 21,877 feet, or 4.1 miles. It has a vertical clearance of 191 feet above the 1,200-foot wide shipping channel.

The bridge is a popular tourist attraction and a favorite among AMI residents and visitors year in and year out. It connects Manatee County (Bradenton and AMI) to Pinellas County (St. Petersburg), passing through Hillsboro County (Tampa) waters. A great place to view the bridge, especially at night, is from the Anna Maria City Pier at the end of Pine Street.

The bridge has a colorful and tragic history: the original Sunshine Skyway was a two-lane cantilever bridge that was opened to traffic in 1954. It was so popular that a similar structure was built parallel and west of it in 1969 to make it a four-lane bridge and bring it to Interstate standards. Opening of the new span in 1971 allowed the original span to be used for northbound traffic and the new one for southbound traffic.

The new span fulfilled its purpose until in the morning of May 9, 1980, when the freighter MV *Summit Venture* collided with a bridge support column during a blinding thunderstorm, sending over 1,200 feet of the bridge plummeting into Tampa Bay. The collision caused six cars, a truck, and a Greyhound bus to fall 150 feet into the water, killing 35 people.

After the Skyway disaster the question was whether to repair the existing bridge or build a new one. Either way, two-way traffic could be maintained on the 1954 span while work was being done. The decision was made to replace the old bridge with a totally new cable-stayed bridge modeled after a bridge in France. The primary factor in the decision was that repairing the broken sections of the old bridge would not have improved shipping conditions.

The new bridge's main span is fifty-percent wider than the old bridge. The support columns (piers) of the main span and the approaches for ¼ mile in either direction are surrounded by large concrete barriers that can protect the bridge from collisions with ships larger than the *Summit Venture*. Today passing under the bridge are tankers, container ships, and the largest of cruise ships.

The main spans of the old bridges were demolished in 1993, but the approaches for both old spans were converted into what are today the world's longest fishing piers: the *Skyway Fishing Pier State Park*. Anglers love to be able to park their car or camper right next to their favorite fishing spot. Access to the piers is located on both the north and the south approaches to the Skyway Bridge. Common catches from the piers include snapper, sheepshead, grouper, Spanish and king mackerel, pompano, snook and more. The piers are lighted at night so that anglers can see to rig a line, bait a hook, and, more importantly, unhook their catch. The lights also attracts many species of fish that would not normally be looking for food at night.

The Sunshine Skyway Bridge is now a part of I-275 (and also US 19). The fishing piers are open 24 hours a day year-round.

# Yer darn tootin',
# I like Fig Newtons

Would it surprise you to know that the man who created the original *Fig Newton*® recipe back in 1891 was also one of the original developers of Anna Maria Island and built the island's first house of worship? It surprised me.

*Charles Roser*, a Philadelphia baker and fig-lover developed the soft cookie filled with fig jam. He sold the recipe to the Kennedy Biscuit Works in Massachusetts which later became Nabisco.

Some credit Roser with also inventing and patenting the machine that made mass-production of Fig Newtons possible but that is not true. The machine was invented by *James Henry Mitchell*. The machine worked like a funnel within a funnel; the inside funnel supplied the jam, while the outside funnel pumped out the dough. This produced an endless length of filled cookie that was then cut into small pieces. The Kennedy Biscuit Works used Mitchell's invention to mass-produce the first Fig Newton cookies.

There is another rumor that Mitchell, the funnel machine inventor, named the cookies after that great physicist Sir Isaac Newton, but that is also just a rumor. The Kennedy Biscuit company had a tradition of naming their cookies and crackers after the surrounding towns near Boston. The cookie was named after the Massachusetts town of Newton. Originally just called the "Newton," the "Fig" was added later after the cookies began receiving good reviews.

Today the Fig Newton is Nabisco's third-largest selling cookie in their product line, with sales exceeding one billion bars a year.

In addition to the original filling, Nabisco now makes several varieties of Newtons, including Strawberry, Raspberry, and Mixed Berry. The Fig Newton also comes in both 100% whole grain and fat-free varieties. They also have recently introduced *Newtons Fruit Thins,* crispy cookies made with real fruit. They come in several flavors. We especially like the lemon crisps.

The story about when Charles Roser, the baker, ended up on Anna Maria Island is covered in one of the historical essays elsewhere in the book.

And, in the recipe section of the book look for *Rachael Ray's* recipe for how to use these delicious fig bars in a Sundae!

# How about some OJ with your Fig Newton?

*Tropicana Orange Juice®,* that is. In addition to a connection with Fig Newtons®, AMI (Bradenton, actually) has an even stronger connection with Tropicana. The company was founded here in 1947 and today daily more than a million gallons of Tropicana Orange Juice are squeezed, bottled and shipped across the country from its plant in Bradenton.

Anthony Rossi, was born in 1900 in Italy. When he was 21-years old he immigrated to New York. He left Italy with the equivalent of a high school education and a reported $30. in his pocket. His is a true American success story. After driving a taxi in New York City and working as a grocer, he moved to Virginia and farmed. He moved again and continued his farming in Florida in 1940. He later tried his hand at running a restaurant. In 1947, he moved to Palmetto, FL and started a company packing and shipping gift boxes of sectioned fruit to New York.

As a natural extension of his product line he began producing frozen concentrated orange juice. The juice business grew so rapidly that he discontinued the production of the fruit boxes in 1952 and concentrated on the juice business (pun intended). The rest is history. Tropicana is the largest selling brand of orange juice sold in the U.S.

Rossi sold Tropicana to Beatrice Foods in 1978 and retired. After subsequent ownership by The Seagram Co., and the Dole Food Company, Tropicana was acquired by PepsiCo in 1998, which combined it with their Dole brands for marketing purposes. Year in and year out, Tropicana buys more Florida oranges than anybody, some 11 billion oranges a year, about one-fourth of the entire Florida crop of oranges.

Mr. Rossi died in 1993. He had been inducted into the *Florida Agriculture Hall of Fame* in 1987.

# Indoor Activities
# and Attractions

Had enough fun in the sun for the day? There are lots of things to do inside, in the air conditioning. Beyond the obvious (you know, reading a book or watching TV or taking a nap), how about going:

**Bowling:** There are not bowling lanes on the island, but on nearby Cortez Road across the Cortez Bridge are the completely renovated AMF Lanes. In addition to the 64-lanes, there is a large bar area with two flat-screen TVs, a 96-inch projection TV, pool tables and dart boards. Overall a very nice facility. Phone 941-758-8838 to check for lane availability and make reservations. Located at 4208 Cortez Road, they are open until midnight most evenings.

**Ice and Sports Complex:** A state-of-the-art 115,000 sq. ft. "igloo-like" facility offering recreational, entertainment and training activities on the ice. Many Olympic figure skaters train here during the off season. Located off I-75, exit 224 in the town of Ellenton. Go to: www.ellentonice.com.

**The Florida Maritime Museum.** Many of the year-round residents have not yet visited this interesting museum housed in a restored schoolhouse built in the early 1900s. Here you will find displays that tell the story of the development of the fishing village Cortez, established in the 1880s. There are ship models, historic boats, pieces from the almost forgotten past and natural history specimens. Located on the grounds of the Cortez Nature Preserve at 4415 119th Street in Cortez. Street West, in Cortez. The museum is open Tuesday thru Saturday from 9 am to 4 pm and is closed most holidays. Oh, and un-expected to be found in a Maritime Museum, there is a butterfly garden. For additional information phone 941-708-6120.

***Sarasota Classic Car Museum*** is recognized as the second oldest continuously operating antique car museum in America. Featuring over 75 automobiles including rare one-of-a-kind, exotic, antique, European and American classics. *Back to the Future* movie fans will want to come see the DeLorean. *Beatle* fans will want to come see Paul McCartney's beloved Mini Cooper and John Lennon's 1965 Mercedes Benz. *Circus* fans will want to come see John and Mable Ringling's collection of Rolls Royces. *Drag Racing* fans will want to come see Don Garlit's dragster Number Two. And many, many more great cars! 5500 N. Tamiami Trail, Sarasota, just across the Manatee County line at the northeast corner of US 41 and University Parkway. Open daily except Christmas 9 am to 6 pm.

***Florida Railroad Museum*** is a truly unique museum experience: you "ride the exhibits!" The museum is open Wednesday thru Sunday from 10 am to 4 pm, year-round. Diesel train excursions operate on Saturdays and Sundays only, departing at 11 am and 2 pm. Special events are scheduled throughout the year featuring themed train rides. Have you ever dreamed of running your own train? The museum has a program that gives you hands-on training in the operation of the locomotive and then lets you take control of the locomotive for an hour. You probably get to blow the whistle too! How about reserving the caboose for you and 15 of your friends? For a flat fee of $200 the caboose is just yours for the entire hour and a half trip. Located 23 miles east of AMI, a few miles past I-75 exit 229. 12210 83 Street E., Parrish, FL 941-776-0906.

# Art Studios
# and Galleries

**The Studio at Gulf and Pine** offers an eclectic display of exhibits, lectures, classes and a place where artists and art devotees can meet and interact. *Rhea Chiles*, former First Lady of Florida, operates the studio. Part of the studio's permanent collection is from the Chiles family's collection of paintings that hung in the governor's office in Tallahassee. Open Tuesday thru Saturday from 1 pm until 5 pm, the studio is located at 10101 Gulf Drive. Telephone 941-778-1906.

**The Artists' Guild of Anna Maria Island** has been an AMI shopping destination for original art and unique gifts for more than 25 years. Artist members of the Guild, a nonprofit arts organization, display their work and take turns staffing the gallery. Popular items include Florida paintings, giclees and photographs by local artists and fine craft gifts. Open 10 to 5 weekdays and 10-4 on Saturday during the season. Summer hours are 10-4 every day. 5414 Marina Drive, at the corner of Marina and Gulf Drives in the Island Shopping Center. Telephone 941-778-6694. When you visit be sure and ask to see *Peggy Potter's* watercolors and *Chris Collins'* photography exhibits.

**Island Gallery West** offers a rich variety of fine art by island and regional artists along with a collection of jewelry, stained glass, fiber art, and pottery. Works of more than 30 artists are on display from 10 to 5 Monday thru Saturday. 5368 Gulf Drive, Holmes Beach, 941-6648. Make sure you ask to see some of *Cecy Richardson's* work; very unusual, very good.

*ArtSpace* is one of the island's newest galleries and is located on the second floor above the Anna Maria Post Office, across from the city pier. It is unique studio/gallery combination where visitors can interact with working artists in their studios. There are also rotating exhibits and you can take a class and purchase art supplies. 101 S. Bay Blvd, Anna Maria. 941-243-3835. Closed for vacation during the month of September. Phone for hours that the studios and exhibits are open.

# South Florida Museum
# Bishops Planetarium
# Parker Manatee Aquarium

Three interesting places, all located together and for a single admission ticket.

**The South Florida Museum** is the largest natural history and cultural museum on Florida's west coast. It houses over 20,000 objects and features exhibits on history, paleontology and archaeology. Included in the collections are decorative arts, textiles, ethnography, minerals, modern shells and more. The first floor contains fossil evidence of Florida's earliest marine and mammal inhabitants. The second floor includes a new medical gallery, the river heritage hall, visible storage galleries and an environmental wing. Exhibits in this wing are designed to educate visitors about Florida's environment incorporating the past, present and future.

**The Bishop Planetarium** is a multi-purpose, all-digital domed theatre boasting one of the most advanced projection systems in the world. It is a remarkable astronomy educational resource, allowing visitors to explore their universe through traditional live star talks and interactive virtual journeys to the far reaches of the cosmos. A favorite planetarium show is the *Ultimate Universe* which takes you on a stunning journey through the cosmos, exploring galaxies, nebulae, and our own solar system. If you could travel at the speed of light it would take 13.7 billion years to complete the trip. The planetarium will have you back home in about a half-hour. The popular children's show is the *Secret of the Cardboard Rocket*. Join two young kids as they speed all the way out to Pluto and back with their rocket ship's navigator, a talking astronomy book.

The ***Parker Manatee Aquarium***, designed to house three adult manatees, holds nearly 60,000 gallons of water, including a medical pool. The aquarium offers both deep and shallow water, allowing the manatees to maintain natural feeding behaviors. An exhibit area within the aquarium helps to educate the public about manatee anatomy and offers above and below water viewing. Manatee Care specialists provide presentations about manatee habitat, nutrition and physiology. Working closely with US Fish and Wildlife and critical care hospitals for manatees, Parker Manatee Aquarium is a second stage rehabilitation facility, providing a temporary home for manatees that will be released back into the wild after having received treatment from an acute care hospital. The Aquarium has housed 27 manatees as part of the rehabilitation program. The facility is also the permanent home to Manatee County's most famous resident and the oldest known manatee in the world, *Snooty*.

Located in downtown Bradenton at 201 10 Street W., the hours of operation vary according to the time of the year. Phone 941-746-4131 for the hours when you plan to visit.

# Florida Manatees and *Snooty*

Manatees are slow-moving marine mammals with large paddle-shaped tails and are an aquatic relative of the elephant. They are grayish brown in color and have thick, wrinkled skin. Unlike blubber, the thick skin does not protect them from very cold water. Rarely do individuals venture into waters that are below 68 degrees Fahrenheit.

Manatees take up residence primarily in Florida's coastal waters during the winter although some migrate as far north as the Carolinas and as far west as Louisiana in the summer.

The average size of an adult manatee is about 1,200 pounds and up to 12 feet in length. Typically females, called cows, are larger than males or bulls, and can weigh up to 3,500 pounds.

Their front flippers help them steer or sometimes crawl through shallow water. Their powerful flat tails help propel them through the water. Well-known for their gentle, slow-moving nature, manatees have been known to body surf or barrel roll when playing.

They only breathe through their nostrils, since while they are underwater their mouths are occupied with eating. A manatee's lungs are 2/3 the length of its body. They are herbivores; they eat marine and freshwater plants. Since manatee fossils have been found from eras as long as 50 million years ago, manatees might be the original vegetarians.

The cows generally give birth to one calf at a time; the gestation period is about one year. Calves are born weighing between 60 and 70 pounds and measuring about 3-4 feet long.

They nurse underwater.

***The Story of Snooty:*** Born on July 21, 1948, at the old Miami Aquarium and Tackle Company, *Snooty* was the first recorded birth of a manatee in captivity. He was moved to Bradenton a year later and since that time has had more than one million visitors.

Snooty is a 9 foot 8 inch male who weighs 1,200 pounds. He has a waist line of 89 inches. He maintains his trim figure by sticking to a diet of mainly salads. His favorite foods are lettuce, carrots, broccoli, bok choy, cabbage and kale. For a treat he enjoys apples and, of course, he takes his vitamins every day.

Even though Snooty is getting along in years he still stays active. He is a participant in the training of staff from the *Mote Marine Laboratory* and *New College* and he is the subject of informative talks given several times daily to visitors of all ages.

He is Manatee County's official mascot and ambassador for manatees and other endangered species. The aquarium's staff helps Snooty "correspond" with students from around the country and the world. These students, in turn, share their knowledge with their classmates.

He loves visitors; come see him while you are visiting the area.

# Mote Marine Laboratory and Aquarium

Marine aquariums are the current rage of the amusement park world. But this is an aquarium experience that is different.

*Mote Aquarium* is part of the *Mote Marine Laboratory*, one of the world's most respected marine research institutes. They have been advancing the science of the sea since 1955. A partial list of current research initiatives include: marine microbiology, ecotoxicology, shark biology and conservation, marine biomedical research, coral reef restoration, and more. *The Sarasota Dolphin Research Program* conducts the world's longest-running study of a dolphin population.

At the aquarium you can explore the secrets of the sea through touch pools, viewable working laboratories, and high-tech interactive exhibits that showcase the world-renowned research of the Mote Marine Laboratory. See sharks, sea turtles and manatees, along with more than 100 other species of marine life. For more information, including the new shark encounter, go to their web site at www.mote.org and click on Aquarium. This will lead you to other programs, including a summer camp program that our granddaughter has attended for the past two summers. She loved it!

The aquarium is located on Long Boat Key, just a dozen or so miles south of AMI. You can take the free AMI trolley and connect at Coquina Beach with the 75 cent Longboat Key Trolley which will take you directly to Mote. Or it is a short drive from the island. Drive down Gulf Drive south across the Long Boat Key Bridge. Keep straight on Gulf of Mexico Drive (the same road; they changed the name.) until you cross a second bridge. Turn left at the traffic light and you are there. It is well marked with signs. Mote is about a mile north of St. Armand's Circle.

***Sea Life Encounter Tour:*** *Sarasota Bay Explorers* at Mote Aquarium offers several types of eco-tours including their renowned Sea Life Encounter Tour. A marine biologist will lead you on this hour and forty-five minute cruise through Sarasota and Roberts Bays. You will observe Florida manatees and resident population of bottlenose dolphins while learning about the ecology, history and folklore of the area. Your guide will lead you on a short nature walk on an uninhabited island where you will have the unique opportunity to view herons, egrets, ibis and pelicans in their nesting habitat. The highlight of the trip is always the collection of a sample of marine life with a trawl net. You'll observe and handle some of the curious residents of Sarasota Bay: puffer fish, sea horses, stone crabs, cow fish to name a few.

For more information on other eco-tours go to their web site at www.sarasotabayexplorers.com/sealife.html. The site will also give you information regarding times of operation, prices and how to make reservations.

# Ringling Museums

This is another off-island experience that you do not want to miss. Whether you are a circus, art or history fan, *The Ringling* has something for everyone in the family.

As with the *Biltmore House* in Asheville, NC, I am not going to write very much about the Ringling; there is just too much to write. Books have been written about it.

Suffice it to say that we try and take every out-of-town visitor there. After flipping through our very large 450-page coffee table book *The Circus: 1870s – 1950s* most of our guests ask if we can go there before they leave.

And that is just the *Circus Museum*. There is also the *Ringling Art Museum* and the *Ca' d' Zan*, the Ringling's dazzling and palatial mansion. All three of which are located on the 66-acre estate located on the shore of Sarasota Bay. It is only about a 45-minute drive from Anna Maria Island. Access to all three venues is covered by a single admission ticket. Open daily 10 am to 5 pm, and to 8 pm on Thursdays.

There is an excellent restaurant in the entrance/reception building and a very nice gift shop. A more casual café is located just outside of the second Circus Museum building. While it is a pleasant walk on the paved walkways there is also a motorized tram to transport you from venue to venue.

Save a day of your vacation just for Ringling. It is truly a treasure and an experience not repeated anywhere else in the world.

Oh, I almost forgot; don't miss a walk through Mrs. Ringling's rose garden.

For additional information go to http://ringling.org.

# Shop, Shop, 'til you drop!

One of the pleasures of vacationing is that there are new and different stores and shops you can visit. And Anna Maria Island has a great number of them. Not your typical touristy souvenir shops you find at many beach communities, where you can buy things you don't need, but quality stores with unique and quality merchandise that you won't find back home or in every department store.

Once again, this list is not all-inclusive; we haven't visited everywhere. We just discovered a jewelry store less than a mile from our home that has some amazing pieces that we have not seen anywhere else.

Shop the ads in our two local (and free) newspapers; many of them contain coupons that will allow you to make a smart buy even smarter.

Here is a listing of a few places that we think you might enjoy shopping:

***Mister Roberts Ladies' and Men's Resort Wear***. They've been on the island for 47 years! S&S Plaza, corner of Gulf Drive and Marina Avenue.

***Irene's Resort Wear.*** Some of the most beautiful clothes on the island. 5308 Marina Drive, Holmes Beach in the Island Shopping Center.

***AMI Outfitters.*** Coastal Gear and Apparel. Where men shop for gear and women shop for men. 505 Pine Avenue, Anna Maria.

***Pink & Navy Boutique.*** An Award-Winning Elite Boutique for women and men. Gift items. 216C Pine Avenue,

Anna Maria.

**Tide and Moon Jewelry.** Featuring the Anna Maria Island Pendant designed and handmade by owner Laura Shely. 314 Pine Avenue. Anna Maria.

**Bridge Street Jewelers.** Island's largest collection of sea life jewelry. 129 Bridge Street, Bradenton Beach.

There are plenty of other interesting shops on the island, especially in the *Historic Bridge Street* area in Bradenton Beach, in *"downtown"* Holmes Beach and all along *Pine Avenue* in Anna Maria. Also try the strip centers along East Bay Drive, between CVS and Walgreen's; lot's of fun stores, including the *Dollar Tree* where you can get a box of three bags of Weaver Microwave Popcorn for a dollar! (We were friends of the Weavers when we lived in Indiana – delicious popcorn.)

A great way to shop on the island is to use the free trolley. You can just pull the buzzer when you see an interesting store, get off, shop, and then catch the next trolley to the next interesting store.

And for those of you who may have gotten "hooked" shopping online: shopping this way you can actually touch the merchandise before you buy it and see the real color, not something that has been distorted in cyberspace. You can even try on the shirt or dress or shorts before you buy them. None of that key punching, waiting for delivery, trying it on to discover that it doesn't fit, repackaging it, mailing it back, etc. You buy something this old fashioned way and you actually get to take the merchandise home with you. Just another part of the wonderful *good old days* on the island!

# Amazingly Beautiful

The jewelry in this small shop is so different, so beautiful, so appropriate for a place like Anna Maria Island, so reasonably priced for the quality of the design and craftsmanship, that my words could never adequately explain it.

If you are ever on Anna Maria Island you MUST go see for yourself. Even if you don't like jewelry, never wear jewelry, or never give jewelry as a gift, you still need to visit **Libby's Island Jewelry and Gifts**. It is like going to a museum of fine art!

I think the secret to their bringing together such an outstanding collection of pieces is their ability to search and find outstanding designers from far reaches of the country. Top designers showing in their store include Chris Bales, Charles Albert, Go Go Jewelry, Echo of the Dreamer and more. Many of the pieces, including those of Chris Bales, are one-of-a-kind originals.

The store is a division of the *Andy Thornal Company*. If you have never visited that store in downtown Winter Haven, Florida you are in for another treat. It's been around since 1945 and is VERY unusual, in a very good way. Go to their web site at andythornal.com for a sample look at their unique merchandise.

You can see a large representative sample of Libby's pieces on their facebook site, but you should really see the pieces in person. https://facebook.com/libbyislandjewelry, 5537 Gulf Drive North, Holmes Beach. 941-779-0999.

# "Ice Cream," you scream, We all scream for Ice Cream

Is there anything better than ice cream after a day at the beach? In fact, is there anything better than ice cream period? Not much.

There are more than a few places on the island to get a dish or a cone of ice cream, but the following we especially recommend. Four are on the island and one is just off the island on one of the two causeways.

***Two Scoops*** in Anna Maria across the street from the City Pier is the favorite of our eight-year old granddaughter, Clara. She loves to go for a walk on the pier, watch the fishermen, talk to the pelicans and then go across the street for two scoops: usually one each of *Cake Batter* and *Superman*. I wish they would change the name, but my favorite is *Muddy Sneakers*: vanilla mixed with Reese's Bits and pieces of Snicker's candy bar. If I wasn't such a big UM fan I'd try the *Gator Tracks*: chocolate fudge with peanut butter cups and brownie chunks. They also sell hot dogs and a few sandwiches.

***Joe's Eats and Sweets*** in Bradenton Beach makes all of their own ice cream right on the premises. More flavors than you can count. How about Carrot Cake ice cream? Or White Chocolate Peppermint Bark. My favorite is pineapple coconut. And if I really deserve a treat I jazz that up with pineapple topping, shredded coconut, real whipped cream, and a cherry on top. Joe calls it his Hawaiian Delight Sundae. And they serve both sugar-free and lactose-free ice cream. Open 11 am until 10 pm. Upstairs at the rainbow-colored building at 219 Gulf Drive S. 941-778-0007.

The ice cream stand inside ***Anna Maria Island Beach***

*Café* at Manatee Beach in Holmes Beach is not fancy but they serve Edy's Grand Hand-dipped Ice Cream. And equally as important, those that measure such things tell me that they serve the largest scoop on the island. They also make a wonderful banana split, as well as shakes and a root beer float. And it's just ten paces away from the beach.

**Dip's Ice Cream** is an eight-time winner of *Anna Maria Island Sun's* annual Reader's Choice Award. Their specialty is home-made Working Cow ice cream. They also serve Italian Ice and soft-serve. They been satisfying locals and vacationers alike for more than 21 years. 9801 Gulf Drive, Anna Maria. 941-778-1706.

**Tyler's Homemade Ice Cream** is off-island, but just a little way. Cross the Cortez Bridge back to the mainland and it is less than a mile away on Cortez Road, on the right. To have survived at this somewhat off-the-beaten-path location since 1984 more than suggests there is something special going on here. There is: great tasting gourmet ice cream, made on the premises; a friendly staff; reasonable prices; and the place is kept very clean. Feel like over-indulging? (You *are* on vacation.) Try one of the triple scoop sundaes.

# Pamper Yourself

Anna Maria Island offers you numerous opportunities to relax and recharge, to rejuvenate your mind, body and soul. A good way start or end your visit on the island is by treating yourself to some true pampering: visit a day spa, get a massage, get a new haircut and style, have a relaxing facial, treat those neglected nails to a manicure and pedicure, attend a yoga class on the beach. These and more beauty, health and wellness therapies are available all around the island. The following are some of the most popular; ads for other salons and spas can be found in the island newspapers.

Let's start with a massage. Just as food is fuel to our body, massage is food for your muscles, mind and spirit. Massage has many positive benefits. There are numerous types of massage and you should pick one that meets your body needs.

***Ginny's Rejuvenating Massage Therapy*** can help you do that. *Ginny Upshaw* is a Licensed Massage Therapist who is qualified to give Swedish Massage – relaxation; Thai Massage – "lazy man's yoga," stretching while you are passive. Ginny actively stretches muscle groups with a rhythmic compression; Neuro Muscular Massage – deep tissue massage; and Reiki – positive energy for your body. Ginny will present a program about massage to help explain what health benefits are and what type of massage will meet your personal needs. Relax, renew, rejuvenate . . . you will be amazed at how you feel! Call her at 941-448-1879 to make an appointment. She has our highest recommendation! An island treasure!

***Salon Salon Beauty Boutique and Spa:*** As a full-throughout the salons on a daily basis and brings joy to all who visit. Co-owners *Nikita Fosmore* and *Jeff Petitt* are 2nd and 3rd generation stylists. Salon Salon is the sixth salon in the family service hair salon and spa, their team's dedication to hair care, skin care, nail care and body wellness has set them apart. The atmosphere is *beachy chic*. A lust for life and laughter ring nd the most impressive. Two locations: Salon Salon of AMI, 3612 E. Bay Drive, Holmes Beach, 941-778-0400 and Salon Salon on Pine, 313 Pine Avenue, Anna Maria, 941-778-0500. The spa facility is located at the Anna Maria salon. Excellent rating.

*Acqua Aveda:* The 2,600-sq-ft salon and spa, located in downtown Holmes Beach, is a perfect place to experience island renewal. *Amy Welch*, director/owner, says, *"Let our team create services to bring you and the world back into balance."* Acqua Aveda also offers a "Stay Spa" service at your vacation site: enjoy treatments on your private balcony, beach front or poolside. Choose from a range of spa therapies for yourself or the whole group. There is also a men's spa offering essential services. 5311 Gulf Drive, Holmes Beach, 941-778-5400.

*Body and Sol Day Spa*: Locally owned and operated, Body & Sol take pride in providing their clients with professional spa services in a warm and comfortable atmosphere. They offer massage therapy, skin care, waxing and natural nail services in a quiet, intimate setting that will relax your mind, body and soul. They invite you to come in from the beach with bathing suits and sandy toes. They also offer yoga classes for every level with top certified yoga instructors. Open Monday – Saturday, 10-5. 9805 Gulf Drive, Anna Maria, 941-650-5441.

*Aluna Wellness Center:* Aluna Wellness is an eco-friendly holistic center offering acupuncture, massage, wellness treatments, body scrubs, herbal consultation and organic skin care. They bring together authentic ancient healing traditions from around the world with contemporary therapies to nurture your whole being. The center offers four treatment rooms, a relaxation and meditation room and a lovely Zen garden located directly across from the beach. 2219 Gulf Drive, Bradenton Beach, 941-778-8400.

*Sea-renity Spa & Boutique*: Experience authentic island-style relaxation and stress relief in their spa on historic Bridge Street. Try the island's only beach massage in their private tiki hut right on the beach. Their Bodycare treatments are a great relaxing and beneficial add on. And they can bring massage and yoga to your island wedding party, girl's getaway or family reunion. The boutique offers unique apparel, wellness items, local art, books and more. 112 Bridge Street, Bradenton Beach, 941-779-6836. Beach Massage at 1301 Gulf Drive.

*Divine Appointments:* There was a lady in front of me at the Publix checkout who was just beaming; she was obviously very happy and satisfied about something. I glanced down and saw these bright green toenails. *"Great toes,"* I remarked. *"Thanks,"* she said. *"I just had a massage and a pedicure at Divine Appointments. I got my toes done to match our boat!"* Divine Appointments is off-island in Bradenton, but they sure have a satisfied client singing their praises on the island. Call and see what other services they offer besides massage and pedicures. 941-747-5772. 515 36 Street W. Suite E, Bradenton, just five blocks off of Manatee Avenue.

*Attention Men:* It's as close as you can get to being pampered and still be in a good, old-fashioned barbershop, like the ones they used to have before too many of them turned into *styling salons*. Four barbers: Don, Duane, Patsy and Larry. One will talk you ear off; another might cut your ear off. (Just kidding.) Great folks; great cuts; "good old days" atmosphere. In the Island Shopping Center, next to the hardware store. Corner of Gulf and Marina Drives, Holmes Beach.

# Q: What is better than Three Tenors?
# A: Two Divas!

There are a number of different and excellent musical venues and talents on the island. Everything from the *Anna Maria Island Concert Chorus and Orchestra*, to a jazz band playing every week at the Sunday Brunch at the *Sandbar Restaurant*, to a drum circle every Friday night at the *AMI Beach Café* at Manatee Beach, to live popular music every night at several places on Historic Bridge Street and at Bradenton Beach. There is even a periodic Bluegrass Festival. And several of the island churches hold concerts of various types during the year.

There is always something musical somewhere on the island for everyone. When you are in town check both of our excellent island newspapers, *The AMI Sun* and *The Islander*, for the musical opportunities that exist while you are visiting.

But whatever your taste in music, you'll be thrilled and absolutely amazed if you ever have the opportunity to hear either of the island's two "divas" sing. And if you hear the two of them sing together, which they frequently do, they'll knock your socks off. (Does anyone know exactly what that means?)

I know what I mean when I say these two young women are great talents. Not only do they have marvelous voices, but they each have wonderful but different personalities and love to perform and entertain. Oh, did I also mention that they are both beautiful?

***Carole Cornman-Fetterman***, is a highly talented

soprano. After earning her bachelor of music degree from Butler University she subsequently earned a masters of music degree in vocal performance and a graduate performance degree in opera performance from the Peabody Institute of Johns Hopkins University. Carole has performed as a soloist with many churches in the midwest and the east coast as well as some cathedrals in Europe with the Butler University Chorale. She has been a member of Sarasota's professional singing ensemble, *Gloria Musicae*, for eight years. For the past ten years she has been soloist and choir director for the *Episcopal Church of the Annunciation*. What a treat to hear her sing almost every Sunday. In great demand, she performs regularly throughout the Sarasota-Bradenton area as well as on the island, including jazz/gospel concerts with jazz pianist *Tom Benjamin*. She is also a private vocal instructor. Oh, and she plays the saxophone and knows how to snowboard!

***Deborah Polkinghorn-Suta*** is an amazing mezzo-soprano who is currently in her dissertation of her Ph.D. in Music Education and teaches at several Universities and privately. I think she is wonderful, but don't take my word for it: *RoseMarie Freni*, of the New York City Opera has described her as "possessing a full rich voice with excellent range and a true talent on stage." A conductor referred to her as "a rare breed of singer; a virtuosic performer." She has toured Europe and the United States on Vocal Tours and has performed with numerous symphony orchestras. I get chills, and often tears, every time I hear her sing.

You can look for their performance schedules on either *Facebook* or *Linkedin*. And you can hear Carole on any given Sunday at *The Episcopal Church of the Annunciation* on Holmes Beach. Deborah, when she is in town, is section leader at the *Church of the Redeemer* in Sarasota.

p.s. Thank you, Pam. It was great while it lasted.

# Renew Your Spirit, Soothe Your Soul, and Give Thanks to God for this Wonderful Place.

When we first moved to the island we were pleasantly surprised at the high level of attendance for Sunday worship services at all six of the churches on the island. One might expect that some visitors might feel that "since we are on vacation we can skip church this week." Not so on AMI. Sure, there are some folks who chose to do their worshiping in the water or on the beach, but it seems that a great number of our visitors sense that they truly are at one of God's special places and look forward to giving Him thanks and praise. And many of our permanent residents feel the same way.

The following is a listing of the six island churches and their location and service times. Included are telephone numbers to verify the service times as some change depending upon the season of the year. Locations of denominations not located on the island are listed in the Appendix.

*CrossPoint Fellowship*. 8605 Gulf Drive, Anna Maria. 941-778-0719.

*Episcopal Church of the Annunciation*. 4408 Gulf Drive, Holmes Beach. 941-778-1638.

*Gloria Dei Lutheran Church*. 6608 Marina Drive, Holmes Beach. 941-778-1813.

*Harvey Memorial Community Church*. 300 Church Avenue, Bradenton Beach. 941-779-1912.

***Roser Memorial Community Church***.  512 Pine
Avenue, Anna Maria. 941-778-0414.

***St. Bernard Roman Catholic Church***.  248 South
Harbor Drive, Holmes Beach. 941-778-4769.


**All Island Denominations:**

Founded in 1982, All Island Denominations (A.I.D.) is a
non-profit organization run by the six churches on Anna Maria
Island.   Its governing board includes both clergy and lay
leaders from each congregation – all are volunteers.

Through A.I.D. the churches offer emergency charitable
assistance to island residents or members of Island churches
in circumstances of financial need.

This enables the churches working together to assist
their neighbors in ways they could not do separately.  That
includes organizing and encouraging ecumenical and
interfaith activities of a religious and/or community service
nature.  A.I.D. includes: accepting requests for financial help;
screening assistance requests through the A.I.D. client
assistance record book; assisting Island residents individuals
or families with groceries,; sponsoring and organizing annual
worship services for Ecumenical Week of Prayer for Christian
Unity, Thanksgiving Eve, and the National Day of Prayer.

A.I.D. receives regular support from the participating
congregations on the island and gladly accepts donations from
individuals and groups in the community.  Their support is
always appreciated.

# Finding the Best Restaurants in an Unfamiliar Town

I've learned several things about selecting restaurants in areas frequented by tourists and how to find the good ones when you are new to a community. As I mentioned earlier, I spent most of my life working for newspapers, living in a number of towns in a number of states. With every move came the challenge of finding the best restaurants in the new area.

In every town there are always a lot of restaurants, and not all are national chain fast-food joints. And the ones that are there this year might not be there next year. Many restaurants don't make it past the first or second season. I saw the same restaurant building in one town change names three times in five years.

Running a successful restaurant business is hard enough in any town, but it is even more so in areas frequented by tourists; having to deal with the large swings in the volume of business between in-season and out-of-season makes the job even more difficult.

Being able to cook great tasting food and being able to manage a profitable business are two different things. To be successful you have to be able to do both. Some failing restaurants deserve to fail; others don't.

But when you are new to town or just visiting, how do you know which places to try?

First, don't get lazy and fall back on chain restaurants, even if they are not fast food. If you enjoy an occasional visit to a *Chili's* or an *Applebee's* or an *Olive Garden*, that's fine, but you can do that back home.

Don't waste the opportunity to visit some of the small, local, individual culinary gems found in almost every town and city. It just may take a little effort to find them. There are dozens of them on and around Anna Maria Island and throughout the mountains of North Carolina. This book will help you find them.

You cannot always judge by the number of cars in the parking lot. Lots of cars may be the result of good marketing, not necessarily good food. But, if you find a parking lot full of cars with local, in-state license plates you can be fairly certain that the food is good and is being sold at value-sensitive prices.

Next, if a restaurant has been around for ten or twenty or forty years, unless the waitresses are both unbelievably beautiful and scantily clad, you can bet they didn't make it for that long on their marketing expertise. No business survives and thrives unless it is producing a good product, at a fair price, and providing exceptional customer service. So, longevity is an important criterion.

I began my newspaper career selling ads. I still read them and shop them every day. But don't always believe what you read. Often restaurant ads are filled with hyperbole (known in some areas simply as BS). I've yet to enjoy an "all-you-can-eat" meal of any sort, or a buffet with 250 different items, or anything from a menu that takes half-a-dozen pages to list their 100 different offerings. All three of these were advertised in a recent edition of one of our island publications. Shop the local papers, but be discriminating. And most good restaurants do not hesitate to post their menu in the window.

In order to even have a chance to succeed, new entries into the market must have people give them a try. We've done some of that trying for you. Throughout the book you will find restaurants we recommend that have been around for many years and you will also find new places that we have tried and enjoyed. Hopefully, they will still be there when you arrive.

# Eating Out on the Island

I mentioned earlier that good food is an important part of a good life. You will find plenty of opportunities to experience that while you are on Anna Maria Island. There are fine-dining and award-winning restaurants; middle-of-the-road, just good cookin' places; a variety of ethnic restaurants; seafood shacks and burger joints. Something and somewhere to satisfy palates and pocketbooks of every sort.

What you will not find on Anna Maria Island are fast-food and chain restaurants; there just aren't any*, and most of us like it that way. If you have children and they are experiencing Whopper-withdrawal you'll just have to drive back across the causeway to Bradenton.

As I also mentioned earlier, the list of restaurants in this book is not all-inclusive. Even after three years of living here we are still discovering new dining experiences. Dee and I recently had lunch at a seafood restaurant that we had driven past dozens of times and never considered stopping. It's been there for years. From the outside appearance and the signs we thought it was just a bar. Wrong. They have a bar, but they also have a restaurant that served us one of the best dolphin (mahi-mahi) sandwiches we can remember eating.

The next number of pages will give you a snapshot look at the amazing variety of restaurants that await you on AMI. Some that we consider "extra special" will receive more space than a snapshot. Since Dee and I do not eat red meat I have had to depend on several local friends to advise me on where to find the best steaks and ribs, and barbecue and hamburgers.

*There is a small Domino's Pizza and a Subway, but that's it.

***City Pier Restaurant***. Located at the end of the City Pier in the town of Anna Maria, there is not a better view from the island of Tampa Bay and the Sunshine Skyway Bridge. While walking your way out to the end of the pier, stop and watch the pelicans waiting for a handout from the fishermen or watch the fishermen reel in a sheepshead or a mackerel. Then enjoy a casual lunch or dinner. They serve everything from sandwiches and burgers to fresh fish and vegetarian dishes. Draft beer by the pint or pitcher; 20 other beers by the bottle. Wine by the glass and half or full carafe. Open 11 to 9 Sunday thru Thursday and from 11 to 10 on Friday and Saturday. 941-779-1667.

***Anna Maria Island Beach Cafe.*** We can't decide if we enjoy it more for breakfast or for dinner (or lunch). It's close enough for us to walk to and we often do. It is located at Manatee Public Beach, right on the beach, in Holmes Beach. It is casual and reasonably priced. More importantly, they serve very good food. For breakfast I go for an omelet, grits and a biscuit. For lunch or dinner we like the fish tacos, the clam strip baskets, and their wraps, especially the chicken Caesar wrap. You can see their complete menu at www.amibeachcafe.com. Sit inside or outside. And they have live entertainment every night. Another reason we like the cafe so much: *John Goodhue* is a great manager and a very nice guy who always puts his customers first!

***Old Hamburg Schnitzelhaus.*** Located just two blocks south of the Manatee Causeway (turn left at the first traffic light once you are on the island – East Bay Drive), this is the island's only purely German restaurant. The menu contains just about everything that you would expect to be there: potato cakes, spatzle, Jager schnitzel, schweinebraten, and more. A friend raves about the Bavarian platter. Very friendly service, neighborhood atmosphere. 3246 East Bay Drive, Holmes

Beach. 941-778-1320.

***Rudy's Subs and More.*** What a cute store and what a fun menu. Open just for breakfast (8-11) and lunch (11-3). Two gals from Colorado with years of restaurant experience "retired" a few years ago, discovered AMI after much searching for the "perfect" place to land, bought a home and opened *Rudy's*. And we are so glad they did. A sub for breakfast? How about a Veggie Roo: a fried egg, mushrooms, onions, tomatoes, cheese and peppers on a toasted sub roll. Looking for something more traditional? How about a home-made muffin or cinnamon roll or a Jerry Seinfeld-made-famous muffin top? The lunch menu offers about eight different subs but it is the Philly Cheese Steak sub that gets the most raves. Colorado chefs preparing a Philadelphia tradition on an island in Florida? Go figure. I figure you'll love this place. 9906 Gulf Drive, Anna Maria. 941-896-7844. By the way, while you are there pick up one of their hats or visors or T-shirts; great island colors!

***Sandbar Restaurant.*** One of the island's premiere dining destinations and one of three restaurants owned by one of the sons of the late Lawton Chiles, former US senator and governor of Florida. The Sandbar has recently completed renovations of the interior dining area and they made a good situation even better. But it is the outside, right-on-the-beach-seating that is the big pull. A little pricier than some of their competition, but part of what you are paying for is the location and the view. And it's worth it. Too often restaurants "with a view" think they can slack off on the quality of the food or the size of the servings or the level of service and "get away with it", letting the view compensate for shortcomings in other areas. Not so with the Sandbar. It seems their attitude is "we've got the best view and location on the island, let's make sure all of the other parts of our business are the best also." They do not accept reservations, but that seems to work. We've had guests who waited over an hour during the winter season Visit the combined web site for all three of the restaurants: www.groupersandwich.com and click on *The Sandbar* for a current lunch and dinner menu and for dining hours, which change during Daylight Savings Time. 100 Spring Avenue, Anna Maria. 941-778-0444.

*Beachhouse Waterfront Restaurant* is one of the three "sister" restaurants, along with the *Sandbar* and the *Mar Vista,* that are under the same ownership. You might say that the *Sandbar* and the *Beachhouse* are "twin sisters" as both have inside dining and a covered deck with dining right on the beach. The *Sandbar* is located at the far north end of the island; the Beachhouse is at the south end, in Bradenton Beach. The menus are very similar but the *Beachhouse* may be a little more suited for family dining. Check out the www.groupersandwich.com web site and click on *The Sandbar* for their menus and hours. 200 Gulf Drive North. 941-779-2222.

*Sign of the Mermaid:* An excellent place for dinner, but it is the breakfast and lunch specials that are so popular. How about Crème Brulee French Toast? And they serve breakfast until 2 pm for you late-risers. You'll want to make reservations for dinner. We have a soft spot in our heart for the Mermaid. It was here that our friend *Marietta* received an on-his-knees wedding proposal. She said, *"Yes!"* 941-778-9399. Located at 9707 Gulf Drive, Anna Maria.

*Mr. Bones:* What a great name for a BBQ joint! All home-made, all of the time. Open seven days for lunch and dinner. 3007 Gulf Drive, Holmes Beach.

*Oma Pizza and Italian Restaurant:* They claim to be the maker of the world's largest pizza, but they serve veal, chicken, fish and pasta as well. My wife usually orders the eggplant parmesan. They are open from 11 am until midnight, seven days a week. And they deliver until midnight as well. 201

North Gulf Drive, Bradenton Beach. 941-778-0771.

**Banana Cabana:** A Caribbean restaurant serving some of my favorite flavors and dishes: Jerk Chicken and Ribs, Mango Crab Cakes, Macadamia Nut Grouper, and more. We like this place a lot. They make their own jerk sauce and a Habanero hot sauce that they should patent and sell to sinus doctors. It's a family-run affair: father, mother and son, who's the chef. Great server named Kelly, who has been there for eight years. The family is originally from New Jersey and are big-time Philadelphia Eagles fans. Live music on Friday and Saturday nights from 7 to 10 and an open mic on Sunday from 3-6. They serve lunch on Tuesday thru Sunday and dinner every night beginning at 5 o'clock. 103 Gulf Drive, Bradenton Beach. They take reservations. 941-779-1930.

**Paradise Bagel Café:** A nice place for a light breakfast, brunch or lunch, and for dinner Wednesday night only. There are a variety of New York deli-style platters, salads, and egg dishes plus blueberry pancakes. Dee usually orders the whitefish salad platter. I usually go for the lox platter with a Black Russian bagel. Lots of cream cheese smeared on the bagel and served with a large portion of smoked salmon, sliced tomato, red onion and capers. You order at the counter and pour your own coffee (limit 12 refills), but your meal is served to you. Wednesday night is Pasta Night from 5 to 8 pm. Greek salad, spaghetti and meat balls, garlic parmesan bread and a complementary glass of beer or wine. The café is open from 7 am until 2 pm Monday thru Saturday and from 7 am to 12:30 pm on Sunday. 3220 East Bay Drive, next to Walgreens, Holmes Beach.

**Ginny's and Jane E's Bakery, Café and Costal Gifts:** A truly unique place to shop and eat. They are located in a converted grocery store in the town of Anna Maria. Here you also order your meal at the counter and then go find yourself a seat at one of the tables mixed in and among the

161

antiques and unusual collection of local art pieces. They call your name when your order is ready. The food is good and the atmosphere is fun and relaxing. After your meal wander around the shop; they really have some interesting, fun and unusual items. Open seven days from 8 until 5. Located at 9807 Gulf Drive in Anna Maria. 941-778-3170.

***Anna Maria General Store and Deli:*** Located just a few blocks further north and to the right, on Pine Street, heading toward the Anna Maria Pier. Look for the attractive green and purple store. Great deli sandwiches, local juices, nice selection of wines. They will prepare a picnic basket for your day's outing. 307 Pine Avenue, 941-779-9200.

***Solo's Pizza.*** How about a sports bar/pizza joint where you feel comfortable bringing the kids. Solo's offers numerous TVs, games and pool table along with sandwiches, pizza and salads. We usually each order a small Greek salad and then split a large Veggie Pizza. Open daily 4 to 11 pm. 3244 E. Bay Drive, Holmes Beach.

***Tortilla Bay.*** This is a southwest grille with an island twist. Eat in or take out. We can't get enough of the mahi-mahi tacos, soft or hard or mix and match. We also enjoy the Sunshine Salad served in a fried tortilla bowl. Open 11 am to 9 pm. 5318 Marina Drive, downtown Holmes Beach. 941-778-3663.

***Island Spice.*** They serve delicious and authentic Indian cuisine made by excellent chefs. Some American dishes are also on the menu. Open for breakfast, lunch and dinner. 1701 Gulf drive N., Bradenton Beach. 941-527-0123.

As I mentioned earlier, this list of good places to eat is not all-inclusive. There are other good places to eat on the island. Do some exploring yourself; it will be hard to go wrong. One of the *good things* about *bad restaurants* is that they usually do not stay in business for very long.

# Duffy's Tavern

*Bruce Hunt* is a native Floridian who has authored eight books on Florida travel and history. It was in the 3rd Edition of his book *"Visiting Small-Town Florida"* that I read his comments on the towns of Anna Maria and Holmes Beach and Cortez. Guess what? He thinks as highly of them as I do.

It was through the encouragement of Bruce, and our shared good friend, *Andy Duncan*, that we first visited *Duffy's Tavern*. In his book Bruce refers to Duffy's as "a beer and burger joint icon that has been on the island since 1958."

I've mentioned before that Dee and I do not eat red meat, so what are we doing patronizing a burger joint? Because of the ambience; because some of our friends enjoy eating there; and because they also serve garden burgers, grilled cheese and tomato sandwiches, and PBJs (peanut butter with your choice of grape or strawberry jelly). The first two go well with any of the two dozen or so beers that they pour. The PBJ goes down better with the chocolate milk.

But our friends who do eat red meat rave about the burgers, the chili dogs and the BBQ pulled-pork sandwiches. The pork is hickory-smoked and basted with a vinegar sauce. As with the burgers, the meat is piled so high on the bun that you need both hands to eat it.

Our friend *Ed Upshaw*, who introduced us to Jose's Cuban restaurant, sings Duffy's praises: *"It's not just the delicious hamburgers that keeps bringing us back, but the colorful local characters as well."*

Further along in the book, in the North Carolina section, I

joke about sleeping in the bedroom of seven sisters in Black Mountain. Only five sisters, and their momma, run Duffy's.

Miss Duffy (the momma) bought the business in 1971 and she and her five daughters have run it ever since. And have run it well: Duffy's was named by *USA Today*, as one of the ten best "hamburger heavens" in the country! My two brothers-in-law, Avery and Chuck Bennett, with their highly-experienced burger palates, graded Duffy's burgers at A and A-. Confirming high praise indeed from these two.

Don't plan on eating there on Tuesdays; they are closed. But they are open the rest of the week from 11 until 8, except on Sundays when they are open from noon until 8.

They are located in the heart of "downtown" Holmes Beach at 5808 Marina Drive, across the street from the City Hall. 941-778-2501.

*What do you say to a hamburger?*
"How now, ground cow?"

# The Feast Island Restaurant

Do you have a favorite neighborhood restaurant where you eat frequently and know that every time you go there the food will be good and the service efficient and friendly? We do.

It is *The Feast Island Restaurant* also located in the heart of "downtown" Holmes Beach in the *Island Shopping Center* at the corner of Marina and Gulf Drives. Owned and operated by two brothers who run the kitchen, the restaurant serves all of the types of food one would expect at a neighborhood restaurant located on an island.

I had better stop here and explain the "neighborhood" thing. I refer to it as a neighborhood restaurant because it's in *our* neighborhood. And we feel a sense of neighborly pride in having them so close to us. People drive from all over the island and off the island to eat at our neighborhood restaurant. In fact, if you will look at the large map of the world on the wall next to the cash register you'll see by the push pins that people have traveled from all over the world to eat here. Well, maybe they didn't travel here specifically to eat at The Feast, but they did eat here while they were in town. And they felt good enough about the experience to leave their mark.

Back to what you might expect: a variety of fresh, local seafood items; three great soups; six terrific signature salads; about a potential three dozen or so pasta dishes depending upon how you mix and match the selection of noodles, sauces and toppings. Oh, and a grilled Black Angus filet, two veal dishes, and a rack of ribs.

With all that to choose from you still can't decide? How about a pizza? There are seven signature hand-thrown pizzas on the menu and the combinations to design your own are almost limitless. We order either the Margarita, the Vegetarian, or the White Pizza. I'd enter any one of the three in a "Best Pizza on the Island" contest and expect to win. If there is a better pizza on the island we have yet to find it.

Dee often makes a meal out of the Tropicale Salad with a piece of salmon, or shrimp or chicken on top. The salad is baby arugula with sliced avocado, hearts of palm, and Parmesan Reggiano cheese with a balsamic vinaigrette dressing. Outstanding!

After grouper, Florida lobster and dolphin (mahi-mahi), my favorite seafood is shrimp. The Feast prepares them in a variety of ways: Firecracker Shrimp, tender popcorn shrimp tossed in a spicy sauce; Coconut Shrimp, rolled in toasted coconut and flash fried, served with a delicious orange-ginger sauce; Moroccan Curry Shrimp, jumbo shrimp seasoned with yellow curry and sautéed, and finished with a reduction mango sauce; or Key West Shrimp, a dozen large shrimp either fried, grilled, blackened, or jerk style. I've tried them all and enjoyed them all. But, ever since returning many years ago from our honeymoon in Jamaica, I have been a sucker for any seafood prepared with jerk sauce.

They have an extensive menu and I am often leery of that. Can they prepare all of those dishes fresh? In this case, yes, they can and they do.

Open seven days a week from 11:30 am 'til 9:00 pm. Dinner reservations are suggested. Call 941-778-5092.

By the way, if you are interested in college basketball ask if server *Ken* is working that shift. He played college ball for the University of Connecticut and loves to talk hoops!

# The Waterfront Restaurant

One of the most popular eating establishments on the island and one of our favorites is *The Waterfront Restaurant* across from the City Pier in Anna Maria. It is on the smallish size compared to some restaurants on the island, but that is a good thing. While it may be difficult to obtain a table at certain times of the year, the atmosphere does not feel "busy" even when they are.

A growing genre in the restaurant business is those serving "locally sourced seasonal and sustainable" food. The Waterfront has taken that to a higher level. While there are always excellent and dependable "standards," one page of the menu is updated each day.

Some dishes may be of limited availability and may have to be "86'd" before the end of the dinner service. Local fishermen provide them with hard-to-catch and underutilized local species that larger and more commercial restaurants would have little use for.

They pride themselves on following an old formula: finest product, classic presentation, with the addition of rare and seasonal items, utilizing original and cutting-edge techniques.

One of the first axioms I remember from one of my early cooking classes is that "Diners also have taste buds in their eyes." That is, food that looks good does not necessarily mean that it is going to taste good, but food that tastes good always tastes even better if it looks good. Food at The Waterfront not only tastes good but it is always beautifully presented and graciously served.

I want to tell you about some of our favorite dishes. Let me begin with lunch. I almost always order the *Grouper Tacos*.

Made with seared Black Grouper (my favorite grouper prepared my favorite way) served on grilled soft flour tortillas with fresh pico de gallo, shredded cheddar jack cheese and topped with jicama tartar slaw. I wish they would give me the recipe for the jicama slaw. I've tried to duplicate it but have not been successful. If I could just find that "secret" ingredient I'd make it at home and eat it every day. It is that good.

Dee switches around depending upon the daily specials, but often falls back on a Classic Caesar Salad topped with Calamari Curls. The two items are listed separately on the menu but they are always happy to serve the two items together. The calamari is some of the best we have ever eaten. Two things take it above the ordinary: how the squid is cut and with what it is dusted before frying. Instead of the usual cross-cut rings you are usually served. These squid are cut in-house into thin strips and dusted in seasoned semolina flour and quickly fried, which causes the strips to curl up. They are extra light and tender.

For a non-seafood luncheon dish I recommend the Turkey and Brie Croissant. It also is prepared differently than what you may have been served elsewhere. There are not many seafood restaurants that smoke their own turkey (and salmon) over apple wood. The turkey breast is then thinly sliced, topped with an ample portion of high-quality brie cheese and baked on a flaky croissant. Honey mustard is served on the side, along with your choice of fries, slaw or the side special of the day.

It seems like Dee and I each usually order one of the daily dinner specials when we come in for dinner, but when ordering from the regular dinner menu I have had the Crab Cakes, the Pollo Calabrese and the Bay Boulevard Sampler. Dee has more than once ordered the Lobster Ravioli.

The Pollo Calabrese is a boneless chicken breast that has been stuffed with a mixture of spinach, roasted tomatoes and goat cheese. It is then seared on the stove top and finished by roasting it in the oven. It comes served sliced and drizzled with a delightful lemon butter sauce and with a side of that evening's starch or grain. It's our daughter-in-law's favorite.

The Bay Boulevard Sampler is a combination of Gulf Shrimp, Black Grouper, and large Sea Scallops that have been prepared to your choice: grilled, blackened or fried (go for the grilled). Of course I had to add the optional crab cake. They nearly had to roll me to the car.

As mentioned earlier, Dee and I do not eat red meat, but I often overhear one of the other diners order the Lamb Shank Colorado. It certainly looks good when being served. It is a large fore shank that the menu says "has been braised in red wine with herbs and caramelized onion until fork tender, and served over tonight's potatoes with its own sauce."

And get this: *Sarasota Magazine* named The Waterfront Restaurant in 2013 the "Best Restaurant for Steak." Amazing, with all the true steak restaurants around a primarily fresh seafood restaurant is voted the best place to eat steak! It must be their 16-oz. Bahi Rib-Eye which has been marinating for three days in their Polynesian seasoning and glaze, then char-grilled the way you like it. Our friends Liz and Bob Lang agree that the recognition is well-deserved. When I asked them who serves the best steak on the island they both quickly replied, "The Waterfront!"

If you are into beers and wines The Waterfront has an-extensive a selection as anyone on the island. They offer 10 imported and hand-crafted microbrews on tap along with 20 additional ales and lagers available by the bottle plus all of the popular domestic beers. In addition, they offer an extensive wine list with more than 80 choices from around the world. Plus there are daily wine specials. They are open daily for lunch from 11:30 am until 4:00 pm and for dinner Sunday through Thursday from 4:30 until 9:00 pm, and Friday and

Saturday evenings from 4:30 until 10:00 pm. Eat inside amongst the warm wood paneling or outside on the covered open-air patio overlooking Tampa Bay. Call 941-778-1515 for reservations.

# Off-Island Restaurants

There are a number of restaurants that we enjoy that are not on the island, but are close enough to warrant driving to them. A couple are just across one of the causeways and really could have been listed as one of the island restaurants. The following are some of our off-island favorites.

Our friend *Ed Upshaw* was eating regularly at **Jose's Real Cuban Food** before it was featured on *Food Network's* hit show *Diners, Drive-ins and Dives*. Maybe it was Ed that told show host *Guy Fieri* about Jose's. Guy said that Jose *"serves excellent Cuban food, at reasonable prices, in a friendly family environment."* Having spent much of my life in Miami, I know Cuban food. This is the real thing. Roast pork, piccadillo, arroz con pollo, and much, much more. Located at 8799 Cortez Road West, just a couple of miles east of the Cortez Causeway, *Jose's* is open Monday thru Thursday from 11 to 8 and Friday and Saturdays from 11 to 9. The restaurant is closed on Sunday. Telephone 941-795-4898.

**Walt's Fish Market and Restaurant**, claims to "have the freshest and best selection of seafood in the world" and you know what? I believe them. I have fished and cooked fish, shopped at seafood markets, and eaten at seafood restaurants most of my life. If it gets any better than *Walt's* I haven't found it. The history is too long and interesting, and the menu is too extensive, to write about all of it here. Go to their web site at www.waltsfish.com. And then go to the restaurant and market. Casual dining. They have been serving the Sarasota and surrounding market since 1918. They are open daily from 9 to 9. 4144 Tamiami Trail, south of downtown Sarasota.

***Crab & Fin***, located at St. Armand's Circle on Longboat Key, is another outstanding seafood restaurant. If you are looking for a little more formal and upscale dining experience but still would like a large selection of fresh seafood expertly prepared, try here. The menus are printed daily to reflect the freshest seafood available. In a way different from *Walt's*, which specializes in serving seafood caught by local fisherman every day, the Crab & Fin is committed to offering pristine and unique seafood from around the world, shipped in by air daily. At a recent visit they were offering fresh raw oysters from Washington State, Prince Edward's Island and Nova Scotia, Canada. They only buy from ecologically responsible fisheries who promote only sustainable seasonal or aqua-cultured varieties. Of course, they always offer a selection of locally-caught items. Open daily from 11:30 am to 10:00 pm. Telephone: 941-388-3964. Or go to their web site www.crabfinrestaurant.com.

***Star Fish Company Dockside Restaurant***, is sort of like a mini-Walt's, but the dining is even more casual. The catch is more limited than at *Walt's*, but is just as fresh as the seafood market and restaurant are located right on the commercial fishing docks. You eat outside next to the water where the pelicans land and take off regularly. The fresh seafood market is inside. You order from a window; the menu is printed on the wall. Then you find yourself a picnic table which may or may not be in the shade. When you respond to your name being yelled out, your meal is brought to you in a paper box and you eat with plastic utensils. During the winter season you might have to stand in line for as long as forty-five minutes just to place your order and then you may have to wait even longer to find a place to sit. Why in the world would people do that, you might ask? Because the food is great and it is a fun and enjoyable dining experience, if you are into that kind of thing. We are! 12306 46 Avenue W. In Cortez, just two blocks from the east side of the Cortez Causeway Bridge, three minutes from Anna Maria Island. 941-794-1243.

**_Riverhouse Reef & Grill_**, is at the end of the marina pier on the north side of the Manatee River, across from downtown Bradenton. The view is terrific in all directions. You can choose from inside or dockside seating. Fresh seafood aplenty on the menu, but this is not just a seafood restaurant. Chicken, ribs, pork chops, steaks are on the menu as well. I feel I must give you this warning, however. I was disappointed to see more than a few negative comments on the web about their food and service. I was surprised. Every time we have eaten there we have had a very satisfying experience. It can get a little crowded during the season, but few good places don't, and they do not take reservations. We have never had to wait for very long when have had to wait and there has always been a seat at the bar. Give them a try; I'll be very surprised if you are not very satisfied. Open Sunday thru Thursday from 11:30 until 9 and on Friday and Saturday until 10. 995 Riverside Drive. Take the first left immediately after crossing the Business-41 Green Bridge from downtown Bradenton. 941-729-0616.

"Claw your way to **_Moore's Stone Crab Restaurant_**, on Longboat Key for a feed of delicious stone crabs." _Moore's_ is the oldest seafood restaurant under the same ownership in Manatee County. In 1927, Papa Jack Moore started walking the flats of the bays of Anna Maria Island and Longboat Key getting stone crabs by hand and selling them. As business grew he was able to purchase a small boat and an outboard motor so that he could fish for the crabs using traps. He worked about 50 to 75 traps. Today _Moore's_ has a fleet of boats that work as many as 140,000 traps. The traps are all hand-made. The claws of the crabs are carefully removed and the live crabs are returned to the water to regenerate new ones. During the season, which runs from October 15th to May

15th, Moore's will serve between 350,000 and 400,000 pounds of stone crab claws. The stone crabs are seasonal but always on the menu are other seafood dishes, sandwiches, steaks, pasta and chicken dishes. Open every day from 11:30 until 9:30. 800 Broadway Street. Cross the Longboat Key Bridge (now becoming Gulf of Mexico Drive) and turn left on Broadway Street, just a little ways south of the bridge. *Moore's* is located next door to the *Mar Vista*. 941-383-1748.

**Mar Vista Dockside Restaurant and Pub** is the third of restaurateur Ed Chile's trio of fine island-dining restaurants. It is located on the bayside of the northern part of Longboat Key (next door to *Moore's Stone Crab Restaurant)* in the heart of Longboat Village. Originally built in 1912, the restaurant is housed in one of the twelve oldest surviving structures on Longboat Key. Enjoy a delicious Old Florida-style meal in the inside dining room or outside on the covered deck overlooking the lovely Sarasota Bay. For a look at all of their menus go to the shared web site at www.groupersandwich.com and click on *Mar Vista*. Open every day, lunch is served from 11:30 until 5 and dinner served from 5 until 10. 760 Broadway Street. 941-383-2391.

Finally, a fairly new restaurant that we enjoy very much. The **Sage Biscuit and Café** opened in December 2012 and has been a hit from the very beginning. Open 7 days a week from 7 am until 3 pm for breakfast and lunch only, they have a very interesting menu featuring traditional breakfast and lunch fare, but with delightful twists. Not just French Toast, but how about Apricot Stuffed French Toast with sourdough bread, vanilla egg batter and apricot cream cheese. Not just an omelet, but a Seafood Omelet with crab, shrimp, tomato, green onions and Monterrey Jack cheese. Not just a Steak Sandwich, but a Sage Biscuit Steak Sandwich:   marinated char-grilled skirt steak  topped with caramelized onions, arugula and tomato served on fresh baked baguette with horseradish cream sauce. Dee likes the Eggplant Bruschetta Sandwich: buttermilk fried eggplant topped with diced tomatoes, garlic, fresh basil, goat cheese, and drizzled with balsamic reduction, served on a grilled baguette. I enjoy the black bean chili and a fried green tomato grilled cheese sandwich on sour dough bread. We won't need much for dinner tonight! And there are many other interesting dishes from which to choose. Usually busy (a good sign), but the co-owner father, son and daughter-in-law-team keep things moving like a well-oiled machine. Having a motivated and well-trained staff of servers helps too. Part of the servers' success is that they willingly help each other. In addition to many other duties, daughter-in-law Nichole also makes the homemade pies, which are a big seller. They are like old-time diner pies: lemon meringue and coconut cream pies! Just about six miles across the Cortez Bridge at 6656 Cortez Road West in Bradenton. See the complete menu at www.sagebiscuitbradenton.com.

# The Lazy Lobster of Longboat

Our friends *Gerry and Thibaut Brian* introduced us to The *Lazy Lobster of Longboat* and are we glad they did! The Brians live half the year in Pennsylvania and half the year here. The first stop they make after opening their home when they return here each fall is at The Lazy Lobster. They miss it that much when they are gone. Fortunately we can enjoy the place all year, although they are closed for lunch in the summer.

As a native Floridian I have always favored Florida lobster, or crawfish as we call them, over Maine lobster, but The Lazy Lobster has taught me that properly-prepared one can be just as good as the other.

Thibaut's favorite is the Lazy Man Lobster. No bib necessary! The lobster is, of course, fresh and steamed. It is served out of the shell (hence the name) with drawn butter, potato gratin and the day's fresh vegetable. A really smart idea is that you can order the dish in three different sizes: 4, 6 or 8 ounce portions of the lobster.

Lobster is also served in most of the other traditional ways: whole steamed, broiled tail, baked with seafood stuffing, or Thermidore and Newburg style, as well as lobster mac & cheese, and the old stand-by, a lobster roll.

But it is not just the lobster that brings folks back again and again. My wife's favorite is the potato Crusted Grouper, fresh grouper crusted with shredded potatoes, sautéed crisp and served with a heavy-grain mustard sauce and the day's fresh vegetable.

My favorite dinner dish is Seafood Fra Diavolo, sautéed shrimp, scallops and mussels with spiced marinara sauce served over linguine and topped with a grind of fresh Romano cheese. I enjoy anything Fra Diavolo but am cautious ordering it when eating out. Too many restaurants under-spice the sauce, while others make it so hot that my brow breaks out in perspiration and I have to request an additional glass of water to put out the fire. Lazy Lobster's chef has just the right touch, to my taste, and serves a properly spiced and balanced dish.

Our favorite lunch dishes include a cup of lobster bisque or seafood gumbo and either the Coconut Shrimp Salad or the Fried Grouper Po' Boy. The salad is made with mixed greens tossed with dried cranberries, diced papaya, tomato, and toasted coconut. It is then topped with gorgonzola crumbles and coconut fried shrimp and a wonderful raspberry dressing on the side.

The Grouper Po'boy consists of select cuts of fresh grouper that has been lightly fried and served on a split, buttered and grilled roll with tartar sauce and a side of coleslaw and French fried potatoes. Along with the cup of bisque or gumbo it makes a very satisfying lunch. Or, skip the soup and order the Grouper Sandwich. You receive a larger portion of grouper than with the Po'boy and you can have the grouper grilled instead of fried, if you prefer. Cole slaw and fries are included also.

If someone in your party is not a fan of seafood don't let that discourage you; the menu offers a variety of meat and poultry dishes also, including: Chicken Marsala, Liver and Onions, Wiener schnitzel, Baby Back Ribs, Veal Scaloppini, and a Filet Mignon. If you want the best of both worlds order the filet and lobster tail combo or the Veal and Lobster.

The mission statement of the restaurant is *"to be the neighborhood choice for our guests and their families; providing a casual atmosphere that consistently exceeds their expectations. Great food, high energy, and honest friendly people are the keys to our success. We're a fun place to go where you can get anything you want and it will always be great!"* Quite a challenge, but they live up to it in every way.

The only thing I disagree with is the "neighborhood" part. The atmosphere and the staff and guests are neighborly enough, but people drive from far further than the neighborhood to eat this outstanding food.

They are open daily for Early Dining from 4:00 to 5:30 PM and for dinner from 4:00 to 9:00 PM. Beginning in October through spring they serve lunch from 11:30 AM until 3:00 PM.

For reservations phone 941-383-0440 or go to their web site at www.longboatkeylazylobster. You can also download the complete lunch and dinner menu from there. Located at 5350 Gulf of Mexico Drive, Longboat Key (on the left 2½ miles south of the Longboat Key Bridge coming from Anna Maria Island).

# Every Church
# Should be so Blessed

I wrote in the introduction to this book that I was going to mention some of the "extra special" people that we have met during our time on Anna Maria Island and in the North Carolina Mountains. Here are two of them:

*Terry and Dick Hussey* are members of *The Episcopal Church of the Annunciation* on Holmes Beach. Every church should be so blessed.

The Husseys are basically from the northeast but visited Anna Maria Island off and on beginning in the 1970s when visiting Terry's parents. They moved to the island themselves in 1999 and later moved to a home in Bradenton. They were still just six miles from the island and the church.

Dick has served on the vestry and as Senior and Junior Warden for several terms. Terry for a number of years was the Vestry Clerk and is now on the vestry herself. Terry is also editor of the monthly church news publication and Dick is the production manager. Terry also produces the weekly e-mail to the parishioners containing details of the upcoming Sunday services and the church activities for the coming week.

The two of them also serve once a week as office volunteers, assisting the parish administrator. And if there is a church event or activity, you know who you can always count on to be there working or assisting. Need a wheel chair pushed or a table cleared? Dick will gladly do it. Need someone to design a poster or sell the tickets or keep the list? There's Terry happily doing it. Need a ride to church? Terry and Dick will pick you up and take you home.

They are not only hard workers, they are intensely spiritual. We should all be so diligent in our church attendance. They both are Eucharistic Visitors, taking Holy Communion to people that are in the hospital, nursing homes or home bound.

Would you like to meet the Husseys? Just come to church any Sunday. Dick will spot you as a newcomer before you get comfortable in your pew. Following the service he'll find you, introduce himself, invite you to coffee hour, and then bring other people around to meet you.

Terry and Dick Hussey: extra special people! Like I said, every church should be so blessed.

# The Quiet Ones in Church

Everyone knows we should be quiet when we are in church and most of us are. But these are not the people I am writing about. I'm writing about the <u>really</u> quiet ones, those that, week-in-and-week-out, quietly go about their work for the church and for the community and for humankind in general. The unsung heroes, if you will.

These are usually the humble ones who never enjoyed singing *"This little light of mine; I'm gonna let it shine."* There is, of course, a difference between "letting your light shine before others" and "shining your light in the face of others."

The purpose of this little piece is twofold: first to shine a little light of appreciation on these that quietly do so much and often receive so little credit (not that they want it), and secondly, to encourage those of you who may be reading this to think about those quiet ones in your life, in your place of worship, or your community. Maybe there is an appropriate way for you to shine some light their way. Even if they are not seeking or expecting it, they will appreciate it.

Like other lists in the book, this list is not all-inclusive. There will be at least one person I have overlooked or don't even know about. Some of you may have so effectively hidden your light under a basket that I've missed seeing it. I apologize. But don't worry; realize that there is someone far more important than me who recognizes and appreciates what you are doing. I'm the one that has to worry, worry about how to respond when, standing outside the Pearly Gate, I am asked, *"How come you didn't include Stephanie, or William, or whomever in your book?"*

Here is my list of unsung heroes from our church. I purposely have omitted mentioning the things that they so quietly and regularly do in hopes that some of you might ask them what it *is* they do and if you may help them do it.

Bea Alpaugh
Jeanne Akers
Larry Albert
Molly Bengtson
Tom Benjamin
Judy Bennett
Mary Jo Bopp
Thibaut Brian
Carol Carter
Chris Collins
Luanne Collins
Jeanne Colwell
Suzie Cowgill
Mary Cullinan
Gretchen Edgren
Jeff Endean
Ann Fletcher
Bruce Gillies
John Goodhue
Margaret Jenkins
Dean Jones
Karen Jones
Pam League
Don Lind
Julie Lind
David Lowe
Wendy Lowe
Irv Maranville

Joyce Maranville
Jack Messmer
Joan Oster
Jackie Pepka
Regina Percy
Barry Peterson
Caroline Powers
Vivian Ragsdale
Ruth Richardson
Kelly Rubino
Addie Sanders
Mary Saunders
Barbara Smith
(the late) Ed Smith
Pam Stewart
Thom Tenny
Dick Turner
Ginny Upshaw
Ed Upshaw
Bill Wait
Sue Wait
Cecil Warf

God's blessings on them all.

# Who Woulda Guessed?

What is one of the last things you might guess an island would be famous for? How about a pickle!

The ladies of the *Episcopal Church of the Annunciation* on Holmes Beach have been preparing, jarring, and selling pickles for at least forty-years as a fund raiser. And twice a year permanent residents and visitors alike line up at the door when they go on sale.

The sliced pickles have a unique flavor and texture all of their own. I guess you could describe them as a sweet dill pickle. They are different and delicious. They are crispy and made in very small and limited batches, that is, as pickle batches go.

In all the years that the church has been making these pickles there have been only a very few women who have had access to the actual recipe, which is as closely guarded and protected as is the formula for *Coca-Cola*®.

*Jeanne Colwell* is the current keeper of the recipe and has been for a good number of years. Each year she recruits a limited number of parishioners to help her prepare the pickles and a few more to help her jar them. *Cecil*, the church sexton, is charged with the task of guarding the "vats" while the pickles are being "cured." But none of the volunteer workers have access to the recipe.

I heard Jeanne tell one of the women that she would show her the recipe but that she would then have to kill her. Or was that a line I once heard in a movie?

Anyway, as they say, the pickles are "to die for." If you happen to be in town on the first Saturday in December, when the pickles go on sale at the church's Holly Berry Bazaar, stop by and  get in line to buy a jar or two. If you miss out then, try the *White Elephant Sale* in late February or early March. If there are any pickles left unsold in December they go on sale again at the White Elephant event.

# North Carolina Mountains

# An Overview of the
# North Carolina Mountains

Rutherfordton, where my wife's former church is located, is in the foothills of the North Carolina Mountains, about half way between Charlotte and Asheville. Shortly after we moved to Rutherfordton we purchased a home at *Lake Tahoma* in McDowell County, about thirty miles to the north of Rutherfordton, just west of the town of Marion, and about thirty miles east of Asheville, just off of U.S. 70 and I-40.

Lake Tahoma is a wonderful little community of just fifty homes, situated on a 165+ acre lake with the Blue Ridge Mountains in the background. From our dock we can see the peak of *Mt. Mitchell*, the highest point in the U.S. east of the Mississippi River (6,684 feet at the summit). Only a handful of the homes are occupied year-round. Most of the homeowners live in Asheville or Charlotte or Shelby or Morganton or some other nearby North Carolina town or city. One of our favorite couples live part of the year in Atlanta. Located more or less in the southeast corner of the mountain region, it is a perfect spot from which to head north or west into the heart of the mountains. From Lake Tahoma it is less than ten miles up a twisting NC-80 to an entrance to the Blue Ridge Parkway and Mt. Mitchell State Park.

The mountains of North Carolina begin at the western end of the state and flow from the South Carolina and Georgia state lines to the borders of Virginia and Tennessee.

As vast an area as this may seem, the mountain areas only make up about 20 percent of the total land mass of the very large state of North Carolina. The extreme length of the state from east to west is 503 miles; its breadth from north to south is 187 miles. The total area of the state is in excess of 52,000 square miles. The mountains encompass about 10,000 square miles, or an area close to the size of the states of Vermont or Massachusetts.

When one hears mention of the mountains of North Carolina most immediately think of the *Great Smoky Mountains,* probably because of the *Great Smoky Mountain National Park*, the most-visited park in our National Park system. The second most-likely reference would be the *Blue Ridge Mountains* because of the *Blue Ridge Parkway*, the 469-mile scenic drive that connects the Great Smoky Mountain National Park to the Shenandoah National Park in Virginia. These two mountain ranges, the Great Smoky Mountains and the Blue Ridge Mountains, form the highest part of the *Appalachian Mountains*, the range that extends for about 1,500 miles from central Alabama to southeastern Canada.

But there are a few smaller mountain groups in the area as well. All told, there are some 125 peaks that exceed 5,000 feet and 43 that tower above 6,000 feet, while some of the valleys drop to as low as 1,000 feet above sea level. Geologists most typically segment the North Carolina Mountains into three divisions: the Southwest Mountains, the Central Mountains, and the Northern Mountains.

The *Southwest Mountains* are any mountains west of Asheville and include the National Park and the towns of Maggie Valley, Sylva, Waynesville, Franklin, Highlands, Cashiers, Dillsboro, Cherokee, Bryson City, and others. The high spots of these towns follow.

The *Central Mountains* basically include all of the mountain areas surrounding Asheville, encompassing the towns of Black Mountain, Hendersonville, Lake Lure and Chimney Rock, Rutherfordton, Saluda, Tryon, Brevard, and others.

The *Northern Mountains*, also known as the High Country, include the towns of Burnsville, Spruce Pine, Linville, Blowing Rock, Boone, Banner Elk, Little Switzerland, West Jefferson, Valle Crucis, Wilkesboro and Glendale Springs. These towns, as well as those in the Central Mountains, will also be highlighted in pages that follow.

When is the best time to visit the mountains? The State says it best: *"Let the seasons guide your way to an unforgettable visit to the mountains. Fall offers spectacular views along the Blue Ridge Parkway, America's Favorite drive. Winter creates a snowy wonderland at High Country ski resorts (the Northern Mountains). Spring brings crisp, fresh air perfect for hiking the Appalachian Trail. Summer offers water sports ranging from kayaking tranquil rivers to rafting Class IV-V whitewater rapids."*

I guess the correct answer to the question is *"anytime."* There is something special and magical every season of the year in the mountains of North Carolina.

Come see for yourself.

# The Southwest Mountains

The Smoky Mountains is the primary range in the southwest but touching on the Blue Ridge Mountains as well. Major towns include: Bryson City, Cherokee, Dillsboro, Sylva and Maggie Valley. Each of these towns will be covered individually on the following pages.

But there are other smaller communities in the southwest mountains that deserve your attention as well:

*Franklin:* The "Gem Capital of the World" is a favorite of gem enthusiasts, rock hounds and tourists. A group of middle-schoolers from our church spent a week in the mountains. The overwhelming number of them answered "gem mining" in response to the question "What was your favorite experience on the trip?" Bring your kids here; they'll love it! There are more than a half-dozen mines to visit. And take them to the *Franklin Gem and Mineral Museum* to see the 2¼ pound ruby. There's more to do than gem mining: hiking trails galore, three major waterfalls, and a variety of art galleries and craft studios. Consider staying at the *Blaine House Bed & Breakfast.* Located in the southernmost mountains, Franklin offers easy access from US Highways 23/441 and 64, as well as from Interstate Highways 26, 40 and 85.

*Highlands:* An upscale community in the high elevations of the Southwestern Mountains, Highlands is a favorite destination for golfers. There is a variety of country clubs with courses thoughtfully designed to blend in with the natural beauty of the area. More a residential community than a tourist destination, the permanent residents refer to the "Highlands Way of Life," an easier pace that allow one to take the time to smell the wildflowers and gaze in awe at the fall colors and lush foliage and the inspiring views of the beautiful Blue Ridge Mountains. Downtown Highlands features unique upscale shops, several delightful inns and a number of excellent dining options. Consider staying at the *Old Edwards Inn* and eating at their AAA-rated Four-Diamond restaurant, *Madison's.* You'll also want to stop by *The Stone Lantern,* a unique home décor shop and largest importer of *Ikebana* supplies and equipment.

**Cashiers** (pronounced KASH-erz). Located just a few miles northeast of Highlands, on US-64, Cashiers is one of North Carolina's premier resort destinations. As with Highlands, the views of the Blue Ridge Mountains are breathtaking and the life-style might best be described at "elegant." At the same time true Southern Hospitality abounds. Try lunch at *Café 107,* a quaint bistro serving great homemade soups and hummus and more. For dinner head to *The Orchard*, serving "American Cuisine with a Southern Flavor." The restaurant is housed in a 100-year-old farmhouse serving dinner-only in an atmosphere of "rustic elegance with mountain charm." I love the menu which has divided their offerings by food from "The River and Sea, the Garden, the Pasture and the Barn."

**Waynesville:** Located just off I-40 at US-19 as it begins its way west toward Cherokee and Bryson City. If you are headed that way don't just drive through . . . stop for an hour, or a day, or a week. There is plenty to do and enjoy and Waynesville is a convenient "home base" about half-way between *Asheville* and *The Great Smoky Mountain National Park.* The town has been referred to as a "quaint mountain retreat". As with other towns in the area, there is plenty of Southern Hospitality here too. One of the "special" places is the *Waynesville Inn Golf Resort & Spa,* featuring 27-holes of championship golf, two restaurants, rooms and suites and spa services. Smaller but equally as outstanding is *The Sway*

*Mountaintop Inn,* with 14 guest rooms, suites and cabins on top of a mountain with amazing views of the Smokey Mountains. No golf, but you can play racquetball, croquet, badminton and horseshoes. The *Wall Street Journal* named The Sway one of the nation's best getaways. Open late April through November.

**Murphy:** One could say Murphy is the first and last town in North Carolina, depending upon whether you are coming or going. If you are headed to the mountains from Atlanta or Chattanooga it is worth a stop. The Chamber of Commerce says that this is where "*the forested mountains touch the sky, the lakes sparkle, the air is crisp and clean, and the charm of small town America still exists.*" That alone warrants a visit. But there is more: Murphy is a beautiful small town in the mountains – its population of 1,700 resembles a Norman Rockwell painting. Two lakes, Hiwassee and Apalachia, offer a variety of activities for the entire family. There are dozens of cabins available for rental, as well as other accommodations. Go to www.cherokeecountrychamber.com for a listing.

# Bryson City

Bryson City is a small town in the western half of western North Carolina. If that is too confusing get out your GPS: it is located at 35/25'37"N 83/26'52"W. That's on Highway 19, 66 miles west of Asheville. You can drive there from Asheville in an hour and a half, but don't do it. There are too many good places to stop on the way, like in Cherokee (pg. 211). Take your time getting there. But plan to stay a while once you arrive. Before you decide where to spend the night, however, be sure and check out the *Hemlock Inn* (pg. 201), which is a couple miles east of town.

The town is surrounded by mountains on all sides. The boundary of the *Great Smoky Mountains National Park* is just north of the town and the boundary of the Nantahala National Forest is just to the south. Native Americans have been living and hunting in the area surrounding what is now Bryson City for 11,000 years. The Cherokees believe that their oldest village, Kituhwa, was located just upstream from Bryson City. The Qualla Boundary, which makes up the largest part of the reservation of the *Eastern Band of Cherokee Indians*, dominates the area to the east.

Bryson City and the Great Smoky Mountains National Park have a long history together. A Bryson City resident for a number of years, Horace Kephart, an author and outdoor enthusiast, was one of the early proponents for the establishment of the park. The main eastern entrance to the park, which opened in 1933, is located about 12 miles east of town, in Cherokee.

One of the main attractions bringing people to Bryson City is the *Great Smoky Mountains Railroad (GSMR),* which offers a variety of excursions and rides. The railroad has 53 miles of track and crosses over 25 bridges and goes through 2 tunnels. Norfolk Southern Railways ended freight traffic in the area in 1985 and the state of North Carolina purchased the tracks. The GSMR was established in 1988 as a scenic line with its depot and departure point in Bryson City. One of the most popular excursions is the annual *Polar Express* where young and old enjoy an hour and fifteen minute ride to the North Pole to visit *Santa*. This special Christmas activity runs from early November up until a day or two before Christmas. Also very popular are the Mystery Theatre Dinner Trains which operate every Saturday evening from May thru September. Passengers participate in a hilarious 3-hour performance trying to solve the mystery while enjoying a three-course dinner. For a complete schedule of all of the excursions download their brochure from their web site at www.gsmr.com.

Bryson City is an experience unto itself. Lots of interesting shops and things to do, as well as good places to eat. That mountain air does build one's appetite.

For the past two years (2012 and 2013) Bryson City has hosted the *ICF Canoe Freestyle World Championships*. Held on the Nantahala River and aided with a wave machine, in 2012 athletes from 17 different countries and 5 continents participated in the championships.

In other pages of the book, I will describe two other interesting and enjoyable experiences available to you while you are in the Bryson City area: *whitewater rafting* on the *Nantahala River* (pg. 207) and a visit to the *Fontana Dam*, the highest dam east of the Rockies (pg. 205). Check them out.

# Hemlock Inn

Have you ever visited or stayed at a place that you just couldn't get enough of and had to keep returning? That place for us is the *Hemlock Inn*. We first stayed at Hemlock Inn in 1969 and have been returning every few years ever since. It is just that special.

Hemlock Inn is a country bed and breakfast inn, run by a family that treats their guests as family. John Shell owned an insurance brokerage business in Marietta, Georgia, and Raymond and Georgia Johnson, then owners of the inn, were among his clients. The Johnsons had purchased the property from the Haynies, who had founded the inn in 1952. It was during a visit to the inn in 1969 that the Johnsons told John Shell that they were ready to retire and asked his advice on selling the property. After a short discussion John said "Sell it to me and my family! We'd love to own and run it," and he took off back to Marietta to get his wife Ella Jo and their two young daughters.

It was a match made in heaven; the Shells were perfect for Hemlock Inn and Hemlock Inn was perfect for them. Our first visit to the inn was shortly after the Shells took ownership.

The Inn is now operated by one of the Shell daughters, Lainey White, and her husband Mort. Their three sons, all in or out of college by now, used to help out at the inn, just as Lainey and her sister did when they were growing up. Now there is even a third generation helping run the Inn: Chad and Maggie Gilbert, oldest grandson of Ella Jo and John Shell, and his wife.

There are several things that make Hemlock Inn special to us. First, it is one of the most quiet, relaxing and beautiful spots you'll ever visit. Do not come expecting to find a television set in your room, or even in the great room. If there is a television set on the property it is hidden somewhere deep inside the innkeepers private living quarters. The most strenuous activity, besides rocking in rocking chairs on the front and side porches, is shuffle board and skittle pool off the back porch. The inn is located about a mile up the side of a mountain off of Highway 19, a few miles east of Bryson City, and overlooks the valleys and the Great Smoky Mountains. You couldn't hear a car from the highway if you wanted to, and who would?

The food served is a close second; a delicious home-cooked country breakfast comes with your room and dinner is also available, if you choose. Do choose. Meals are served family-style around a half-dozen or so round Lazy Susan tables that sit ten or twelve. There are only 25 units (twenty-two rooms and three cabins) so the Hemlock Inn is never crowded, even when it has full occupancy, which is most of the time. We love it that everyone stands behind their chair before sitting down and waits until Mort says grace, thanking God for this wonderful world and this wonderful place.

Then it's "Dig In!" Some of the best country cooking you've ever put in your mouth, prepared by a cook staff that has been preparing meals at the inn for many years. And, the pleasant wait staff just keeps refilling the bowls of grits and curried fruit and biscuits, and country ham and scrambled eggs and home-made preserves and on and on. Don't dare leave the table without tasting the pumpkin chips and the apple chips. They are so special that the secret recipe is the only dish that is not included in the *Recipes from Our Front Porch* cookbook that Ella Jo prepared before she passed on.

Dinners are even more outstanding than the breakfasts, if that is possible. As with breakfast, dinner is served family-style. Fried chicken like your grandmother used to make.

202

Squash casserole, fried okra, country-style steak covered in gravy. Home-made pies, cakes, cobblers and more.

A limited number of seats at the tables are available for non-guests, but be sure and call before showing up to make certain there is room for you.

Finally, it is the friendly family atmosphere, created not only by the owners and the staff, but by the guests. At most every visit we have made, the majority of the other guests had also been there before.

We'll be recommending places to eat and places to stay throughout this book. There is none that we recommend any higher than Hemlock Inn. I could write an entire chapter about this wonderful place. Go to their web site at www.hemlockinn.com for more information and for a description of the rooms, rates, and availability.

# Fontana Dam

The highest dam east of the Rocky Mountains is located just 35 miles west of Bryson City. Fontana Dam stretches almost a half mile across the Little Tennessee River. Towering 480 feet, the dam is equal to the height of a 50-story skyscraper. To give that some perspective, remember the dam that Harrison Ford jumped off of in the movie *The Fugitive*? That was the *Cheoah Dam*, which is also on the Little Tennessee River but located further downstream from Fontana. Well, the Cheoah could be called a mini-dam compared to Fontana; Fontana is more than twice as tall.

I first visited Fontana Dam as a small child, two years after it was completed. I don't remember the entire vacation trip when this occurred, but I specifically remember the visit to the dam. Thirty years after that we took our two sons to see the dam and now another thirty years later they still vividly remember the experience.

Fontana was built during the Second World War to provide electric power for the war effort. Five thousand people worked around the clock in three shifts to complete the dam in record time, just 36 months. Work began in 1942 and the dam was completed in 1944. The dam today is operated by the TVA, the Tennessee Valley Authority, and provides electrical power for parts of the Tennessee valley.

The dam creates a reservoir twenty-nine miles in length with 238 miles of shore line. The water is used to power the turbines and generators that produce electricity. When power is needed, water is released from the reservoir through a large pipe and into a turbine. The force of the water spins the blades of the turbine, which is connected to a generator that also spins, producing electricity. After passing through the turbine, the water reenters the river on the downstream side of the dam.

In addition to the electrical power, the dam provides flood control and recreational opportunities such as boating, fishing and swimming. The Appalachian Trail, which runs more than 2,000 miles from Georgia to Maine, crosses the Fontana Dam. The hot showers available at the trail shelter have led grateful hikers to name it the Fontana Hilton.

The visitor center is open to the public May through October from 9:00 am to 7:00 pm. The top-to-bottom and inside-and-out tour of the dam is well worth the time and effort. If you have never visited Fontana Dam don't allow yourself to leave the Bryson City area without at least driving across the top of the dam or stopping for some pictures.

*Two fish swim into a concrete wall. One turns to the other and says, "Dam."*

# Whitewater Rafting

The Nantahala River was named by *National Geographic Adventures* as the number one place in the U.S. to spend a wet and wild vacation. They referred to it as "The Nation's Best Place to Cool Off with a Splash."

Located about a dozen miles west of Bryson City, the scenic Nantahala River ranks among the most popular rafting runs in the country, with more than 200,000 rafters and paddlers each year.

Class II and Class III rapids are available. The Nantahala is considered a "family" river suitable for senior citizens and children who are at least 7 years old and weigh at least 70 pounds.

The first time we took our family whitewater rafting it was on this river. The boys were about twelve and fourteen. The four of us were in a self-guided raft. The rafting companies are very safety conscious and before we were allowed on the river we had to attend a half-hour safety video and demonstration. And, of course, we all had to wear helmets and life vests.

One point that was clearly made at the safety demonstration was that every raft had to appoint a "captain" to sit at the rear of the raft and call out instructions as the raft went through the rapids. "Pull to the left, LEFT, to the LEFT, damnit. Now back to the right, RIGHT, RIGHT." Well, you get the idea.

Who but the father would be best qualified to be captain? No one, that's who. David, our youngest son, who even at twelve had more muscles that the rest of us, was sitting on the right front side of the raft; Dee, my wife, was sitting behind him on the right; Philip, our oldest son, was on the left side. I was in the middle at the back.

We did fine in the calmer water and small rapids, but when we reached the larger rapids the roar of the water became louder and louder and it became more and more difficult to communicate. As the raft finally got through this one particularly difficult series of rapids, David all of a sudden began paddling backwards.

*"What are you doing?"* his mother yelled. *"You're paddling backwards! Don't paddle backwards!"*

*"No, no,"* David yelled back at her. *"We have to go back, we have to go back,"* as he continued to paddle in reverse.

*"Back, what are you talking about back? Why do we have to go back?"* Dee exclaimed.

*"To get Dad,"* David answered.

Dad had fallen out of the raft, and David was the only one who had noticed. There I was maybe 75 yards back in the middle of the rapids hanging on to a rock.

Well, there was no way they were going to paddle the raft back up stream against the fast running rapids, but they finally did get the raft up next to the bank on the side of the river and I got up enough courage to let go of the rock and float through the rapids feet first and on my butt as we had been instructed in the video. Once through the rapids I was able to swim over to the raft and get back in. Quite an experience.

It was a number of years later before Dee and David and I attempted whitewater rafting again. He was in college and we were on the Chattooga River, the river where they filmed the movie *Deliverance*. A little different experience this time: Dee fell out of the raft . . . and pulled me out with her.

In the movie *Love Actually*, as the heart-heavy young man standing in the snow said after showing his best friend's wife the show cards which expressed his love, *"Enough . . .*

*enough.*" That's the way I feel: enough, enough . . . river rafting, for me that is. But don't let me discourage you from trying it.

There are a good number of rafting companies along the side of the road next to the river in Bryson City. Go to http://greatsmokies.com/riverrafting.asp for a complete listing.

# Cherokee

The town of Cherokee is located at the south terminus of the **Blue Ridge Parkway** and the eastern entrance to the **Great Smoky Mountain National Park**. It is also the capital of the Eastern Band of Cherokee Indians and the center of the North Carolina's largest tourist center. More than 9 million people a year visit the Great Smoky Mountain National Park and the majority of them also visit one or more of the attractions in Cherokee.

There are at least 20 different tribes of Native Americans associated with North Carolina, including the Creek, the Croatan, the Catawba, and the Tuscaora, but there is only one federally-recognized Indian tribe in North Carolina today: the Eastern Band of the Cherokee Indians. Most people recognize the name Cherokee, making it one of the best known in history.

No one knows exactly how long the Cherokee have lived in western North Carolina, but archeologists have discovered evidence that people lived here at the end of the last Ice Age, more than 11,000 years ago. Some have suggested that the artifacts found may go back 14,000 years.

The Cherokee Indians were the first to be charmed by the natural beauty of the mountains and the clear blue sky. They called the area the "Land of the Blue Smoke", leading to the Smoky and Blue Ridge mountains as we know them today.

Today, the Eastern Band of the Cherokee Indians is a sovereign nation of 100 square miles, with more than 13,000 enrolled members. They eagerly await the opportunity to share their culture with you. The vacation destination has many fun activities – museums, amusement parks, a casino, hiking trails, scenic drives, great shopping and more, but it is the four feature attractions that command the greatest attention.

**The Oconaluftee Village:** As you step into the village you are transported back in history. Visitors are able to take self-guided tours to explore the authentic working village with dwellings, residents, and artisans right out of the 1750's. Visitors can interact with villagers as they make pottery and masks, hull canoes, weave baskets, do beadwork and participate in their daily activities. The village also presents live reenactments and hands-on arts and craft classes. It is truly a living history site. Open daily except Sundays May 1 thru October 20th.

**The Museum of the Cherokee Indian:** Virtual Cherokee storytellers welcome you and serve as your guides to this educational and interactive museum experience. Visitors are taken back to the beginnings of human existence in this area. Modern technology, computer-generated imagery, and special effects are used by the guides to provide you with their own point of view of their heritage. The museum is open seven days a week, but closed on Thanksgiving, Christmas, and New Year's days. Seasonal hours.

**"Unto These Hills" Outdoor Drama:** One of the nation's foremost outdoor dramas. It has been staged annually since 1950 and has been performed for more than six million visitors. The play follows the story of the Cherokee's first contact with Europeans to their infamous and tragic removal, via the Trail of Tears, in 1838. Set against the backdrop of the Great Smoky Mountains, the beautiful outdoor theatre seats 2,800. Performances are scheduled June thru mid-August every evening except Sundays.

**Qualla Arts:** Founded in 1946 with the purpose of pre serving and advancing Cherokee arts and crafts, the Qualla Arts & Crafts Mutual, Inc., is today the oldest and leading

Native American Arts cooperative in the U.S. Unlike most of us, the Cherokees are still in touch with their ancient art and craft traditions. Now you can be in touch as well, by bringing home the available, affordable work of contemporary Cherokee masters. During the summer visitors can indulge their creative sides with live arts and crafts demonstrations. Admission to the showroom and gallery is free and is open seven days a week, except on Thanksgiving, Christmas, and New Year's. 8 am – 4:30 pm, Monday thru Saturday; Sundays 9 am to 5 pm.

A visit to Cherokee should be part of any trip to North Carolina.

# Dillsboro

Dillsboro is another one of those towns where it is like stepping back in time. It has been a tourist town since the 19th century when the railroad first brought visitors to the mountains to escape the summer heat.

Little has changed more than a century later. Its five square blocks of century-old stores, galleries, restaurants and inns are a reminder of small town life from years gone past. No shopping malls, no chain stores, just an interesting collection of mom-and-pop businesses featuring everything from fashion boutiques to arts and crafts.

There are shops with cheeses, coffees, chocolates and confections. There are artisan's studios where you can watch the creation of one-of-a-kind, hand-made works of fibers, glass, clay, metal or precious stones. It is worth the trip alone to visit the General Store with its old-fashioned soda fountain.

Dillboro's old-style charm and cordial atmosphere has made it a home to a growing number of artisans and craftspeople. At the edge of town, a small group of residents are beginning to use green energy, methane gas from a landfill, to fuel blacksmith forges, glass-blowers' ovens, potters' kilns and to warm greenhouses.

The most featured site in Dillsboro is the historic *Jarrett House*. Established in 1884, The Jarrett House is a beautiful bed-and-breakfast inn and restaurant that is noted for its Victorian-style furnishings and traditional family-style dining. The Jarrett House is one of western North Carolina's oldest operating inns, providing lodging for travelers first by train and now by road.

Special features on the menu include, of course, trout and country ham and red eye gravy for over 120 years. Unusual dessert treats are their old-fashioned Vinegar Pies.

Dillsboro has changed very little – the town's founder, Thomas Dills' home still stands as do many of the shops that first opened their doors in the 1800s. Some of the old and the new shops include:

**Bradley's General Store**, open since 1888. It features an old time soda fountain; local honey, jams and jellies; antiques; and Amish-handmade furniture. It's on Front Street.

**The Golden Carp**, with original watercolors by in-house artist, John Miele, and other local artists, as well as locally-made pillows, throws, and tapestries. The shop also carries a large selection of baskets. It's on Webster Street.

**The Cheddar Box** is a leading supplier of locally produced gourmet foods, including homemade butter fudge, locally roasted coffee, apple butter and jams and jellies, as well as chutneys, BBQ sauce, and salsa. It's also on Front Street.

**Dogwood Crafters** is a cooperative of over 80 Smoky Mountain artisans. Showcasing mountain crafts for almost forty years, the shop invites visitors to explore and learn all about the shop's offerings. Exploring, that's my kind of place. Located on Webster Street.

**Shirley's Boutique** is housed in a 100-year old building but carried current and traditional fashions and accessories for the discerning woman. Located at the corner of Church and Front Streets.

**Treehouse Pottery** is a working studio and gallery representing the fine art of clay. It's located on Front Street.

**Oaks Gallery** showcases jewelry, wood, glass, pottery, weaving and more from over 100 of the area's leading craftspeople. The gallery is located on Craft Circle.

Dillsboro is located between Franklin and Waynesville.

# Fat Buddies Ribs & BBQ

How could you not try a place named *Fat Buddies Ribs & BBQ*? Especially when their slogan is *"So Good It'll Make You Squeal."*

With restaurants in both Franklin and Waynesville, NC there is no excuse not to visit at least one of them when you are in the southwest mountain region.

Start off with a Fat Buddies' Onion Loaf: thinly sliced onions, deep fried to a golden brown and served with Chuck's Spicy Ranch Dressing. Or go for the Fresh Fried Mushrooms: juicy, fresh mushrooms, lightly breaded, deep fried and also served with Chuck's Spicy Ranch Dressing. Or try the Fried Dill Pickles or Potato Skins.

Wash that down with a large glass of sweet tea and you are ready to do some serious eating. You'll be in Hog Heaven with a rack of Smoked Baby Back Ribs. "Slow wood smokin' and steady bastin'" gives Fat Buddies' ribs the flavor of the South! Or go for a plate of BBQ Pork or Beef or a Smoked Turkey dinner. All are served with thick-sliced garlic bread and your choice of two sides.

Or go for the combo that is sort of like this book: a combination of mountains and seashore: your choice of a 12-oz. hand-cut Rib-Eye steak or a ½ rack of baby Back Ribs and Fat Buddies' Fried Shrimp.

One of the best sellers on the menu is Fat Buddies' Pig-Out for Two (or for one big boy): you get a ½ Chicken, ¼ lb. BBQ Pork, ¼ lb. BBQ Beef, a full rack of Baby Back Ribs plus two orders of each: French fries, baked beans, coleslaw, and garlic toast. As the locals say, "Boy Howdy!"

But there are lighter fare on the menu as well. There are

five salad choices including a wonderful Special Turkey Salad and Chicken in the Garden, a fresh garden salad topped with a grilled chicken breast that has been brushed with a Honey BBQ sauce.

The BBQ Pork and Beef can be served as a sandwich and can come with or without fries. The Smoked Turkey is also available as a sandwich, along with a Fried or Grilled Chicken sandwich or a Grilled Turkey and Cheese.

Both restaurants are closed on Sundays but open from 11 am until 9 pm Monday thru Saturday. The Franklin store is located at 311 Westgate Plaza, 2 blocks south of Murphy Road (US-64), turn onto Roller Mill Road. The Waynesville store is located at Waynesville Plaza, take Exit 102 A-B (Ross Road) off of the Great Smoky Mountain Expressway (US-23 & 74).

Oh, I almost forgot: everything on the menu is available for takeout and for shipping.

# Maggie Valley

One of the most well-known resort areas in western North Carolina, *Maggie Valley* is a perfect home base from which to explore the *Great Smoky Mountain National Park*. If you can't get a room at the before-mentioned *Hemlock Inn*, to the west in Bryson City, check out the various accommodations available in Maggie Valley. You can choose accommodations ranging from motel and hotel rooms to bed and breakfasts to individual log cabins. The national park is located about half way between the two towns.

Maggie Valley is a little more "touristy" than other mountain towns, but that does not mean that you won't enjoy your visit. Good old Southern hospitality remains in abundance and there are lots and lots of fun things to do. Or, it's a great place to just sit back and relax and enjoy the wonderful beauty that surrounds the area.

In the winter the ski slopes open offering some of the best skiing in the southeast. Other times of the year enjoy golf, whitewater rafting, horseback riding and other outdoor activities. Motorcycling on the Blue Grass Parkway has long been a favorite summertime activity.

For those of you who enjoy dancing or just foot stomping to the beat of the music, Bluegrass and Country Music concerts and festivals are held throughout the year.

If you are in need of a little retail therapy Maggie Valley is the place to shop. From art and antiques, regional and high fashion, crafts and items unique to the area, Maggie Valley is a year-round shopping destination. The shopping district is pedestrian-friendly making it easy to get around.

In a word, Maggie Valley has something for everyone.

There are a dozen or so good restaurants in Maggie Valley and nearby towns. The following are several of the ones we have most enjoyed:

In a lovely setting overlooking the Smokies, eating at the Maggie Valley Inn and Conference Center's **Rendezvous Restaurant** is like dining in an old hunting lodge. They offer a nice selection of appetizers, but a rather limited selection of entrees, although they do offer daily specials. It is worth a trip if for nothing more than a drink (they have a full-service bar) and some appetizer items. The setting is lovely. The Inn and Conference Center is located at the corner of Highways 276 and 19, just 8 miles from the Blue Ridge Parkway. 70 Soco Road, Maggie Valley. 828-926-0201.

**The Legends Sports Grille** brags that they serve the "best hamburger east of the Mississippi River." We'll let you decide that, but you can choose from ten different burger selections, including an Italian Burger with pepperoni and provolone, topped with marinara sauce. Or choose from 13 different styles of chicken wings. The Jamaican Jerk wings are my favorite. With 24 flat screen television sets, it seems like the place in town to hang out and cheer your favorite team. Located at 3865 Soco Rd., Maggie Valley . 828-926-9464.

Earlier in the book I mentioned some tests to use to find a good restaurant. One was the number of locals that eat there and another was the length of time the restaurant has been in business. **Joey's Pancake House** exceeds in both tests! Since 1966, locals and visitors alike have been raving about breakfasts at Joey's. There is nothing "regular" about Joey's famous "regular" golden pancakes, they are outstanding. But many say the specialty pancakes are even better. How about Reeses Cup pancakes! All of the "regular" and slow-cooked oatmeal, and creamed chip beef on toast are outstanding as well. Open every day except Thursday from 7:00 am until noon only. 4309 Soco Road, Maggie Valley. 828-926-0212.

***The Maggie Valley Restaurant*** is another that has passed the test of time. They are celebrating their 60th anniversary this year, pleasing their customers by serving southern cooking at its best. One of the major "pulls" is that they serve breakfast anytime with a variety of pancakes to omelets, and complementary sausage-gravy, red potatoes, or grits with all egg orders. And delicious real, home-made buttermilk biscuits; ask your server to put a couple of pieces of country ham into one. A good variety of just good country cookin' is available for lunch and dinner. Open seven days a week from 7:00 am until 9:00 pm, May thru October. 2804 Soco Road, Maggie Valley. 828-926-0425.

# J. Arthur's Restaurant

A Maggie Valley restaurant that "meets the test" is *J. Arthur's*. You don't survive (thrive) for twenty-five years without doing something right. And, J. Arthur's does it all right! Feed your family, celebrate an anniversary, cater your wedding, J. Arthur's is, as they say, *"the place to be."*

In additional to serving excellent food at value prices, another way to thrive in the restaurant business is to take care of your guests, and the folks at J. Arthur's take pride in doing just that. Not just the owners, but the entire staff not only want you to enjoy the food but they want you to enjoy the experience of eating there as well. That attention to service and the outstanding food is what has brought people back time and time again over the years.

For families with small children, there is a "kid's corner" with coloring books and toys, as well as a children's menu that includes the typical hot dogs and hamburgers, but also fish and chips, barbecued ribs and fried shrimp. All children's meals are served with fries, veggies or applesauce, a drink, and a hot fudge sundae.

On the lighter side, J. Arthur's offers a variety of grill, sandwich, and salad selections. Not to be missed is the amazing and never empty Gorgonzola Cheese salad bowl. You can add salmon, chicken breast, sliced steak or cold shrimp, but only the salad is unlimited.

The extensive dinner menu includes such beef standards as grilled rib eye, filet and Chateaubriand, but also a variety of chicken, pork and seafood dishes. In addition to fresh, local rainbow trout, they serve Basa Bella Meuniere, a mild white fish with artichokes and mushrooms in a lemon butter sauce.

It is one of the most popular items on the menu.

All entrees are served with a choice of homemade soup of the day or salad, potato or vegetable, rolls and butter. The desert menu has always been tempting, but we are usually so full from the generous portions of dinner we've never had room for dessert. Next visit I'm going to ask for a dessert to go!

For a complete and current look at their menu see the web site at www.jarthurs.com. On the web site, you will also find the extensive list of wines that are available by the glass. Last time I checked, the web site also offered a printable discount coupon. Check it out. Located on Highway 19, Maggie Valley.

# Sylva

I first visited *Sylva*, North Carolina as a small child, in 1946. My mother was seven or eight months pregnant with her second child, it was in the summertime in Miami and hot (no AC in those days), and she had had just about all she could take of me running around the house causing trouble. She was already mad at my father, perhaps for getting her pregnant (sorry, brother Steve), so she shipped us both off to North Carolina by ourselves for a little vacation. Vacation for her, I think, from us.

Anyway my father and I spent a week in Sylvia, staying at a farm house that took in boarders. I don't remember very much about Sylvia itself, but having been back there recently I don't think it has changed a lot. And that is a good thing. It is charming.

Sylva is a small town about halfway between Franklin and Waynesville, just south of Cherokee. It is about 45 minutes west of Asheville. Population about 2,500. Nestled in the Great Smoky Mountains, Sylva offers residents and visitors a wide selection of both indoor and outdoor activities.

Designated a *Main Street Town* by the State of North Carolina, downtown has many unique shops you will want to visit and several nice restaurants and downtown cafes. We especially enjoyed Lulu's. While you are downtown you can't miss seeing the Jackson County Courthouse, considered to be the most photographed courthouse in the state.

For outside activities visit the Tuckasegee River, noted for its whitewater and trout fishing. Pinnacle Park, located 10 minutes from   downtown, has waterfalls and hiking trails for its whitewater and trout fishing. Pinnacle Park, located about ten minutes from downtown, has waterfalls and hiking trails (moderate to difficult) and offers a wonderful view of the town from the top of the mountain.

As a point of interest, parts of the movie *The Fugitive* was filmed in Sylva: the hospital scenes following the train wreck and some of the river scenes. The train wreck itself was filmed in Dillsboro, about two miles from Sylva.

Sylva also has its own hometown brewery: the *Heinzelmannchen Brewery*. Their beer is served on tap at many of the local restaurants and cafes, but I have not seen one of their bottles or cans. They must be extra large ones in order to fit all those letters on the label.

*"Not all enchanted forests exist in fairy tales."*
Come see ours in North Carolina.

# Lulu's Café

An article in *Southern Living* magazine claimed *Lulu's* as "our favorite restaurant in the region." I can understand why they like it so much.

*Fodor's* travel guide wrote that "If you need a break from the Smoky's traditional trout, ham, and gravy food groups, this American gourmet-diner is considered by many locals as the region's finest restaurant." This I cannot understand; who needs a break from gravy food groups? Isn't there a recommended daily consumption of gravy?

Anyway, for lunch if you are in the mood for something that is not covered in gravy, try Lulu's La Bella, fresh grilled portabella mushrooms marinated in a citrus basil sauce served with a hot baguette your choice of a creamy Gorgonzola dressing or lemon-oil for dipping. Or, her Blue Moon Burrito, a tortilla filled with spicy pinto beans, Cheddar and Monterey Jack cheeses and topped with lettuce, tomatoes, black olives, red onions, sour cream and jalapenos. It is served with brown basmati rice and salsa.

Lulu's dinner menu is filled with interesting dishes including Salmon Mojitos Platanos: fresh Atlantic salmon grilled and served over a creamy coconut, rum, and roasted plantain coulis. It is served with black beans and rice and topped with green onions.

The Raspberry Rum Pork Loin is one of the most popular dishes on the menu. Rosemary rubbed pork loin roasted and finished on the grill and then basted with a raspberry-rum semi-glaze. This delicious dish is served with garlic mashed potatoes and the daily vegetable offering.

Hmmm, again . . . citrus basil sauce; creamy Gorgonzola dressing; creamy coconut, rum and roasted plantain coulis;

raspberry-rum semi-glaze: *Fodor's*, it all sounds like gravy to me!

My favorite appetizer is the Artichoke Montrachet Crostini. First artichokes and shallots are sautéed in white wine and then pureed with locally-produced goat cheese. The mixture is then baked on an organic French baquette. Outstanding!

Lulu's is open Monday thru Saturday from 11:30 am until 8 pm in the winter and until 9 pm in the summer. Located in downtown on Main Street, Sylva, North Carolina.

*"I come from a family where gravy is*
*considered a beverage."*
Erma Bombeck

# The Central Mountains

Portions of both the Smoky and the Blue Ridge Mountains are included in the Central Mountains. Asheville is the capital of the North Carolina Mountains and deserves a book of its own. I've included write-ups on two Asheville restaurants and a short piece on *The Biltmore Estate,* but this section of the book is basically about the interesting towns surrounding Asheville: Black Mountain, Brevard, Lake Lure and Chimney Rock, Lynn and Rutherfordton. Each of these towns will be covered individually on the following pages, but there are other small communities in the central mountains that deserve your attention as well:

*Hendersonville:* Named by *Where to Retire* magazine as one of the *50 Best Places to Retire,* it is also a great place to visit. A tour of the 5+ block area that is a *"Main Street National Register Historic District"* is by itself a reason to visit. But there is much, much more. Take either of the two exits off of I-26, less than 20 minutes south of Asheville.

*Saluda:* This historic Victorian mountain village at the foothills of the Blue Ridge Mountains has been a favorite vacation destination since the turn of the twentieth century. Stop by *Thompson's Store*, the oldest grocery store in the state of North Carolina. This family-owned store was founded in 1890 and has been run continuously by members of the family ever since. The store is one of the few places I can find *Zarina Bella* hot sauces. I haven't tried it, but people I trust tell me that their homemade sausage is the best they have ever tasted. You can get a sausage biscuit at *Walt's Grill,* located inside the store.

*Tryon:* Our friend *Ed Richardson* lives in Tryon and loves it. He has lived and traveled various places around the world and counts Tryon as one of his favorites.

The epicenter of equestrian events, Tryon was once the training center for the *US Olympic Equestrian Team*. They continue to hold an annual Steeplechase and nearly year-round horse shows at the *Foothills Equestrian Nature Center*.

Interestingly, *Hernando De Soto*, who you read about in the Anna Maria Island section of the book, reputedly traveled by horseback with a thousand men in search of gold to the area of what is now between Spartanburg, SC and Asheville, NC. (Tryon is just about in the middle of the two cities.) You will recall that De Soto left a few pigs in Florida; perhaps it was the descendants of some of his horses left in North Carolina that led to Tryon becoming an equestrian center. You never know.

If you ever get to Tryon, check out the schedule of events at the *Tryon Fine Arts Center*. Our friend Ed may be performing in one of the local civic theatre productions.

# The Beauty of Nature

The beauty of the Great Smoky and the Blue Ridge Mountains have for many years been an inspiration for writers and artists of all types. From poets to spiritual and inspirational writers to historians and novelists, from potters and weavers to visual artists in all media, the lure of the mountains has been irresistible.

It was for **Alan** and **Robbin McCarter** of Hendersonville. It was the ethereal beauty and spiritual inspiration of the mountains that led them to leave their other careers behind and move to the North Carolina Mountains to become full-time artists. And what a successful second career it has been for both of them.

They say that the gentle yet exalted beauty of the region has enriched, uplifted, and transformed their lives forever. Their purpose in art *"is to find and glorify the divine in Nature, to share this vision with others, and to thereby uplift the human spirit to a realm of beauty and goodness."*

They have fulfilled their purpose every time we have entered their studio. Although we live among this beauty when we are in North Carolina there is something about the art of both Alan and Robbin that takes us to another and higher level. Spend a half-hour in their gallery and I guarantee that you will leave with an uplifted spirit and an expanded appreciation for the beauty of nature. You'll probably also leave with a piece of original art or a print or giclee of their work.

Alan McCarter's style is soft idealized, romantic realism. Robbin also paints in a soft realistic style, but with special attention to small, delicate detail. Alan uses acrylic in a rich classic technique. Robbin generally works in watercolor, but also in acrylic and colored pencil. Alan paints majestic panoramas of the mountains and also light and movement in streams and waterfalls, and woodland interiors. Robbin's favorite subjects are the tiny yet exquisite wildflowers, both as individuals and in their own unique habitats.

Alan and Robbin invite you to visit their gallery, to share in the peaceful and uplifting vision of their paintings and enjoy the atmosphere of a Sanctuary of Nature within. The gallery is located in downtown Hendersonville at 451 N. Main Street. The hours are noon to 5 pm, Tuesday thru Saturday, and by appointment. Morning they are usually out painting, but if you need an appointment for times or days that they are not usually open that can be arranged. Phone 828-689-7117.

Alan also holds periodic workshops. If you will leave your name with the gallery with your phone number or email address he will contact you for future workshops. The Gallery is also on *Facebook*. For a look at their latest paintings go to their Facebook page under the name "McCarter Gallery."

# Brevard and Transylvania County

Transylvania County is home to some of North Carolina's most spectacular waterfalls; more than 250 falls are in the general area surrounding the town of Brevard. Brevard, the county seat, is a charming community in the Blue Ridge Mountains nestled in the middle of the Pisgah National Forest. The town has been named by several national travel publications as "one of America's top ten places to live and play."

Much of Transylvania County is also located in parts of the Nantahula National Forest and the Blue Ridge Parkway. This means that waterfalls in these areas are on public land and access to them is available to anyone. There are at least twenty-five falls that would be categorized as "major falls."

Our favorites include: *Bridal Veil* and *Triple Falls*, both of which were filmed in the movie *The Last of the Mohicans; High Falls; Twin Falls* and *Looking Glass Falls*. It will involve some driving and some hiking, but you can see them all in a single day.

Not just the beautiful waterfalls, streams, and mountain trails, but a wide assortment of other activities await you, such as biking, fishing, kayaking and climbing. And, you are close to some of the area's other major attractions including the *Biltmore Estate* (pg. 243) in Asheville and *Chimney Rock Park* at Lake Lure (pg. 261).

But, next to the waterfalls, it is the *Brevard Music Festival* for which the town is most noted and revered. For more than seventy years the Brevard Music Center has been providing young musicians with the opportunity to develop their talents.

Each summer, four hundred students, seventy-five guest artists and faculty members, and a staff of technical and support personnel assemble in Brevard, creating a community of learning, teaching, and performing. The intensive summer study is for gifted high school students, college, and pre-professional musicians.

The combination of studying with distinguished professional musicians and an intense performance schedule sets the Brevard Music Center apart from other summer music institutions and gives students the opportunity to experience, first hand, the world of a professional musician. A festival of more than eighty public concerts brings major orchestral, chamber, and operatic repertoire to tens of thousands of listeners each year.

For interested students, applications are available online at www.brevardmusic.org. The web site also lists the performance schedules and ticket information.

There are a number of very nice places to eat in Brevard. We think you will especially like these:

*Marco Trattoria* is an Italian Mediterranean-style restaurant open seven days for lunch and dinner. On Saturdays and Sundays they also have a brunch menu. Go for lunch and order the Roasted Vegetable and Goat Cheese Panini and a cup of tomato and fennel soup. You won't want dinner that night; you'll want to go back and have another sandwich and cup of soup. It's that good. Open 11-3 and from 5-9, seven days. 204 W. Main Street – 828-888-4841.

*Mayberry's.* There are any number of good reasons to stop in here, but there are two in particular. You must try the apple slaw. They serve in on top of their Sweet Hot BBQ sandwich, but it available as a side and you can order it on any sandwich. The second reason is that they are conveniently located just down the street from the White Squirrel Shoppe, and you *must* go into there when you are in Brevard. Oh, I guess there is a third reason: they serve a great Bloody Mary. 30 West Main Street, 828-862-8646. Open Monday-Thursday 11-9, Friday & Saturday 8-9, and Sunday 8-3.

***Bracken Mountain Bakery*** is the perfect spot to start building the picnic lunch you will want to take with you when you plan to spend the day visiting the falls. For being located in a relatively small town they produce an amazing variety of products. Among the more popular are: Bracken Harvest Brown – their own multi-grain made with cracked rye, yellow corn grits, oats, wheat germ, brown sugar and molasses. The Cinnamon Raisin Bread has a unique and special flavor as it is made with a buttermilk dough. They also have a variety of flatbreads including a Greek Olive. You'll want something sweet for dessert. They make sweet croissants, scones, Danish, muffins and cookies. The Peanut Butter Chocolate Chunk cookie is amazing. Open Monday thru Friday from 7:30 'til 5 and on Saturday from 8 until 5. Except that they are closed on Mondays during the winter season (Nov-April). 42 S. Broad Street, 828-883-4034.

Since I mentioned the *White Squirrel Shoppe* I guess I need to mention the now-famous white squirrels of Brevard themselves. Supposedly some fifty years ago two of these rare variants of the Eastern Grey Squirrel escaped from a circus that was visiting Brevard. Apparently one was a male and one was a female because today there are hundreds (thousands?) of white squirrels jumping through trees and running around Brevard. Cute little buggers. So is the *Shoppe*, located at 2 West Main Street. 828-877-3530.

# Apple Mill
# Whole Apple Butter

A couple of years ago Dee and I went on a hunt for sources for pure North Carolina honey. As often happens when you go hunting or exploring you find things you were not expecting or looking for. We found the honey, but we also found this wonderful apple butter.

I am normally a proponent of "home-made", and in spite of finding a number of good-sounding recipes for homemade apple butter, I'm recommending this instead. I doubt that any of the recipes could create an apple butter any better than the whole apple butter produced by the Apple Mill in Saluda, NC.

Made from sound ripe apples, fresh cider, spices and cider vinegar, with no sugar added, it is cooked in the Colonial style: very slowly to thicken, no pectin added. The Apple Mill cooks the butter in stainless steel and stirs it with sassafras paddles. They suggested we try making a Swiss cheese and apple butter sandwich. We did and it was delicious.

Apple products are prepared on-site six months of the year. Glass windows separate the processing area from the retail area allowing customers to view production. Apple Mill products 'taint cheap, but are worth it.

Since we were last in the store they have added some apple baking mixes, including Apple Crisp Mix, Apple Fritter Mix, Apple Nut Bread Mix, and an Apple & Spice Cake Mix.

If you can't stop by the store, just off the Saluda exit of I-26, the apple butter and other apple and fruit products can be ordered online at www.ncapplemill.com. Online prices include free shipping. The store is closed on Tuesdays.

Our friend *Dean Jones* of Bradenton makes a pretty darn good apple butter too, but it is for friends only; too bad it's not for sale. I sure am glad we're one of his friends! Although it has been a while since we've been given a jar. (Hint, hint, Dean.)

# Apollo Flame Bistro

When we lived fulltime in North Carolina we used to drive fifty miles to get to the Apollo Flame Bistro and then drive fifty miles back home. And we'd do it at least once a month. And it was worth every mile! The food is that good. When we are back for our short visits this is our first stop!

This family operated restaurant was started in 1974 and serves the best Greek and Italian food we have found in the mountains. The family recipes have been passed down for three generations. The portions are large, the prices are low, and the service is excellent. What a combination for success! And successful they have been. Readers of the Mountain Xpress, a local tabloid newspaper, voted the Apollo Flame the "Best Greek Restaurant" in the Asheville area for 13 straight years.

We've tried many of the dishes on the menu and all have been good, but we keep coming back to our favorites: the famous Greek Salad with grilled chicken breast and then a white pizza with spinach. A small platter, not a dish, is heaped high with greens, olives, feta, pepperoncini and tomatoes. The homemade Greek dressing is served in a bottle and on the side. We usually do not eat chicken, but we do here. The salad can be topped with sliced chicken breast that has been marinated in the Greek dressing. Talk about tender and talk about flavor! It is wonderful.

After splitting the salad we order a large white pizza. A wonderful thin crust, which we order "extra crispy," is topped with mozzarella and feta cheeses and either spinach or fresh tomato. No sauce. We choose the spinach. After the large salad we usually can eat just a slice or two of the pizza. So why order a large pizza? Why not order a small one? Because then we wouldn't have any to take home with us. Happy to box up the rest of the pizza, the wait staff also always offers us a large to-go cup of whatever non-alcoholic beverage we were drinking.

Other items on the Greek portion of the menu include: the Big Fat Greek Platter, with chicken, meatballs, lamb, lots of Greek salad and pita with Tzatziki sauce (a Greek cucumber sauce); a Combo Gyro Platter or a Chicken Gyro Platter; and Greek Spaghetti, served with olive oil and feta cheese, along with garlic bread and a salad.

On the Italian portion of the menu such standards as lasagna, manicotti, meat or cheese ravioli and tortellini are anything but "standard". All are exceptionally well prepared. Spaghetti with all types of sauces is available, as well are a handful of vegetarian dishes. The Vegetarian Pita is served with a healthy portion of Greek Salad. If it is lighter fare you are after, a variety of hot oven subs or a chef's salad are good choices.

Pizza is another of their specialties. In addition to the white pizza, all of the usually expected pizza toppings are available for you to design your own small, medium or large pie. When we brought an out-of-town friend with us one afternoon he ordered the Apollo Supreme pizza, topped with sausage, pepperoni, hamburger, ham, mushrooms, green peppers and onion. *"The best pizza I've ever eaten,"* he exclaimed! When we were there one time our server apologized and said that it would be a few minutes before our pizza would be ready. The cooks were just finishing up an order for thirty pizzas to go. No one, no one would order thirty pizzas at one time unless they knew they were going to be great. They are!

There is a limited choice of decent house wines available for about $3.50 a glass, as is a nice selection of domestic and imported beers. And there are always daily specials on the blackboard. And did I mention the wait staff? Well-trained and outstanding! If you ever get to or even near Asheville, don't leave the area without visiting the Apollo Flame Bistro. They are open from 11 am until 10 pm Monday thru Saturday. As *Melina Mercouri* once said, *"Never on Sunday."* She was Greek, wasn't she? The bistro is located less than a mile from the entrance to the *Biltmore Estate,* at 485 Hendersonville Road, Asheville. (They have another location in town, but THIS is the one!)

# Biltmore Estate

There has been so much published about the Biltmore Estate in Asheville that I hesitated including anything about it in this book. But my wife, our son David and our daughter-in-law Chasity had such a wonderful experience at the Biltmore one Christmas that Dee encouraged me to include it. Actually we've had an enjoyable time every time (five or six) we have been there.

Those of you who have visited the Biltmore Estate know that it is a truly magnificent and beautiful home. But if you haven't been there at Christmas time, at night when it is all lit up, and when every room of the house has been decorated, and singers in costume are serenading the guests with Christmas Carols, you haven't experienced the estate at its most glorious.

The largest home in America, completed in 1895, George Vanderbilt's 250-room chateau is as impressive today as it was more than 100 years ago. The self-guided tour will take about an hour and a half and you will want to spend time visiting the gardens and the winery.

Our favorite restaurant following the tour is the *Stable Café*, which has been transformed into a restaurant from what used to be the horse stable in the 19th century. It is the perfect place to relax and reminisce about the amazing rooms and furnishing and art work we just saw on the tour of the estate. Ask for one of the horse stall booths; even though the seating is a little tight, it is fun to eat where the horses ate before you. Open just for lunch, the restaurant serves traditional Southern fare, including slow-cooked rotisserie chicken, barbecue, salads and desserts. There are about a half-dozen places to eat on the estate. For dinner we especially enjoy the *Bistro* at the

Winery.

We are looking forward to spending the night at the *Cottage on Biltmore Estate.* Originally serving as the residence of Biltmore's market gardener and afterwards as lodging for visiting VIPs, the 2-bedroom, 2-bath cottage is now available to the public.

If you have never been to the Biltmore, be sure and visit it when you are in North Carolina. If you have been there before, but not recently, visit it again. It just keeps getting better and better.

For additional information about the estate, the inn and cottage, days and hours of operation, reservations, etc., go to www. biltmore.com.

# West End Bakery and Café

What a fun place! This Asheville bakery and neighborhood café offers not only some excellent home-baked breads and pastry items but also offers breakfast (served all day), lunch and a Sunday brunch.

The two women owner-operators, Cathy and Krista, started the business almost 15 years ago. Both had a passion for healthy eating and were committed to opening a bakery and café that offered well-prepared dishes and bakery products made from the best locally produced and organic ingredients. They have met that commitment in spades!

The bakery produces a daily variety of pastry items, including their signature cinnamon roll, the recipe for which is a closely guarded secret. But who cares, as long as they keep baking them.

Breads are made with organic flour and many are whole grain. They also sell a variety of wheat-free breads. An assortment of breads is baked daily, but not every bread is baked every day.

Some of the more popular loaves include: French Batard, Whole Grain Spelt, Flax Almond, Potato Bread, Multi-grain Sesame, Black Turtle Bean Bread, Peasant Sourdough, and our favorite, Spinach Feta. The weekly schedule showing which breads are baked on which days can be found on the bakery's web site at www.westendbakery.com.

A variety of cakes are baked each day and special cakes and wedding cakes can be ordered. Brides-in-waiting are invited to stop by and pick up a copy of their wedding cake brochure and make an appointment to meet with the baker to discuss the perfect cake for their special event.

The bakery and the café open daily at 7:30 am and on Saturdays and Sundays at 8:00 am. They close at 6 pm daily and at 3 pm on the weekends.

Breakfast items include something as simple (ha) as their famous cinnamon roll and a cup of espresso or a scone and a cup of coffee to a bacon, egg, and cheese sandwich or a bowl of granola with fresh fruit or yogurt. They also offer a daily smoothie.

Lunch can be soup or salad, or a hot or cold sandwich, or you can mix them together as a combo. The soups change daily and are made from scratch. Look for Cathy's award-winning Curried Pumpkin Apple Soup.

Hot sandwiches include a nice variety, including a tuna melt and a turkey panini which Dee and I tried when we were there. And there is always a daily special. Cold sandwiches include a gourmet chicken salad, hummus and veggies, and even a peanut butter or almond butter and jelly sandwich.

We enjoyed our sandwiches, but Dee's cup of soup, while tasty, was lukewarm. We also took home two loaves of bread: the black turtle bean and the whole grain sourdough. We especially liked the latter, but the black bean was just so-so to our taste. My sandwich was made on the spinach-feta bread and was excellent.

We have not yet been able to make the Sunday Brunch, but I can't wait to try the smoked trout on a bagel, the veggie sausages, and the cheese grits.

For meetings or parties, the café can cater a variety of breakfast items including cinnamon rolls and other pastry items and an egg, veggie and cheese casserole that can be served warm. For lunch, salads and sandwich platters are available. They also offer a selection of hors d'ouevres including finger sandwiches and a variety of dips and chips.

The Bakery and staff strive to give back to the community by volunteering with local schools and other not-for profit organizations to promote healthful eating.

The West End Bakery and Café is one of the most popular gathering spots in West Asheville. Give them a try.

And wander around West Asheville while you are there. The small neighborhood is sort of a mixture of bohemian, artsy, and organic, with a little music thrown in. The bakery and cafe is located at 757 Haywood Road, in West Asheville. 828-252-9378.

# Black Mountain

Whenever we have guests from out-of-town we always take them to Black Mountain. Located about half way (15 miles) between our home on Lake Tahoma and Asheville, Black Mountain is one of those just about perfect little stops. The Swannanoa Chamber of Commerce says it best: "*The beautiful mountain scenery, variety of recreational activities and friendly hometown feel continues to attract many visitors each year. Take a walk through historic downtown and discover numerous upscale gift shops, galleries and Appalachian-style craft stores, with local craftsmen demonstrating iron works, dulcimer making and hand thrown pottery.*"

One of the highlights of our visit to Black Mountain is always a stop in at *St. James Episcopal Church*. The church has an amazing collection of memorial stain glass windows that date back to 1921. The original St. James Parish Church was constructed in 1912 and served the congregation until 1994 when they moved to a new location and a new building. When the congregation moved to the new building, 16 memorial windows were moved as well and an additional 13 windows were added. The enormous and majestic window of the Risen Christ that surmounts the altar is lit from inside the church so that in the evening it is a striking witness to people driving into town. St. James is affectionately known as the church of the "Jesus Window" and wonderful stories have been told of people receiving comfort and strength from sight of the window.

There are lots of good places to eat in Black Mountain are mixed in between the quaint and interesting shops downtown and throughout other parts of town. Those that we think offer a little something extra include:

**Morning Glory Café**:  6 East Market Street, in the Village of Cheshire, 1 mile south of downtown on NC9. Three years ago they were just serving breakfast, but until 2 pm. It was perfect for those who like to sleep in in the morning but didn't want to wake up to lunch.  Well, they were such a hit that they now serve breakfast and lunch seven days a week, from 8 until 3 and dinner Wednesday thru Sunday. Want a super lunch? Try the BLFGT (smoked bacon, romaine lettuce, fried green tomatoes on toasted wheat bread with lemon-caper remoulade.) Brave? Top it with a local fried egg. This isn't just mountain food; this is gourmet of the highest order! Reservations suggested.

**Black Mountain Bistro**:  203 E. State Street. The bistro is locally owned by a family that has been natives of the Black Mountain area for five generations. Everything on the menu is freshly made daily and recipes for many of the dishes "have been around for ever". Their commitment is to *"Serve the best quality food at reasonable prices."* Not a bad motto. The bistro is open every day except Sunday, Monday thru Friday from 11 am until 9:30 pm, and on Friday and Saturday until 10:00 pm.

**Veranda Café and Gifts**: 119 Cherry Street. Amazingly delicious food! The soups and sandwiches are outstanding. I may have tasted a better soup than their Hungarian Mushroom Soup, but I can't remember where or when. While you are in Black Mountain, stop by here and have a cup of the soup; you'll love it. Open for lunch only, 11 to 3, daily except Sunday.

**Dynamite Roasting Company**:  Hwy 70, just west of downtown. Amazing coffee! The two musicians and former bandmates fire up their old-school, small-batch roaster every day.  Drink  it in at the Dynamite Coffee Bar or take a pound of fresh-roasted beans home. Open Monday thru Friday, 7 am to 7 pm, on Saturday 7 to 6, and Sunday 8 to 6.

***Berliner Kindl German Restaurant and Deli:*** 121 Broadway. This German-owned and operated restaurant and deli offers a wide selection of German food to eat in or take out. Super sauerkraut; lots of rye seeds. The deli has imported meats, chocolates, cookies, and breads, as well as German beers and wines. Open Monday thru Saturday 11 am to 8 pm. Reservations accepted. 828-669-5255.

# Red Rocker Inn

In the introduction to the dining section of this book I mentioned that one of the criteria that can be used in selecting a good place to eat is for how long has the restaurant been serving food.

Red Rocker Inn certainly meets, no, sets the standard. How about since 1897! Yes, eighteen ninety-seven, not nineteen ninety-seven.

This lovely and historic Victorian house that has been converted into an inn has seventeen beautiful rooms decorated in period-style, each with central air conditioning and private baths. Each of the rooms is named, not numbered. When Dee and I stayed there I thought it would be fun to stay in the Seven Sisters Room. "*No*, said Dee, "*I think we'll stay in either the Anniversary Room or the Preacher Room.*" Well, I guess she had a point; it was our anniversary and she is a preacher.

The inn is owned and operated by Jenny and Doug Bowman. One of their four daughters (plus one son) is the head chef, and girl can she cook! The Red Rocker is one of our favorite places to stay in the mountains. If it wasn't for the fact that the inn is located only about twenty minutes from our home at Lake Tahoma, we'd stay there more often.

But being close is only a plus when having dinner there. We'd drive a lot further to eat there if we had to. I would classify the experience as gourmet southern cooking served in a casual fine-dining style.

At a recent visit for dinner our server was named *Mazy*, short for Margaret, she told us. It should have been short for *Amazing*; an amazing server, serving amazing food.

We each began our meal with a pleasant and reasonably-priced glass of Merlot and the "Christmas in July Salad": an assortment of crisp, fresh salad greens covered with a good handful of red raspberries that Mazy had hand-picked that morning from the berry bushes in her parent's nearby back yard. The red and green salad was then sprinkled with a dusting of "snow", crumbled Feta cheese from the *Looking Glass Creamery*, a local culinary gem. A home-made creamy raspberry dressing was served on the side. If I had made the dressing it would have been a little sweeter, but the salad was enjoyable just the same. Oh, I forgot to mention the hot biscuits and apple butter that was brought to our table shortly after we sat down. Both home-made, of course.

You will read elsewhere in the book that Dee's favorite fresh water fish is mountain trout. She will seldom pass it up for something else when she sees it on a menu. She didn't pass it up this time either, and is she glad she didn't. The fileted trout had been lightly coated in a mixture of Panko bread crumbs and Parmesan cheese, then quickly sautéed and topped with buttered toasted almonds. The light crispiness on the outside was in perfect balance with the sweet, tender fish inside.

All entrees come with your choice of two side dishes, of which there are usually five or six from which to choose. And they vary night-to-night depending upon what locally-grown produce was available earlier that day. With the trout Dee ordered the herb-seasoned mashed potatoes and the sautéed fresh zucchini.

I ordered the Stuffed Chicken Breast – stuffed with local goat cheese, sautéed spinach, roasted shallots and black mission fig jam and then finished with a garlic demi-glaze sauce. I selected as one of my sides the Gouda cheese grits, a perfect pairing for the chicken breast. My second side was succotash, but succotash like I have never eaten before. I make succotash with fresh or frozen baby limas and corn, along with a little onion and fresh tomato. This succotash was made with dried baby limas and fresh corn, but mixed with mustard or turnip greens. I am forever hereafter changing my recipe.

We finished the meal by sharing a slice of Bumble pie accompanied by a large scoop of vanilla ice cream drizzled with raspberry sauce. The "bumble" was a mixture of apples, rhubarb, red raspberries, blackberries and strawberries. The tart fruit was in good balance with the sweetness of the ice cream and raspberry sauce and the flaky pie crust is what you'd expect from a good southern cook. I think I'll skip the ice cream next time and ask them to substitute a large dollop of sour cream.

A couple of weeks later we were back again. And again Dee ordered the mountain trout, but this time she substituted one of the sides for a salad and then selected the sautéed kale. I ordered the large dinner salad with crab cakes. I thought I might be taking a risk ordering crab this far away from the coast. It turned out that there was no risk at all. They don't serve better crab cakes in Charleston. Nice crisp crust on the outside and moist, flavorful crab inside. If there was more than a tablespoonful of bread crumbs for binding I sure couldn't find it. And, of course, I couldn't pass up the Gouda grits as a side. There was no room for dessert, so we took home a plate of chocolate-dipped macaroons for later. Yummy.

In the past month we've had two very enjoyable meals and at reasonable prices. I have only one complaint: don't worry about leaving home without your American Express card, they don't accept them. I don't understand why an operation of this caliber and size will not spend the extra percentage point or two in fees. If expenses are this tight I'd add an extra fifty cents or dollar to the entrees to cover it. Accepting American Express Cards in this day and age is just good  customer service as far as I am concerned. But not accepting Am Ex is certainly not so big a deal that we would stop coming here, but I wish they would change their policy.

I asked Mazy about the availability of the Looking Glass cheeses and she directed us to the Black Mountain Farmer's Market held every Saturday between 9:00 am and noon. The creamery is represented most Saturdays. "While you are there," she said, "look for me. I usually have a booth myself. I paint portraits." A recent art graduate from UNC-Asheville, Mazy is working at the Red Rocker Inn to help support her art career until she gets established. If she paints as well as she serves, she has a great career ahead of her.

I could write more about this special place, but why don't you just log on to www.redrockerinn.com and read about it yourself. Or phone them at 828-669-5991. They are located in Black Mountain off I-40 and the Blue Ridge Parkway and just 15 minutes east of Asheville. The inn is open but the restaurant is closed on Sunday.

# Lynn

I was wandering through the web one day and came upon what appeared to be an interesting site: epodunk.com. We've never lived in East Podunk, but we've lived in places that must have been close. Epodunk, the web site, was launched in 1999 and founded by journalists with years of experience in newspapers, online publishing and demographics; my kind of people.

The site provides in-depth information about communities, large and small, from around the country. We've visited most of the "larger" communities in Western North Carolina, so I was more interested in finding small ones we had not visited – places like the real Podunk, located outside of Ithaca, New York.

Wandering thru the site I found a great new place to visit: Lynn, North Carolina.

On the web page of each individual community listed on the epodunk web site is a feature the editors refer to as "Listed Places near _____". Listed places for Lynn, North Carolina included 10 cemeteries, 1 hotel, 3 libraries, and a winery! Wow, what more could one ask for? Imagine spending your last days on earth living in a hotel and surrounded by three libraries and a winery. What a way to go. I had to visit there.

One of the South's favorite poets, Sidney Lanier, must have liked it there: he spent his last days in Lynn. The house where he died of TB in 1881 is still standing there and is occupied. Lynn is located on NC State Highway 108, just southwest of Columbus, NC, where US Hwy. 74 meets I-26. The nice little town of Tryon is just 1.4 miles south of Lynn.

I checked the zip-codes.com web site to get a count of the current population of Lynn and it said "zero." Apparently the day they took the census everyone had driven over to Shelby, NC to attend the Livermush Festival (pg. 345). Either that or they were all at a funeral at one of the ten neighboring cemeteries.

Anyway, let me tell you a little about the winery that is located nearby: **Overmountain Vineyards.** The winery has a Tryon mailing address, but it is actually located out in the boonies, near East Podunk. To reach it from Lynn, you need to go back to Hwy. 74 and head east (toward Rutherfordton and Charlotte) until you reach Exit 167 (Hwy. 9). Turn right on Hwy. 9, heading south, for three miles until your reach the flashing light and Sandy Plains Road. Turn left here and the winery is on your right about two miles up the road.

The vineyard and winery are located on an absolutely beautiful 75-acres of land at the foothills of the Blue Ridge Mountains. Two miles of the Overmountain Victory National Historic Trail crosses the vineyard. This Certified Protected Segment is open for the public to hike. The trail, operated by the National Parks Department, commemorates the military campaign that led to patriot victory at the battle of King Mountain in the fall of 1780.

Overmountain Vineyard is open to the public year-round on Thursdays through Sundays from 1 to 6 p.m. While visiting the winery you may take a walking tour of the vineyards with a glass of wine in your hand, or enjoy your tasting sitting in a rocking chair on the porch. Or, take a more formal approach to your tasting in their cozy new tasting room where you can learn more about their production process. There is a $5 tasting fee. They have five varieties of grapes planted: Cabernet Sauvignon, Merlot, Cabernet Franc, Petit Verdat, and Petit Manseng. From these they produce a Petit Manseng, their estate and premium wine; a King's Mountain  Rose; a Revolutionary Red; and several fruit wines.

At last count the vineyard had some 12 acres under cultivation. Frank and Lita Lilly are the proprietors.

A walk through the Overmountain Vineyards alone is worth a visit... and the wines are pretty good too! Plus you can say you've been to Lynn, or at least close to it.

# Lake Lure/Chimney Rock

Sitting in the foothills of the Blue Ridge Mountains, *Lake Lure*, at the center of the Hickory Nut Gorge area in northwestern Rutherford County, has been referred to by *National Geographic* magazine as "one of the most beautiful man-made lakes in the world." The gorge has spectacular walks, a 400-foot waterfall and the famous 1,000-acre *Chimney Rock State Park* (see below). Lake Lure itself covers 720 acres and has a shoreline of 20 miles. The mountain lake communities of the Hickory Nut Gorge area are well-known destinations for thousands of visitors each year from around the country, Canada, and abroad.

The recently restored and historic Lake Lure Inn and Spa is one of the original North Carolina landmarks. It is also home to a museum of classic cars. Covered boat tours of the lake are available in the summer, as is swimming at the Lake Lure beach. There is a bevy of other attractions and activities available in the area.

But it is about the film *Dirty Dancing* that many visitors from around the world inquire. A number of scenes from the movie were filmed in the area, but it is the scene where Johnny (the late Patrick Swazey) lifts Baby (Jennifer Grey) out of the waters of Lake Lure that gets the most attention and inquiry. The covered boat tour will take you to the exact location where that scene was filmed.

*Dirty Dancing* is just one of several notable films shot here. Almost all of the forest scenes from *The Last of the Mohicans* were shot in the woods surrounding Lake Lure. Many scenes from *My Fellow Americans*, *A Breed Apart*, and *Firestarter* were also shot here.

## *Chimney Rock State Park:*

Chimney Rock State Park is the natural fulfillment of your trip to the North Carolina Mountains. In May 2007, the State of North Carolina acquired Chimney Rock from the Morse family, whose four generations of family members shared the park with millions of guests for over 100 years.

The Park is a perfect place to reconnect with nature and spend time with family and friends. Chimney Rock offers the best of the mountains in one place – spectacular 75-mile views, hiking trails for all ages, a 404-foot water fall, a variety of special events and much, much more.

All said, however, it is the stunning natural beauty of the Chimney Rock and Lake Lure area that has been drawing visitors here since the early 1900s. Just 15 miles from downtown Rutherfordton (pg. 263), Lake Lure is also close to Vanderbilt's famous *Biltmore Estate* (pg. 243) in Asheville.

# Rutherfordton

*"Small Town Friendly."* That's the motto for Rutherfordton, one of the oldest towns in western North Carolina and the seat of the oldest continuous government in the region. The downtown area is listed on the National Register of Historic Places as a historic district and is a beautiful representation of a small town in rural western North Carolina. Its "old time charm" abounds.

Located in the foothills of the Blue Ridge Mountains its elevations offer great views in almost all directions. The population is around 4,200, but Rutherfordton is the county seat for Rutherford County which has a population of about 60,000.

There more than a few good reasons to visit Rutherfordton, but one of the best is to drive by and observe the only remaining cluster of antebellum houses and public structures in this part of the state. *Robin Spencer Lattimore* is an award-winning author, journalist and historian and in 2008 was named as an official Rutherford County Historian by the County Board of Commissioners. Robin's latest book, *Columns & Porches: Architectural Treasures of Rutherford County* describes 66 of the county's significant homes, churches and public buildings constructed from the antebellum period up until World War II. The text and principal photographs by the author and *Lesley M. Bush* detail the architectural significance of these historic places and encourage readers to view each one for themselves. I also encourage you to come and visit and view them all.

Robin has published almost a dozen books on various segments of the history of the area, including *Gold & Glory:*

*North Carolina Gold and the Bechtler Heritage* and *Across Two Centuries: The Lost World of Green River Plantation.* His books are available from various online sources.

Another good reason to visit Rutherfordton is *KidSenses Children's InterACTIVE Museum.* The exhibits and special workshops stimulate the imagination and educate the mind. Children and adults experience hands-on fun as they play, learn and create things together in this exciting environment. Some of the most popular exhibits include:

*Virtual Reality Ride* – go on an exciting ride without leaving the museum! The ride uses a state of the art DLP projection system and hydraulic motion simulation platform to provide an authentic-seeming roller coaster experience.

*WFUN-Studio* – sit at the anchor desk, report the weather, interview celebrities and check out yourself via a video camera and monitor.

*Bubble-Ology* – become Bubble-ologists when you enter the exciting world of bubbles!

*Discovery Garden* – an opportunity to discover the miracles of nature. Children will discover how nature works together in an interwoven network of bees, birds, butterflies, beetles, ants, earthworms, soil, rocks, rain, sun, water and more.

*Dr.DeSoto's Dental Office* – experience positive role-playing in a setting where the child becomes the dentist and the patient is Mr. Fox.

KidSenses is open Tuesday – Thursday 9 am – 5 pm, Friday 9 am to 8pm and Saturday 9 am to 5 pm.

Finally, do not leave Rutherfordton without visiting the church where my wife, Dee, was rector for seven years: *St. Francis Episcopal Church.* Located just a few blocks from downtown, on North Main Street near the *City Cemetery,* the historical structure was completed in 1899. It is considered to be the finest Gothic-Revival church building in western North

Carolina. The walls are built from local granite, and the exposed oak rafters support a steeply pitched blue slate.

The main sanctuary is adorned with an exceptional collection of religious art glass windows including three windows crafted in the 1920s by the *Louis C. Tiffany Company* of New York. Other windows were crafted by the English firm of *J. Whipple & Company* of Exeter, England.

St. Francis is one of the few churches in the country that never close their doors. The church is open and available for prayer and meditation 24-7.

*The Carrier Houses* on Main Street in downtown Rutherfordton is one of our favorite bed and breakfast operations in the state. Built between 1835 and 1879, and standing side-by-side, the homes are two of the town oldest dwellings and both are listed on the National Register of Historic Places.

There are a total of eight guest bedrooms, all with private baths; five in the Carrier-Ward house and three in the Carrier-McBrayer house, which is also the residence of Lynn and Dan Hegeman. You won't find two nicer hosts. And the breakfasts are great! 255 Main Street, Rutherfordton. 828-287-4222 or www.carrierhouses.com.

# The Northern Mountains

The Blue Ridge is the primary range in the northern mountain area. The most familiar of "High Country" towns is probably Blowing Rock, but there are other smaller communities in the northern mountains that deserve your attention as well:

***Banner Elk:*** A quaint mountain town best known for its High Country activities such as skiing, hiking, horseback riding and rafting. The town is surrounded by some of the highest mountains east of the Rockies including Grandfather Mountain and Beech Mountain. Located just 30 minutes from Boone, NC, it is a highly desired destination for those who love the outdoors and southern culture.

***Linville:*** Popular for both golfing and skiing. Linville has three golf courses that are open from late spring until early fall. In the winter, nearby *Ski Beech, Ski Sugar, and Ski Hawknest* are popular skiing and snow tubing destinations. The very popular *Linville Caverns* is close by, as is *Grandfather Mountain*. And don't miss stopping by the *Old Hamilton General Store and Grist Mill* (pg. 285).

***Wilkesboro*** and ***North Wilksboro:*** Wilkesboro is the county seat but North Wilkesboro is the largest town in Wilkes County. Long known as *"Key to the Blue Ridge."* A popular and unusual attraction is the *Barn Quilt Trail*. As you travel through the area look for the barns of local residents who have decorated them with centuries old quilt patterns to ensure the legacy of this form of folk art. You will notice that residents in other areas of the Northern Mountains have picked up on this nice tradition and are beginning to similarly decorate their barns. Look especially for them when traveling north on US 221 toward Lineville and Boone. Some of the best mountain biking in the Blue Ridge can be found in Wilkesboro. Over 40 miles of sweet single track has been built by mountain bikers for mountain bikers and more miles are under construction. Finally, a little bit of infamy about Wilkesboro. You that are NASCAR fans will remember the name *Junior Johnson.* The story is that before becoming a legend on the racetrack, Junior was a legend in Wilkesboro. He is rumored to have developed his driving skills back in the 1950s by outrunning the revenuers and the local sheriffs. It seems that Junior's car was usually filled with moonshine. Wilkes County is known as the "Bootleg Liquor Capital of America."

***Valle Crucis:*** *"Nestled high in the Appalachian Mountains is a peaceful rural community untouched for over 200 years. Its name is Valle Crucis."* The history of the Episcopal Church is woven through the modern history of the Valle Crucis community. In 1842, the Episcopal Bishop of North Carolina visited the town and gave it its name. Visit the *Church of the Holy Cross* and view the suite of 14 original woodcuts depicting *"The Way of Sorrows, the Final Journey of Jesus down the Via Doloroso."*

***Spruce Pine:*** Located off the Blue Ridge Parkway at Mile Marker 331, Spruce Pine is located in the heart of the Blue Ridge Mountains. Once called an outdoor enthusiast's winter wonderland, the spectacular NC Ski Resorts are just a short drive away. But during the other months there are plenty of other outdoor activities: fish the North Toe River, hike or bike on one of the hundreds of trails, or pan for the gem of your dreams at one of the many gem mines in the area. There is also a rich blend of music and other arts throughout the area.

***Glendale Springs*** and ***West Jefferson:*** For a small town in a sort of away corner of the mountains, West Jefferson has a surprising number of art galleries and studios and a bustling downtown arts district featuring regional and local artists. The town is also the site of more than 15 murals that create a downtown walking tour that reflects the area's history and character. It will be hard to miss seeing the painted pedestals and fire hydrants all around town. But with all that, it is the frescoes of *Ben Long* that are the highlight of a visit to these two towns.

### *Frescoes of world-famous artist Ben Long IV:*

Ben Long is one of a few artists today to be recognized as a Master of the art of fresco-painting – painting on wet plaster, the process used by Michelangelo in the Sistine Chapel.

There are three of his frescoes, including *Mary Great with Child,* at *St. Mary's Episcopal Church* in West Jefferson, 400 Beaver Creek School Road.

A fresco of *The Last Supper* can be seen at *Holy Trinity Episcopal Church* in Glendale Springs, 120 Glendale School Road.

Long prefers to paint from life and uses local people for models for his life-size frescoes. Other of his frescoes in North Carolina can be found in Charlotte, Statesville, Morganton, Wilkesboro, Crossmore and Montreat.

If you have time to do nothing more than visit the frescoes while you are in the area, it will be worth the trip.

# Burnsville

Burnsville has changed quite a bit in recent years. There is a lot of new commercial development, especially on Highway 19 coming in from Spruce Pines and points further east. But the downtown is still as quaint as it was when the stagecoach from Asheville would come into town and stop at the *Nu Wray Inn*.

Travel was tough in those days, but it is an easy 35-mile drive from Asheville today. The Nu Wray is no longer an inn but has been converted into a house and venue rental. It's the perfect place if you have a very large family: 7 bedrooms plus two 2-bedroom suites. Or what a great idea to put the entire wedding party in one house. Did I mention that Elvis spent the night at the inn one time?

Burnsville has been called the *"Heart of the Blue Ridge"* and the *"Gateway to Mount Mitchell"* and *"Base Camp for High Mountain Adventures."* We call it the town where our friends *Carol and Ron Thomas* live; at least they do part of the year. They spend the winters in *The Villages* in Florida.

Carol and I worked together years ago at *The Miami Herald*. She held various newsroom management positions before being named Publisher of the Broward County Edition. We had sort of lost touch for ten or so years until Dee and I ran into her at *St. Thomas Episcopal Church* in Burnsville.

I was very excited to see her. I had not spent much time in Burnsville and was interested in how she and her husband felt about the place. They love it!

Burnsville is located in Yancy County, the home of Mount Mitchell, the highest elevation point east of the Mississippi River. Yancy County itself has the highest average elevation of any county in the state.

If you have a chance to visit in August, try and make it the first weekend of the month. That's when the annual Mount Mitchell Crafts Fair is held. First started in the mid 1950's, the fair has been held continuously each August ever since. But, there is something worthwhile to do in Burnsville and Yancy County every month of the year. Come anytime.

Carol and Ron recommended three area restaurants to us, all of which we tried and all of which are worth recommending to you. See the following write-ups for the **Garden Deli** and **Mary Jane's Bakery and Café**, in Burnsville, and the **Knife and Fork**, in Spruce Pines.

# Garden Deli

What has been one of the most popular lunch places in town with locals and visitors alike is now also one of the most popular dinner restaurants as well, at least on Thursdays, Fridays, and Saturdays, which are the only evenings they are open for dinner. They are open for lunch from 11 am until 2 pm every day except Sunday; dinner hours are 5 to 8.

The *Garden Deli* is run by Greg and Hiroko Yuziuk. Greg's father, Ed, opened the restaurant and Greg and his wife have followed in his footsteps. The food is very similar to the delicatessen food that Ed enjoyed when he was growing up in New York City.

Most familiar are the big deli sandwiches, like pastrami and roast beef, piled high with the highest quality meats. But such standards as hot ham and Swiss, and Reubens and tuna melts are also always on the menu. There is a soup of the day that can be served with or without a side salad.

Our friend Carol brags about the homemade chili. Just like in New York delis, all sandwiches are served with coleslaw, kosher pickle, and your choice of potato salad, macaroni salad, or potato wedges.

Salad selections include a garden Cobb salad, topped with white meat chicken salad, crisp bacon, crumbled bleu cheese and a hard boiled egg; or a Caesar salad which can be topped with sliced breaded chicken or turkey and bacon.

The dessert menu is limited, but with a choice of apple pie, plain or ala mode; a chocolate sundae; or New York cheesecake, do you really need anything else?

The dinner menu includes many of the lunch items but also offers Baby Back Ribs, a Greek Chicken plate, and a couple of seafood items. And there are always items for vegetarians, at lunch and at dinner.

A patio wraps around a huge weeping willow tree and is covered by a dense canopy of wisteria vines. No wonder they call it the *Garden* Deli. Outdoor dining on the patio is available when the weather is nice, but there are a fair amount of tables inside. Located downtown, just across the Town Square from the Nu Wray, in Burnsville.

*I once asked a waitress at a different restaurant what was the soup of the day.*

*She answered, "du jour."*

# Mary Jane's Bakery and Café

Mary Jane's Café is our friends *Carol and Ron's* favorite breakfast spot in Burnsville. Mary Jane makes "*out of this world biscuits and sausage gravy.*" Also very popular are their quiches, which are available all day. There are four different ones on the menu, but the most interesting-sounding is the Brie quiche, with bacon, green apples and cinnamon. They also serve Arbuckle Coffee, known as the "cowboy coffee."

Arbuckle Coffee was first established in 1864 by John Arbuckle as the first coffee roaster to package whole bean coffee in sealed one-pound packages. Their unique dry-roast process brings out all of the flavor oils and sugars without causing the coffee beans to stale. Carol and Ron enjoy the coffee so much that they order it by mail from Arizona, and at $16.95 per pound. You can order some also by going to Arbuckle's web site at www.arbucklecoffee.com.

Another satisfied diner, remarking about lunch, said that "*the lasagna is better than my wife and I make, and we make a good one.*" It is served with a full-flavored meat sauce and a side salad. We suggest you try the balsamic vinaigrette.

Mary Jane prides herself on using local, organic fruits and vegetables and grass-fed beef. The fresh baked goods available for sale in the bakery and served in the restaurant are all made from scratch. The sweet rolls are fabulously rich … and good.

The bakery and café are open from 8 until 11 am Monday thru Saturday for breakfast and from 11 until 3 pm for lunch. On Thursday, Friday and Saturday nights they are open from 5 pm until 8:30 pm for dinner. Dinner is a variety of pizzas, salads, and a nightly dinner special. This place is special.

Located at 110 East Main Street, Burnsville. Take Main Street from the Town Square heading east. Mary Jane's is at the bottom of the hill, on the right.

# Knife and Fork

The *Knife and Fork* was one of those new places that we hoped would make it and they did! The restaurant opened in July 2009 and we first ate there that same month and I included it in my North Carolina book a year later. It has since been written up and reviewed in both state-wide and national magazines as well as in newspapers. The *Knife and Fork* and the *Apollo Flame Bistro* in Asheville were the two restaurants we missed most when we moved back to Florida.

The menu offers "only seasonal and sustainable dishes that reflect the traditions and culture of the mountains of North Carolina," exactly the type of restaurant Dee and I were seeking when we would travel throughout the mountain region.

The Knife and Fork is located in the small mountain town of Spruce Pines, with a permanent population of less than 3,000. Yet they prepare and serve food that could hold its own in New York or Los Angeles or San Francisco.

It is owned and operated by Chef Nathan Allen and his wife Wendy and their new baby. They believe that the dining experience should be free of gimmicks and clutter so the focus can be on the food and the company.

The Knife and Fork strives to minimize its impact on the environment and maximize its impact on the local economy. All of the restaurant's ingredients are sourced locally from small farms within the community, which occasionally means limited availability of certain dishes. This practice also means that the menus change frequently to adapt to the changing availability of ingredients. The following is a sample of some of the recent offerings:

Most restaurants	limit their brunches to Sundays, which, given Dee's occupation, makes it difficult for us to sample brunch offerings at other than local restaurants. We have not been able to eat brunch at the Knife and Fork, but there are some dishes on a recent brunch menu that any of the *Iron Chefs* would love to try: eggs a cheval: grilled biscuit topped with pulled pork, duck confit, spinach, cheddar cheese and two sunny side-up eggs; or braised rabbit leg over red quinoa pilaf with blueberries and baby carrots; or grilled stuffed pork belly with greens and grilled cornbread.

A recent dinner menu included a grilled flatiron steak, roast leg of lamb, sautéed mountain trout, braised rabbit leg, and home-made sweet potato gnocchi. Lighter items and sides included potato soup with crème fraiche, poached duck egg on waffle, sautéed ramps and shitakes with quail eggs and crispy potatoes.

Dee and I were there recently for lunch and thoroughly enjoyed our meal. No wonder we missed it so much when we moved. Dee had the grilled mountain trout sandwich and I had the fried chicken sandwich, an enormous piece of fried boneless chicken breast. I don't usually carry a ruler with me, so I had to estimate, but my sandwich must have been at least five inches tall.  I had to "deconstruct" it (a current culinary fad) in order to get in my mouth.

It seems a little silly to brag about hash browns, but those served with each of our sandwiches were outstanding – large chunks of Yukon Gold potatoes that were perfectly fried. I don't know if it was the seasoning or the oil or both, but the flavor was amazing.

As a starter we shared an order of sautéed squash. Obviously cooked quickly over very high heat, the slices of zucchini, and yellow and green squashes were nicely browned on both sides but still very crispy.  Seasoned with fresh herbs and some sautéed baby greens, the squash were finished with a light coating of melted Greyere cheese on top.

There were several other interesting starters on the menu, but it was the cucumbers, tomatoes and cracklin' that caught my eye. In the recipe section of the book you will find a recipe for Cracklin' Corn Bread. Cracklins are the crispy residue left over from the rendering lard from pork fat. Using them in a salad was "genius," as a certain judge on *Chopped* might say.

Finally, how about some of the unusual beverages on the menu: New Holland Dragon's Milk Stout, Stone Sublimely Self-Righteous Ale and a gluten-free farmhouse cider. We'll have to come back soon when we have a designated driver.

Since we were last there (prior to our most recent visit) Nathan and Wendy have expanded the restaurant by purchasing an adjoining building and have added an outdoor patio area. Positive additions and a good indication of their success.

*Sarah* (and *Vic*) *Hansen* (the Lake Tahoma couple from Atlanta I mentioned earlier) says that the Knife and Fork is her now-favorite restaurant. That's quite an endorsement since Sarah herself is one of the best cooks in western North Carolina and is a wonderful hostess. If the homeowners at Lake Tahoma ever decide to elect a "mayor" I want to be Sarah's campaign manager; it would be an easy job to get her elected.

Lunch is served on Tuesdays thru Fridays from 11:30 am until 3:00 pm, with dinner served on Tuesdays thru Fridays from 5:30 until 9:00 and on Saturdays from 5:00 until 9:00. Sunday brunch is served from 10:30 am until 3:00 pm. The restaurant is closed during the months of January and February. Located at 61 Locust Street (Lower Street) in Spruce Pines, North Carolina. Call 828-765-1511 for reservations.

# Switzerland Café

*Little Switzerland* is a small summer colony high in the Blue Ridge Mountains, off of the mile post 334 exit of the Blue Ridge Parkway. Little Switzerland has only 8 shops within the town limits but it has both an uptown and a downtown. Uptown shops include a wonderful store with an outstanding collection of glass and other art objects for sale, a gem shop, a children's clothing store, a Swiss ice cream shop, and a couple of others. Uptown is also where *The Big Lynn Lodge* and the *Alpine Inn* are located. Dee and I spent a night at the Alpine Inn in 1969. It is as lovely a place now as it was then.

*Switzerland Café* is downtown, along with the general store and bookseller. Unfortunately the Café is a seasonal business, open from mid-April until the end of October. If it were open year-round we would eat there more often. When we lived in NC we would eat there several times each summer.

Most noted for their homemade soups, salads, and classic sandwiches, the café also offers exceptional dishes for dinner. Several times I have mentioned North Carolina trout and how it is available at most mountain restaurants, large and small. But no one that we have found serves trout the way Switzerland Café serves it: a whole trout, literally, head and all, smoked in their on-site smokehouse and served chilled with red onion, capers, cilantro yogurt dressing and crackers. Two or even three can share one as an appetizer before ordering a salad, a sandwich or a daily homemade quiche.

Our favorite sandwich is the flatbread turkey panini: roasted turkey, tomato, red onion, pesto, and feta cheese all grilled on herbed flatbread. We also often order two Grown Up Grilled Cheese sandwiches. You can have one for $5.99 or two for $7.99. The "grown up" part is from the smoked Gouda, blue cheese, tomatoes and red onion grilled on marbled rye bread. A great sandwich.

There are two other items on the menu that we especially enjoy. First is a Persian Chicken Salad Sandwich. I'm not sure where the Persian part comes in but I like the addition of green apples, not grapes, in the salad. They also include apricots, almonds, and onions in a lightly curried mayonnaise. (I guess the curry is the Persian part.) It is normally served on toasted wheat berry bread with lettuce and tomato, but you can select a different bread if you prefer.

The other item is New South Pimento Cheese, served as an appetizer. I'll bet our friend Marion will like this pimento and cheese as much as she likes the one from *Fresh Market*. This one has scallions and apple wood bacon in it!

Dinner is served on Friday and Saturday nights (the café is open for lunch seven days a week) beginning at 5:00 pm. There are usually just six items on the dinner menu: rainbow trout; baby back ribs, with a secret recipe of 15 herbs and spices rubbed on before being smoked over hickory; a hand cut rib eye steak; Amish Chicken Pot pie; Chicken Fried Steak; and Spinach Fettuccini, with Gorgonzola cheese.

Switzerland Café offers a limited but representative list of wines and a nice selection of beers and ales. The general store is connected to the restaurant; an interesting place to wander around if you have to wait a while for a table (a good sign, not an inconvenience). Reservations are not accepted for lunch, but if you will call ahead for dinner a table will be waiting for you (828-765-5289). Just off the Blue Ridge Parkway in Little Switzerland.

# Penland
# School of Crafts

Founded in 1929, the school is a national center for craft education and is located just a few miles from Spruce Pines. The mission of the school is *"to support personal and artistic growth through craft."*

The school was an outgrowth of a craft-based economic development project that the founder of the school, Lucy Morgan, had begun several years earlier. "Miss Lucy," as she was known to just about everybody, was one of the few Craft Revival Leaders who was actually born and raised in the western North Carolina mountains.

Today, Penland encompasses about 400 acres and 49 buildings, and more than 1,200 people come each year seeking instruction. The classes are so popular that many of them are filled by a lottery drawing. If a class is over-subscribed by a certain cut-off date all of the applicants will be treated equally and the class will be filled by random drawing of names.

The school's workshop programs combine excellent instruction by outstanding practicing craft people, exposure to different media, a secluded and inspiring physical setting, and a collaborative, community atmosphere.

Students and teachers are encouraged to think, experiment and play. The programs are based on years of successful experience that has proven that exploring materials and working intently with the hands has the power to change lives. Each class is structured by the instructor, but most are a mix of lectures, demonstrations, individual studio work, and field trips.

Students can expect to work hard, learn a lot, make new friends, and forget about the rest of the world in an isolated setting without the distraction of television, phones, or daily newspapers. They can expect to have fun, eat good food, and get the kind of rest that comes from immersing oneself in something you love. Unfortunately they can only house those who are enrolled in classes. It sounds like a wonderful place to stay even if you are not "crafty".

In the interest of protecting the focused atmosphere of the classes, Penland's teaching studios are not open to the public, but you are welcome to visit the campus and walk around the grounds. You are also welcome to view the classes from open doorways or participate in one of the guided tours offered on Tuesdays and Thursdays. Reservations for the tours are required.

But it is well-worth a visit to Penland if you do nothing more than tour the Penland Gallery and Visitor Center. This is one of the finest showcases for contemporary craft in the Southeast. Attracting over 14,000 visitors each year, the gallery displays and sells work by current and former Penland instructors, resident artists and students from around the country. The Gallery and Visitor Center are open seasonally, from March through early December: Tuesday thru Saturday 10 am to 5 pm and Sunday 12 noon to 5 pm.

Call 828-765-6211 for additional information or visit www.penland.org.

# Old Hampton General Store and Grist Mill

Built in 1921, with a grist mill added in 1934, this old general store is located off US-221, just south of the junction of US-221 and NC-105, at the foot of *Grandfather Mountain* in Linville, North Carolina.

The store carries rows and rows of various unusual house wares and unique decorating items, along with an assortment of old time candies. It is a fun place to visit. Don't miss climbing the stairs to the second floor to see the antique and craft pieces for sale.

But, what keeps us coming back at least once or twice a year are the special stone-ground flours and meals and grits. The store operates the only working grist mill in North Carolina. They have an amazing assortment of jams and jellies and such unusual and wonderful things such as dilled garlic cloves, and pickled asparagus, and candied jalapeño peppers. In addition to the grits and flours, they also offer packaged pancake and waffle mixes, including buckwheat. If it's grits you're after, make sure you call ahead before driving up. We recently made the hour-drive to arrive and find out that they were out of grits. Darn!

In the back of the store, you'll find a food counter offering sandwiches and barbecue served on homemade sourdough bread. Banana Pudding is truly a mountain "staple". They make one of the best you've ever put into your mouth. You can eat in or take out. If you're lucky, you will arrive on a day when one of the local bluegrass fiddle groups is there to entertain.

# Blowing Rock

One summer maybe 20 years ago we were traveling north for some reason or another and we spent a night with some friends who had a summer home in Blowing Rock. At the time they lived most of the year in Coral Gables. They took us to dinner at the country club. We had a great dinner, but it was like we were back in Coral Gables. At least a fourth of the people at the club that night were people we knew from Coral Gables and Miami. Another fourth were people from Coral Gables and Miami that our friends knew, but that we didn't know. At least half of the people there that night were from the Miami area. I never could figure out why all these people kept coming to Blowing Rock. If you are going to just be with the same people why not stay home and be with them there.

Well, now I understand. It's because Blowing Rock is a GREAT place. In a way you can have the best of both worlds here also. You can escape the hassle and traffic and stress of South Florida, or anywhere else, and still be with people whom you enjoy, but in a quiet, relaxed and more peaceful atmosphere. You can enjoy your friends so much better up here. Blowing Rock is a perfect place to "get away from it all" and still be with friends. Maybe not your friends from your hometown, but you'll make new friends there soon. Nice people live in and visit Blowing Rock.

Speaking of friends and nice people, two sets of our friends have also discovered the best of two worlds and divide their time between the North Carolina mountains and the west coast Florida beaches. *The Rev. Sam Tallman*, an Episcopal priest, spends the winter months living in St. Petersburg and serving as an assisting priest at *St. Peter's*

*Episcopal Cathedral.* The rest of the year he serves as Curate at *St. Mary of the Hills Episcopal Church* in Blowing Rock.

*Dr. Richard Kitchell,* a practicing dentist in Blowing Rock, and his wife *Luanne* have for many years spent part of the year on Anna Maria Island. This year they made plans to spend even more time in Florida and purchased a place on St. Petersburg Beach. When they are in Florida, Fr. Sam and Dee "share" the Kitchells.

Blowing Rock is a small town, only three square miles, but it has an amazing number of shops, restaurants and places to visit. The downtown area offers antique shops, art galleries, upscale boutiques, clothiers, craft shops and more.

Blowing Rock claims to have been named *"The Prettiest Small Town in North Carolina."* I'm not questioning that, but a friend named our motel in the Florida Keys the *"Best Place to kiss in the Keys."* We used that as a marketing gimmick for years. But the town is pretty, and well-maintained. We enjoy ourselves every time we visit.

In Blowing Rock, there are many fine restaurants and cafes, about two dozen in total. One you should not miss is **The Best Cellar Restaurant** at The Inn at Ragged Gardens. Offering upscale mountain casual dining for lunch and dinner, this fine restaurant has been serving Blowing Rock residents and visitors for over 35 years. The inn is located just two blocks off of the main drag in downtown Blowing Rock.

Another of our favorites is the **Storie Street Grille**. Located right in downtown Blowing Rock on Main Street, the Storie Street Grille is owned and operated by Joan and Bernie Keele. They will be celebrating the 13th anniversary of the restaurant in 2013. Most would classify the Grille as a contemporary American bistro, with an emphasis on regional dishes and locally produced ingredients. Joan says that the secret to their success is their emphasis on quality, value, creativity, and flavor. It must be working; it's one of the most popular restaurants in the area. Serving hours are Monday thru Saturday from 11 to 3 for lunch and 5 to 9 for dinner. Be sure and call ahead to make certain they will have a table for you when you arrive. Located at 1167 Main Street, Blowing Rock.

To learn about the other dining choices in Blowing Rock go to www.blowingrock.com and click on "Dining" for a description of each and a link to their individual web sites. We have not eaten at every restaurant in Blowing Rock, but we have never had a bad dining experience.

In response to a vegetarian:
*"If we aren't supposed to eat animals,
then why did God make them out of meat?"*

# Waterfalls in the High Country

Transylvania County (Brevard) is the North Carolina County most noted for its waterfalls, but there are some amazingly beautiful falls in the Northern Mountains as well, several of which are often overlooked.

Following is a brief description of three of the most interesting falls in the High Country and how to reach them.

Not overlooked are the ***Linville Falls***, which may be the favorite waterfall in North Carolina and certainly one of the most beautiful. The falls are easily accessible from the Blue Ridge Parkway. Take the exit at Milepost 316.3 and follow the signs to the Linville Falls Visitor Center, about a mile and a half off of the Parkway.

There are five viewpoints from which to observe the falls. The trail lengths are all less than a mile and all but one trail is easy to moderate difficulty. The Linville River, on which the falls are located, starts at the top of Grandfather Mountain.

***Stone Mountain Falls*** are in Wilkes County between the towns of Sparta and Elkin, off of US 21, about ten miles south of the Blue Ridge Parkway. Look for signs for the *Stone Mountain State Park*. The trail to the falls is 1.2 miles long and is of moderate difficulty. There are three other falls within the State Park. And while you are at the falls you will want to visit Stone Mountain itself, a single great stone rising 600 feet from the floor of the valley. There is a trail to the top of the mountain. Stone Mountain is a National Natural Landmark.

***Harper Creek Falls*** in Caldwell County (Lenoir) is a little difficult to find but well worth the hunt. There are several ways to get to the trailhead but the easiest is off of NC 90 coming from Lenoir to the town of Edgemont. Stop for a soft drink at *Coffey's General Store* and they will give you directions for the rest of the way. The falls are second only to Linville Falls in terms of beauty. You can view the falls from both the bottom and the top. The trail is about one and a half miles long. It's a fairly easy climb to the top; the hike to the bottom is a good bit tougher.

There are numerous other falls in the Northern Mountains worth visiting, including the *Waterfall on Little Lost Cove Creek,* the *Hunt-Fish Falls* and the *North Harper Creek Falls.*

# Essays, Stories
# and
# Regional Recipes

# Apples

Apples grow abundantly in North Carolina. Most people will be surprised to learn that North Carolina is the seventh largest apple producing state in the union. That's because almost all of them are grown in a single western North Carolina county. More than 4 million bushels of apples are grown in the state each year.

There are over 200 commercial apple operations in the state comprised of 9,000 bearing acres of apple orchards. Henderson County produces about 85% of the state's apple production and is home to about 150 apple orchards. We try and visit the annual Apple Festival held in Hendersonville each fall.

The major varieties grown in North Carolina include: Honeycrisp, Gala, Fuji, Rome and Cameos. Smaller production comes from Staymens, Granny Smith and Jonagolds. One of the newest apples on the market is the Pink Lady with a crisp sweet/tart flavor. The name is derived from its pink blush over yellow overtone. The apple is a cross between a Golden Delicious and a Lady Williams and was originated in Australia in 1973. Our friends *Jane* and *Bill Vaughan* sent us some dried and candied Pink Lady Apples from Meduri World Delights and they were outstanding.

As Americans we each consume about 18 pounds of apples a year on average because they taste so good. But do you know how good they are for you? The age-old adage, "An apple a day will keep the doctor away" is being more and more clearly substantiated. Apples are a good source of bulk in the diet for the proper functioning of the body's digestive and regulatory systems. Studies have shown that persons eating apples regularly have fewer headaches and other disorders associated with nervous tension. Other studies have shown an association of regular apple consumption with a reduced evidence of colds and upper respiratory illnesses.

Even dentists encourage apples for snacks and for ending the meal for better nutrition and for better dental health. That's why it is said that, "North Carolina apples are good – and good for you."

With 4-million bushels of apples grown each year in North Carolina, it's no wonder so many apple recipes show up in North Carolina homes and on restaurant menus. Included throughout this recipe section of the book are a couple of apple recipes I consider to be especially good.

There are two major apple-related events each year in Henderson County: the *Apple Blossom Tour* in April and the *Apple Festival* on Labor Day weekend. Don't miss them if you are in the area.

But it is not just during festival time that you should visit. There are several dozen apple farms that are open to the public from August through the end of fall. Many of them are located on US 64, east of I-26 at Hendersonville, but there are others scattered around the county. For more information go to ncapples.com.

One of the farms that we especially recommend is *Grandad's Apples*. U-pick or they-pick, they also have a corn maze, a pumpkin patch, a little petting zoo with a llama and a goat and all kinds of apple products in the gift shop. When my daughter Pam and her friend Marianne were there in mid-October lots of people were also there, gobbling down hot apple cider and just-cooked apple donuts. And there was a bluegrass band playing in the yard. They drove up and thought there must be a festival going on. Nope, just a typical fall afternoon in apple country. Grandad's has a web site also: www.grandadsapples.com.

# Apple Cake with Rum Caramel Sauce

I've taken a cake recipe from an old country cookbook and combined it with a rum caramel sauce from a new fru-fruey one. The cake recipe called for a butter cream frosting; the rum caramel sauce was to go with an ice cream dessert. They both seemed better suited to each other.

1 ¼ cups vegetable oil
2 ½ cups sugar
6 eggs
3 ½ cups all-purpose flour
1 ¾ T baking powder
1 t salt
1 t ground cinnamon
1 t ground ginger
1 t ground nutmeg
½ t ground cloves
5 cups Granny Smith apples, peeled, cored and diced small
1 ½ cups walnuts, toasted
1 ½ cups sugar
½ cup water
¾ cup whipping cream
2 T unsalted butter
1 T dark rum

Preheat the oven to 350 degrees.

Mix together the vegetable oil and the sugar. Beat in the eggs, one at a time, beating well after each addition. Sift together the flour, baking powder, salt and spices. Gradually add the dry ingredients to the egg mixture as you continue to mix until the batter is well mixed and smooth. Fold in the apples and the nuts. Divide the batter in two prepared cake pans (greased and floured) and bake about 45 minutes or until a toothpick inserted in the center comes out clean.

While the cakes are baking make the rum caramel sauce by combining the sugar and the water in a medium saucepan and bring to a boil over high heat, stirring constantly until the sugar dissolves. Reduce the heat to medium and cook without stirring until an amber sauce forms, about 5 minutes. (Be careful and don't let it burn.) Remove from the heat and quickly stir in the cream and the butter. (Be careful, the caramel is very hot.) Reduce the heat and return the pan to the stove. While continuing to stir, simmer the sauce over medium heat for 2 minutes. Remove from heat and stir in the rum. The sauce can be refrigerated and reheated in the microwave if you decide to make it ahead of time.

When the cakes are done and cooled, remove from the pans and smooth half of the warm sauce over one of the cakes, top with the other half and pour the rest of the sauce over the top. The cakes will be sticky and gooey, but will taste so, so good. Cut and serve with some whipped cream, or a scoop of vanilla ice cream, if you desire.

# Apple "Coffee" Cake

The coffee in this coffee cake is actually *in* the cake! It can be served with coffee, but it is a regular apple cake that has cold coffee as one of the ingredients.

2 cups sugar
1 cup unsalted butter, at room temperature
4 large eggs
½ t salt
3 cups all-purpose flour
2 t ground cinnamon
½ t ground nutmeg
¼ t ground cloves
2 t baking soda
1 cup cold, black coffee
3 cups Granny Smith apples, peeled, cored and
    roughly chopped
¾ cup raisins
1 cup chopped pecans or walnuts

Preheat the oven to 350 degrees. In a large bowl cream together the butter and sugar. Add the eggs and beat some more until well-blended. Sift together the flour, spices, and soda. Re-sift over the egg/sugar mixture. Fold in gently as slowly adding the coffee. Do not over beat. Gently fold in the apples, nuts and raisins. Pour batter into well-greased and floured tube or Bundt pan. Bake for 50 minutes to an hour or until a skewer inserted into the cake comes out clean. Cool in The pan for 10-15 minutes and then turn out onto a rack to finish cooling. When cool, sprinkle with powdered sugar.

# Batter Fried Chitterlings

It was really, really cold one Sunday a few years ago in North Carolina and *Bobby Wall*, a good friend from church and a good ol' boy in the best sense of the word, said to me, "*It's hog killin' weather.*" That reminded me of a story I had not thought of in a long time.

I knew a man years ago that decided to run for the state house in Georgia. He believed that his best chance of winning the election would be to personally call on every home in his district and ask for their vote.

He quickly learned what most country preachers know: try and end up at a nice home around dinner time as you'll likely be invited to stay and eat. Well, he was invited into this one home and was immediately hit with an unusual smell. "*Oh my gosh,*" he thought, "*It smells like they're cooking chitlins* (chitterlings)."

He was invited in to sit at the kitchen table and then he realized that not only did they have a pot of chitlins parboiling on the stove, but there also was a big pot of turnip greens cooking. He told me later that that was the only house he had ever been in where there were more flies inside trying to get out than there were outside trying to get in.

I've never tried a chitterling; they fall into that diet category of "*No, thank you, I don't think I'll have any of those.*" (For those of you from Rio Linda, as Rush would say, chitlins are hog intestines.) It's a brave person who puts one in their mouth; it's an even braver person who's willing to stink up their house to prepare and cook them.

I looked up chitterlings on *Wikipedia* (the new gospel; not!) and learned that "the dish known as chitterlings can be found in most pork-eating eating cultures, as well as in dog-eating cultures." Well, maybe that explains a few things. Anyway, they are eaten frequently by some mountain folk, hence I am including the following recipe I picked up in a small mountain grocery store whose name or town I neglected to write down.

2 lbs. of chitlins, prepared for cooking*
salt
black pepper
buckwheat flour
soda
1 egg

*How you prepare them for cooking is beyond me; you'll have to figure it out for yourself. I don't even want to think about it.

Cover the chitlins with water and parboil until tender. Cool. Make a batter of remaining ingredients; dip chitlins in the batter and fry in 1-inch or more of hot lard fat in a heavy cast iron skillet until golden brown. Serve and enjoy.

Some apparently do. But maybe only after consuming a half-dozen or so swallows of moonshine!

# Black Bean
# and Rice Salad

I developed this recipe about twenty-five years ago and it still gets rave reviews every time I serve it. Whenever you think you want to make some potato salad, for a cookout or a picnic, make this instead. I usually double the recipe so that we have leftovers; its taste even better the second and third day.

4 16-oz. cans black beans (Goya brand is best)
1 1/2 cup raw white rice
1 cup medium finely-chopped white onion
1 cup medium finely-chopped curly parsley
1- 1 1/2 cup Lime Vinaigrette dressing (see below)
1 T Tabasco sauce
2/3 cup pimento strips
Salt and pepper

Drain the beans, reserving the liquid. Put beans in colander and rinse well under running water, then let the beans drain on several layers of paper towel.

Add enough water to the reserved bean liquid to total 3 cups. Put in medium sauce pan with the rice and 1 teaspoon of salt; bring to a boil. Cover tightly, lower heat and let simmer for 15-20 minutes or until liquid is absorbed. Remove from heat, keep covered, and let sit to cool for 10-15 minutes.

When cooled a little remove the rice from the pan and place in a large bowl. Allow the rice to come to room temperature before adding the beans that have dried, the onion and the parsley. Toss and mix well to blend. Mix the

Vinaigrette dressing, add the Tabasco sauce, and pour 1 cup full over the bean-rice mixture. Toss again until dressing is well-dispersed. Cover with plastic wrap and refrigerate for an hour or more.

Toss salad again and check for seasonings and add salt and pepper, and/or more tabasco to taste. You may also want to add an additional ½ cup of the lime vinaigrette dressing, depending upon your taste (I usually do). Add the pimento strips and toss again.

The salad can be served now, but it will taste even better if allowed to come back to room temperature.

All this "rinsing and drying" may seem like a lot of unnecessary steps, but they make a difference. Each ingredient maintains its own texture and the flavors blend evenly.

# Lime Vinaigrette

1 cup good quality olive oil
2/3 cup lime juice, key limes if you can get them
2 t Dijon mustard
4 cloves garlic, crushed and minced
2 T finely minced onion
2 T chopped pimento
Salt and pepper to taste

Whisk together the first three ingredients until well-blended. Pour into a Mason jar, add remaining ingredients, screw on the top and shake the jar like the devil for twenty seconds. Recipe will cover one recipe of black bean and rice salad.

While developed especially for the bean salad, this tangy dressing works well on almost all cold seafood salads, as well as on any tossed vegetable or green salad.

# Classic Chocolate Pie

*Hospitality* is the middle name of most of the folks who live in the North Carolina mountains and their welcoming nature is often expressed through food.

The first such expression was delivered to our door the day we arrived in Rutherfordton by *Ruth Henson*, long-time member of St. Francis Episcopal Church. Her Chocolate Pie is as loved as she is. (And her daughter, Sherry, is just as sweet as the pie.) The recipe was handed down to Ruth from her mother, Alma Hovis.

This is a classic chocolate pie with meringue. Can you get anymore *"classic"* than butter, sugar and *Carnation Evaporated Milk®*?

Recipe:
1 ¾ cups sugar
4 T corn starch
4 T cocoa powder
½ stick butter
4 eggs, separated
1 can Carnation Evaporated Milk
1 can water (just fill milk can with water)
¼ cup sugar
2 baked pie shells

Preheat oven to 400 degrees.

Combine all dry ingredients: sugar, corn starch and cocoa in a heavy sauce pan. Add egg yolks, milk and water to dry mix and cook over medium heat, stirring constantly until the mixture begins to thicken. Add butter and continue cooking and stirring until thickened. Pour mixture in baked pie shells.

For the meringue: beat egg whites, gradually adding ¼ cup of sugar, until meringue comes to a peak and holds. Smooth the meringue over the pies and place them in the oven until browned.

Remove and let cool before serving. Makes 2 pies.

*"Carnation milk is the best in the land;*
*Here I sit with a can in my hand.*
*No tits to pull, no hay to pitch,*
*You just punch a hole in the son of a bitch."*
Author Unknown

# Collard Greens

My brother *Steve* complained to me after reading my North Carolina Cookbook that I did not include a recipe for collard greens.

I was surprised. I thought anyone who was born and raised in Florida and had live more than half of their life in Gainesville, Florida would certainly know how to cook collard greens. If he doesn't, it is one of the few things that he does not know. Maybe he was just looking to try something a little different.

Well, bubba, here is a different recipe. My family enjoys greens and I cook them often. But my way of preparing them is different than most recipes, in a number of ways.

First, I do not cook my greens to death, for a couple of reasons. First, slow cooking for forty-five minutes or an hour takes too long. And, I think greens cooked my way taste better.

Next, most recipes instruct you to cut away the tough center stalks of the collards and then roll up the leaves and slice them chiffonade-style. Come on, this is a southern dish, not some fancy Yankee dish. I just tear the leaves away from the center stalks, leaving the leaves in 3-4 inch-size pieces. One thing you do not want to do is buy those "conveniently prepared" bags of greens that you see now in most grocery stores. They just machine cut the collards, tough stems and all. Finally, since Dee and I do not eat pork or beef or other red meat, you will not find a piece of streak-o-lean or ham hocks or salt pork in my greens. But you will occasionally find smoked turkey wings. Or, if I can't find the wings in the store I'll cook the collards veggie-style, adding two large vegetable bouillon cubes to the pot for extra flavor.
Here is my recipe:

Large bunch collard greens
2 garlic cloves, smashed
1 T whole black peppercorns
2-3 T of olive oil
3-4 smoked, cooked turkey wings or
2 large cubes of vegetable bouillon
½ large Vidallia or other sweet onion, sliced

Fill the kitchen sink with cold water and wash the greens thoroughly to remove any sand. Hold the center of each leaf in your left hand and strip the leaf away from the center stem with your right hand, tearing the leaf into 3-4 inch-size pieces; set them aside.

In a large pot over medium heat add the olive oil, onion slices, garlic and the whole black peppercorns. If using the turkey wings you can add them to the pot now also. Sauté everything for a few minutes to soften the veggies. Fill the pot about ¾ full of water and bring to a boil. If using the bouillon cubes add them now. Don't use the bouillon and the turkey both, just one or the other. Reduce the heat and let the turkey wings simmer for 10-15 minutes. Bring water back to a boil and add the collard pieces. Again reduce the heat to medium and let the greens and wings cook at a slow boil/hard simmer for about 15 minutes. This is cooking for far less as long as most recipes call for. When the leaves are tender but still firm, remove the pot from the heat and add salt to taste and then at least ¼ cup of vinegar. Stir, cover and let sit for 10 minutes or more before serving.

It may seem a little odd to serve a dish which still has whole peppercorns in it, but that is fine. Most of the flavor has cooked out of them and they have softened.   Let the folks eat them or pick them out, it's no big deal.

Two things absolutely must be served with this pot of collards: home-made corn bread and a bottle of pepper-sauce. See if you can find some cracklings at the store and make the cracklin' cornbread recipe shown on the next page.

Pepper-sauce is not a bottle of hot sauce, although you could put a bottle of that on the table as well. Pepper-sauce is that little bottle of small green hot tabasco peppers sitting in vinegar. You'll find them in the condiment section of most every grocery store. Let each person splash on as much of the pepper-sauce (the vinegar) as they like. I usually pry off the plastic inner-cap and pick out a half-dozen or so of the peppers themselves.

If you used the turkey wings you don't need to serve much more with them than the collards, the cornbread and maybe a plate of sliced tomatoes. If no turkey, I often broil a couple of tomatoes topped with a little cheese and bread crumps to go along with the greens and the cornbread.

# Cracklin' Corn Bread

When we moved from Macon, Georgia and away from the *S&S Cafeterias*, I thought cracklin' corn bread would be lost to us forever. But low and behold, they serve it in North Carolina as well, but it is hard to find.

Cracklings are the crisp residue left after the rendering of lard from fat or the frying or roasting of pork skins. When writing about pork skins, I do not mean those fluffy, mostly air, fried pork rinds that are found in the potato chip section of your grocery store. These little pieces of pork are hard and crunchy and a little chewy . . . but oh so good when cooked in cornbread.

If you can find a small little country grocery store that sells lard, and boiled peanuts, and RC Cola, and Moon Pies, they probably sell packages of cracklings as well.

1 ½ cups yellow corn meal
1 t salt
2 T flour
1 T baking powder
1 egg, beaten
1 ¼ cups whole milk
1 ½ cups cracklings

Preheat the oven to 425 degrees. Sift corn meal, salt, flour, and baking powder together. Mix egg and milk and add to the dry ingredients. Mix well and add cracklings. Baked in a greased pan for 20 to 25 minutes. If you have an old cast iron skillet, bake the cornbread in there. Or, if you have one of those round cast iron pans that is sectioned into wedges you'll be eating cracklin' cornbread just like we did at the S&S Caféteria.

Writing about the S & S Cafeteria reminds me of our good friends Anita and Reg Smith, who we would often meet for lunch or dinner at the S & S when we lived in Macon.

I was not going to include in the book any recipes from friends, but Anita's Strawberry-Romaine Salad is just too good not to include. I serve it often to guests and I never fail to get at least one "Oh, my goodness. You must give me the recipe for this salad." It's just a few pages from the back of the book. Do not miss it and don't miss making it.

**Secret tip**: Anita recently shipped me two packages of panty hose. Why? To use to hang the Vidalia onions she and Reg shipped us the week before. They sent the *real thing*, onions actually from Vidalia, GA. How do you keep 30-pounds of onions fresh for the several months that it will take to eat them? Hang them in panty hose. Drop an onion in the toe of one of the legs; tie a knot in the panty hose and drop another onion in and repeat the process. The knots will keep the onions from touching each other. Hang the string of onions in a dark, cool place and simply cut off an onion or two whenever you need one. They'll keep for a long while. Or, wrap each onion in a piece of newspaper and keep them in the crisper section of your second refrigerator, if you have one. Thanks, Nita!

I should have included a recipe in this book for Vidalia Onion Pie. It's too late; I'm adding these few sentences to the final proof copy. Email me at phildem@tampabay.rr.com if you want a copy of the recipe and I'll send you one.

# Crispy Oven-Fried Green Tomatoes

Here is a recipe for fried-green tomatoes that is healthier than the "normal" way of cooking them. But what isn't healthier than something cooked in bacon grease? But, is there anything that tastes better? These taste pretty good, however, and lots of folks prefer the extra crispiness.

6 large green tomatoes, sliced ¼ to ½- inch thick
salt and pepper
3 eggs, beaten
1 cup *evaporated* milk (makes a difference)
2 cups all-purpose flour
1 ½ cup packaged bread crumbs, Italian seasoned
½ cup Parmesan cheese, grated, not shredded

Preheat oven to 400 degrees.

Salt and pepper the tomato slices. In bowl, mix eggs and evaporated milk until well blended. In another bowl, place the flour, and in a third bowl, mix together the bread crumbs and the parmesan cheese. Dip the tomato slices into the egg mixture, then into the flour, then back into the egg mixture and finally into the cheese/breadcrumb mixture. Arrange the slices on a lightly greased sheet pan. Bake for 20 minutes at 400 degrees, turning once after ten minutes. Tomatoes should be golden brown.

# Dave Barry and Doug Spears

This is one of those "I've got to tell it again" stories. I don't apologize for repeating it. The first part of the story is getting a little tired, but the last part is a riot.

I'm on the board of directors of a Canadian media company whose holdings include the *Winnipeg* (Manitoba) *Free Press*. Doug Spears is the humor columnist for *The Free Press* and is Canada's answer to Dave Barry. Both are very, very funny writers. In fact, Dave Barry was so impressed with Doug's writing that he once sent Doug an autographed copy of one of his books.

I'll get back to Doug Spears in a minute, but first let me tell you how and where I met Dave Barry. Dave Barry and I met in a kitchen. In was in 1985 or 1986, shortly after I had returned to Miami to accept the position of President of *The Miami Herald*. A lovely young couple, *Isabel* and *Gene Singletary*, were chairing a fund raiser for The March of Dimes.

The black-tie affair was held at the Intercontinental Hotel in downtown Miami. The main draw for the event was a cook-off competition between a dozen or so "celebrity" chefs. Interior designers from around South Florida were invited to design and build kitchens in the ballroom of the hotel; actual live kitchens with ovens and stoves, refrigerators, and running water.

During the cocktail hour the guests, who had paid a small fortune for their tickets, wandered through the ballroom visiting each of the kitchens, meeting and greeting the celebrities, and sampling the food they were preparing for the competition which would take place during dinner.

Dave Barry and I were invited to cook in one of the

kitchens. Actually, I did all of the cooking. Dave was mad because I wouldn't let him cook *Creamed Chip Beef on Toast*, which he wanted to list in the program as S.O.S., its "generic" name. (Those of you who served in the military will know to what I am referring.) I insisted we prepare some fancy shrimp dish, which, of course, did not win.

So while I was slaving over a hot stove, Dave was greeting our visitors, passing out autographed 8x10 photos and cracking jokes. There were roars of laughter coming from our booth, but I could never tell if they were laughing at Dave's jokes or my cooking.

I don't remember who all of the other chefs were but Dave and I were outclassed by Don Johnson, of Miami Vice fame; Dan Marino, of Miami Dolphins fame; and Donald Trump, fame personified. I also can't remember who won, but it wasn't us and it wasn't Donald Trump, who had flown in some fancy-smancy chef to do his cooking. More important than winning, we had loads of fun and a lot of money was raised for the March of Dimes.

But, back to Doug Spears. A couple of years ago Doug was invited to participate in a similar cooking competition, except that this was cooking deep-fried turkeys. Doug also didn't win, but he had a great time and got a funny column out of the experience. I asked Doug for a copy of his recipe so that I could include it in this book, but he wouldn't give it to me.

His deep-frying turkey experience reminded me of another story. A friend of ours was deep-frying a Thanksgiving turkey for a large family gathering. While no one was watching he inserted a whole Cornish game hen into the cavity of the turkey just prior to plunging the bird into the hot oil. When the meal was ready to be served and the family had gathered around the table, our friend entered the dining room carrying a large platter holding this beautifully prepared golden brown turkey, ready to be carved.

As our friend stood before his relatives and prepared to do the carving he stuck the serving fork into the cavity of the turkey and extracted an equally golden brown Cornish game hen, held it up, and exclaimed, "*Oh, my goodness. This one was pregnant!*"

The family reportedly laughed harder than most folks do after reading columns by Dave Barry or Doug Spears. And that's a lot of laughter.

# Figgy Sundaes

We have two people to thank for this interesting and tasty dessert: *Charles Roser* for inventing the Fig Newton® and *Rachael Ray*, of *Food Network* fame, for creating this unusual and delicious way to use them.

1 cup chopped nuts, such as hazelnuts or walnuts
1 cup chocolate hazelnut spread (recommend N*utella*®)
2 pints rum-raisin ice cream
12 *Fig Newton*® cookies, sliced crossways in quarters
whipped cream*

Toast nuts over low heat in a small pan (I toast them in the oven). Warm the chocolate hazelnut spread in the microwave on high until it reaches the consistency of hot fudge sauce, 40 seconds to one minute. In sundae cups or small bowls, layer ice cream with sliced cookies and toasted nuts and a heavy drizzle of the hazelnut sauce. Garnish with a squirt of whipped cream.

This may seem like an odd combination: rum raisin, figs, chocolate, and nuts; but believe me it works. I tried it with vanilla ice cream and the run-raisin definitely tastes better.

*Rachael uses Redi-Whip; I'd rather make my own. But whatever you use at least use a dairy product, not that stuff in the plastic tub that is made of vegetable oil. Yuk!

# Fresh Tomato Pie

The person in North Carolina who passed along to me this recipe suggested it be served at breakfast, alongside a bowl of grits, a plate of scrambled eggs and cheese and a cup of coffee.

2 T butter
½ onion, thinly sliced
2 cloves garlic, chopped fine
2-3 medium-size ripe tomatoes, peeled and sliced
1 9-inch baked pie shell
½ cup mayonnaise
¼ cup grated Parmesan cheese
2 t dried basil
salt and pepper

Preheat oven to 325 degrees. Prepare and bake a 9-inch pie shell. To peel the tomatoes cut a slight "X" in their non-stem end and plunge them into a pot of boiling water. Boil them for 2-3 minutes and then remove them with a slotted spoon and place them in a bowl of ice water. When cool the skins should slip right off. Sauté the onion and garlic in the butter until softened. Arrange the tomato slices in the baked pie shell; spread out the onions and garlic evenly over the top of the tomatoes. In a small bowl combine the mayonnaise, cheese and basil and mix well. Spread a thin layer of the mayonnaise/cheese mixture over the tomatoes and onions. Bake at 325 degrees for 30 minutes. Let sit for 5 minutes after removing from the oven. Slice and serve warm.

# God Bless School Teachers

At least thirty years ago, sometime in the early eighties, my wife and I were on a road trip traveling somewhere; I do not remember where. I was pushing the "scan" button on the radio, trying to pick up a clear station among all the static. Finally a station did come in but I do not know from where it was broadcasting. It probably was a *National Public Radio* station as it became obvious that the program was being broadcast throughout the country.

It was either *National Teacher Week* or *National Education Month* or some sort of special recognition of teachers. The host of the show was asking people from the listening audience to phone in and acknowledge or recognize a teacher that had made an especial difference in their life. Calls were coming in from all over the country, recognizing "Mr. Wilson, my seventh grade science teacher", or "Mrs. Thomas, my high school home room teacher", and so forth.

If I had realized how significant the next caller's story was going to be I would have paid attention to the teacher's name or from where the call was originating, but I didn't and have no idea who the teacher was or where the school was located. The man's story was this:

*"I want to recognize 'Mrs. Green,' my first grade teacher. On the last day of first grade, just before school let out for summer vacation, Mrs. Green asked me to stay behind after school, she wanted to ask me a question.*

*"When the other students had left the classroom Mrs. Green explained to me that next year all of the children that had been in my class would have a new teacher and that she would have all new children in her class. She went on to tell*

*me that when she had all new children it was very difficult for her, having to learn all the names of the new children and everything. She wanted to know if I would be willing to be in her class again next year to help her with the new children.*

*"I, of course, was thrilled to be asked to help and quickly said 'Sure!'*

*"The next year I did get to help; I passed out papers and wiped the blackboard and did other chores for Mrs. Green.*

*"It was a number of years later that I realized that I had failed the first grade. And it was a number of years later than that before I realized what a wonderful way Mrs. Green had handled it."*

Oh, to have more teachers like Mrs. Green! No, we just pass them along these days. How sad.

*Some students drink at the fountain of knowledge – others just gargle.*

# Grilled Dolphin

*Dolphin*, now being called by its Pacific Coast name, *Mahi-Mahi*, so as not confuse the fish with the mammal "Flipper", is one of the most prolific fish as well as one of the best-tasting. Having caught dozens and eaten even more, they are still dolphins to me. (This political correctness thing is just about to drive me "crazy"; oops, I mean about to drive me "into a severe mental disorder.")

Its sweet, not-too-fishy flavor really needs nothing more than salt and pepper and a squeeze of lime, but this recipe does add an extra something good, without taking away from the flavor of the fish itself.

6 to 8-oz. piece of dolphin fillet per person
salt and pepper
freshly ground nutmeg
medium-thick slice of tomato per person
Vidalia or other sweet onion, sliced
olive oil
limes

Preheat your grill, preferably cooking with charcoal.

While this is being done, sauté the onions in a little olive oil and salt and pepper until they are softened, but still hold their texture. Set them aside but keep them warm.

Salt and pepper each side of the fillets and distribute about a half-teaspoon of nutmeg over the top side of each filet. Rub a light coat of olive oil on the bottom side. When the grill is heated, spray it well with Pam® or some other grilling-type cooking spray to further help prevent the fish from sticking. Do not cover the grill with aluminum foil. We want to grill the fish, not *fry* it.

Place the fillets on the grill and DO NOT cover it. We want to *grill* the fish, not *bake* it. Grill the fillets for about 5-6 minutes or until your eyeball tells you it is cooked about three-quarters through (timing will depend upon the amount of heat from your grill.) Carefully turn the fish, squeeze about a half a lime over each, place a slice of tomato on top of each fillet and grill the other side for about 2-3 minutes.

Remove fish from the grill, plate and cover each fillet and tomato with a healthy portion of the onions. Finish the dish with a little more nutmeg over the top.

Served with black bean and rice salad (pg. 303), tropical coleslaw (pg. 383), a hunk of Cuban bread and a cold beer, you have one heck of a good meal!

# Grits

Almost every southerner has enjoyed eating grits over the years: grits with just butter, salt and pepper; shrimp and grits; fried leftover cold grits; grits and catsup with fried fish; cheese grits; etc. But northerners, especially those from the northeast, often have a difficult time acquiring a taste.

I have breakfast once a week with a group of men from our church and I think several of them would eat a big spoonful of beach sand before they would eat even a small spoonful of grits. I'm going to work on them. I like them too much to allow them to end their life (the beach sand would kill them) without ever tasting real, properly cooked grits.

I've never had a bowl of grits that I didn't like; I have just liked some more than others. I take that back. I once was served a bowl of instant grits that had the consistency of Cream of Wheat®. Yuck! I didn't finish it. Grits need some bite, some texture, and coarse stone-ground grits have it.*

Coarse ground grits are harder and harder to find, but they are usually available at the **Old Hampton General Store** in **Linville**, North Carolina (pg. 285). They were out of them the last time we were there, but our friend *Dick Wilkins* of Rutherfordton finally tracked some down for us at a store in South Carolina. (Thanks again, Dick.) On the next page I am going to give you their recipe for cooking grits, and then I am going to tell you how to do it even better.

* "Grain is crushed for bread (or grits) but one does not thresh it forever; one drives the cart wheel and horses over it, but one does not pulverize it."     Isaiah: 28:28

Here is the official Old Hampton General Store recipe:

4 cups of water

1 cup stone-ground corn grits

1 t salt

After supper, put the water and grits in a saucepan and let soak overnight. In the morning bring the water level up to the top of the grits. Add the salt and bring to a boil and cook 15 to 20 minutes, or until tender.

That's their recipe, now I'm going to tell you how to make something good into something even better.

Bring the grits to a boil and reduce the heat to slow simmer and cover. Don't cook for 15 to 20 minutes on high heat, like the General Store recipe suggests, cook for 30 or 40 minutes, on low heat, stirring very frequently and adding more water as needed.

While cooking, turn the pepper grinder about twenty turns and add some more salt, to taste. When you think the grits are about done (taste for tenderness; chewy, but not crunchy) add a half a stick of butter and stir well until it melts and is well combined with the grits.

Serve the grits with a side dish of grated sharp cheddar cheese. Now that's a bowl of grits!

I used to occasionally add a can of chicken stock in place of some of the water. It gave the grits a nice little different flavor. But as I keep getting older I find myself becoming more of a purist and enjoying a more-simple life style. Just water in my grits now days. Maybe getting older isn't so bad.

# Grouper Ceviche

Ceviche, sometimes spelled with an "s", is a popular seafood appetizer that originated in Peru, but that is now served throughout Latin America and Florida.

The first cookbook that I wrote, *Recipes from the Florida Keys,* contained a recipe for Conch Ceviche. The conch (pronounced konk) is the large hard shell used by native Caribbean sailors as a mouth-blown signal horn. Most people will recognize the conch as the shell you hold up to your ear to hear the ocean.

The animal inside is delicious and most often served in conch chowder, or conch fritters, or as cracked conch. But the meat is very tough and takes some work to prepare it properly.

Ceviche is seafood that has been "cooked" by marinating it in citrus juice. The acid in the juice "cooks" the seafood. Most often ceviche is made from shrimp, scallops, conch, or fish, usually a mild white fish such as snapper or grouper.

My conch recipe would work just fine with grouper, but I thought I'd check around and see if anyone was doing something new and extra creative. First I went to my own cookbook collection. Then as a big *Food Network* fan I next went there.

Well, what did I find? I found that there was very little agreement among top chefs as how to properly prepare ceviche. Not only do they not agree on how long to marinate the seafood in the citrus juice, they do not agree on what citrus juices to use.

*Norm Van Aken* uses a mixture of lime and grapefruit juices and marinates for just 10 minutes; *Bobby Flay* says 30 minutes and mixes orange juice with the lime juice; *Giada* mixes lemon and lime and marinates for 3 hours; *Ted Allen* uses lime juice and marinates for two hours; *Alton Brown* sears each side of the fish on high heat and then marinates it overnight in lime juice; *Santos Loo*, a Peruvian chef, mixes lemon and lime juices and marinates for 10 minutes.

Come on, Chefs. Let's have some agreement! Aw, to heck with them. I'm going to use my old and proven conch recipe and substitute grouper for the conch.

8 to 10 oz. grouper filet, well cleaned and trimmed
1 cup lime juice (key lime if available), or more
¼ cup finely minced red onion
2 T finely chopped green pepper
2 T finely chopped sweet red pepper
½ cup olive oil
3 T orange juice
¼ t dried oregano, or 1 T fresh oregano, finely chopped
1 t salt
¼ t freshly ground black pepper
½ t hot sauce, (recommend Matouk's from Trinidad:
            available at *Fresh Market* stores)

Dice the fish in ½-inch chunks and place in a glass bowl; add enough lime juice to cover the fish. Cover the bowl with plastic wrap and place in refrigerator overnight or for up to 24 hours. Unwrap and drain well. Combine remaining ingredients and mix well; add to fish and stir to cover all pieces.

Recover bowl with plastic wrap and refrigerate for 3-4 hours before serving. Check seasoning to taste; it may need some additional salt or hot sauce. Serve in stemmed martini glasses or on a small plate in a lettuce cup. Recipe should make about four ¼-cup servings, which is ample for an appetizer.

# Grouper Fromage

When I first heard of a recipe for grouper with melted cheese I was turned off. No way was I going to "waste" good grouper by covering it with mayonnaise and melted cheese. But then I remembered a fish sandwich I once was served and it had melted Swiss cheese on it and it wasn't too bad.

I also remembered that I prepare a seafood dish that contains a piece of fish, a scallop, an oyster, a shrimp and a mushroom cap and is then covered with a Mornay sauce. Is Mornay sauce really that much different from mayonnaise and melted cheese?

I talked myself into trying it and am I glad I did. The recipe was supposedly originally *Emeril's* but has been modified and updated by another cook, me.

1 T olive oil
¾ cup chopped onion
2 cups grated Pepper Jack cheese
1 cup mayonnaise, not low-fat or lite
1 t bottled hot sauce
1 ½ t Old Bay seasoning
4 pieces of grouper filet, about 6-8 oz. each
1 lemon, halved
1 stick cold butter cut into 16 slices

Preheat oven to 350 degrees.

In a small skillet add 1 T olive oil over medium heat. Add onion and cook until softened. Transfer to large bowl and allow to cool. To the bowl add the cheese, mayonnaise and hot sauce and 1 t Old Bay seasoning. Mix well and set aside.

Grease a large baking dish. Place the fish in the baking

dish and sprinkle with salt, pepper and the remaining ½ t of Old Bay seasoning. Squeeze the lemon juice over the fish and top each piece of fish with two of the butter slices. Bake for 10 to 12 minutes depending upon the thickness of the filets.

Remove baking dish from the oven and cover each fillet with ½ cup of the cheese mixture. Return the dish to the oven and continue baking until the cheese melts, about 8 to 10 minutes.

I can't imagine serving any starch other than rice with this dish and it certainly needs something green to add some color to the plate. Finally, make sure you have a cold, crisp white wine to go along with it.

# Grouper Sandwich

There is an Official Florida State Saltwater Fish: the Atlantic sailfish. That darn sailfish lobby; the legislature should have named the State Fish the grouper.

And there is no Official Florida State Sandwich. And if there was one it would certainly not be a sailfish sandwich. Sailfish have little commercial value as their meat is very tough. You occasionally see smoked sailfish from time to time, but no one would ever consider eating a sailfish sandwich.

If the legislature ever does get around to naming an Official State Sandwich, however, they will probably make it the *Cuban Sandwich*. That already is the official South Florida State Sandwich, and deservedly so.

The *Food Network* once polled its viewers to find the "best" sandwich in each state and what do you know, the viewers named a *Grouper Sandwich* as the "best" in Florida. The "winner" was the grouper sandwich from *Frenchy's Original Seafood Restaurant* in Clearwater, Florida.

I'm sure Frenchy's make a good one, but having never eaten there I am not sure they make the "best". First of all they have six different grouper sandwiches on their menu. In my way of thinking if you make the "best" you shouldn't have to have but that "one" on your menu.

I'll also argue the "Clearwater" connection. If there were ever to be an Official Headquarters for the Grouper Sandwich it should be on Anna Maria Island. My educated guess is that there is no other dish that is offered on more AMI restaurant menus than a Grouper Sandwich. And that includes burgers.

Almost every Florida seafood restaurant makes a Grouper Sandwich – some are fried, some are grilled; some are well-seasoned, some are not; some are good, some are not as good; some come blackened, some are Cajun; some are excellent, some are outstanding.

So popular is the Grouper Sandwich that the web address of one of the island's major restaurateurs (he owns three outstanding restaurants) is www.groupersandwich.com!

My favorite way to prepare a grouper sandwich is what I call "fried, ceviche-style". It's served on a toasted bun with a light smear of garlic tartar sauce and a slice of a heirloom tomato and some shredded lettuce. I used to serve it with coleslaw on the sandwich but I like this way better. The coleslaw often overpowered the taste of the fish.

There is a recipe for Grouper Ceviche on page 329, but this ceviche-style preparation is quicker and simpler. Don't use this one to prepare ceviche itself, however. Just use it in this recipe to slightly pre-cook the fish before frying it. At the end of this recipe is a recipe for preparing the garlic tartar sauce which I think goes very nicely with the fish. Just don't use too much of it; just a light smear.

4 pieces of grouper filet, about 6-8 ounces each
2 t Old Bay seasoning
1 cup lime juice, Key Lime if available
1 cup chopped cilantro
Salt and pepper, to taste
1 cup Canola or peanut oil for frying
2 cups all-purpose flour
1 t Old Bay seasoning

Mix the Old Bay seasoning, lime juice and the cilantro and place in a gallon zip-type plastic bag along with the fish. Refrigerate and allow fish to marinate for 30 minutes to an hour. In a flat bowl mix the remaining Old Bay seasoning and the flour with some salt and pepper to taste. Heat the oil in a large skillet over medium heat. Blot the fish lightly on a paper towel and dip each piece of fish in the seasoned flour; shake off any excess and place the fish in the pan. Cook about 3 or 4 minutes, depending upon the thickness of the filet pieces, turn and cook the other side until the fish is done. Drain on a paper towel while toasting the rolls on a cookie sheet in 350 degree oven.

Give each side of the toasted rolls a light smear of the garlic tartar sauce, add the fish and top with the tomato slice and the shredded lettuce. I usually serve the sandwich with a side of fried sweet potatoes and a dill pickle spear.

I think I'll enter this recipe in the next "Best Grouper Sandwich" competition. It might just win.

### *Garlic Tartar Sauce*

> 2 T finely chopped cornichons
> 2 cloves garlic, finely chopped
> 1 T small capers
> ½ cup mayonnaise, not lite or no-fat
> 1 T white wine vinegar
> pinch of salt
> a few grinds of freshly ground black pepper
>
> Mix together until well blended.

# The Guava,
# Queen of the Tropical Fruits

In Florida there are almost as many varieties of tropical fruits growing on the land as there are varieties of fish in the sea. In Miami, where Dee and I grew up, most neighborhood yards had one or two or a dozen different types of fruit trees growing. In my yard alone we had avocados, mangos, grapefruit, carambola (starfruit), bananas, key limes, and even a pineapple plant. Many of these same fruits are grown on Anna Maria Island and in other parts of Manatee County.

Of all of these I consider the mango as king, but followed closely behind by the guava, as queen. The guava is a round, smooth-skinned fruit a little larger than the size of a golf ball. Green-skinned when they are growing, the fruit turns a pale yellow when ripe. The inside of the fruit is – er – well – uh . . . guava-colored. The color is hard to describe, sort of dark, pinkish, rose-colored – you know . . . guava-colored. (There is a Mexican variety that has a white, pear-colored flesh, but they are not as sweet and flavorful as the variety grown in Florida.)

My favorite way to eat guava is to simply cut the ripened fruit in ¼-inch or so slices, place them in a bowl and sprinkle them with some sugar. Then cover the bowl with plastic wrap and refrigerate for an hour or longer. Then dig in; eat skin and seeds and all.  Or, if you do not need the extra roughage, scoop out the seeds before slicing (see the next page).Delicious!

My second most favorite way to eat guava is Guava Shells with Cream Cheese for dessert.  Guava shells are made by peeling the very thin skin, cutting the guava in half and scooping out the seedy center pulp, leaving the fleshy "shell" which is then candied. Canned guava shells in heavy syrup are available in most Florida grocery stores and in Latin American markets throughout the country.

The famous Cuban restaurant, **The Columbia**, serves a wonderful guava cheesecake, *Torta* de *Quesco y Guayaba*, using guava shells. The Columbia, founded in Ybor City (in Tampa), also has a restaurant at St. Armand's Circle on Longboat Key, just south of AMI.

The most frequent use of guava is to cook it into guava jelly or guava paste. Guava paste is a thicker, more solid form of guava jelly that is used in *Pastelito de Guayaba*, those delicious flaky Cuban pastries that are filled with guava and sweetened cream cheese and then baked.

There are a number of producers of guava jelly and jars can be found on supermarket shelves throughout the country. But the best guava jelly I have ever eaten is packaged right here in Palmetto, Florida, not twenty miles from the island.

We have our friends, *Shirley Ann* and *Dick Turner* to thank for our introduction to **Palmalito Guava Jelly**. The *Palmetto Canning Company* has been producing *Palmalito* brand guava jelly since the company was founded in 1927 by John Greenlow. Shirley Ann and Dick are friends of the Greenlow family, who have owned and operated the company since it was founded. Shirley Ann even has one of her guava recipes printed on the lid of the jar.

The company originally only produced and sold guava jelly. Today the diversified company has increased the product lines into many other flavors of tropical jellies and a BBQ sauce. My other favorite is Mango Jam. Publix Super Markets and other grocery retailers carry the *Palmalito* brand or you can order a six-pack of the product online from the *Parksdale Farm Market* at www.parksdale.com.

Shirley Ann Turner was raised in Lakeland, Florida and Dick was raised here in Bradenton. They met when they were students at the University of Florida.  They are blessed, as we are, to enjoy the *"best of two worlds."*  In addition to  their home in Bradenton, they also have a home in the North Carolina Mountains, in a golf course community between *Highlands* and *Cashiers* in the southwestern part of the state. While Dick's business interests take him back and forth during the year, they basically enjoy the mountains in the summer and Florida in the winter.

If you were to look up *Southern hospitality* in a dictionary you'd find a picture of Shirley Ann Turner. In Georgia we'd say she's "as sweet as a peach." Here in Florida we say she's "as sweet as guava jelly!"

# I've Got Rhythm . . . in my Two Right Feet

One of my favorite old-time songs is George Gershwin's *I've Got Rhythm*. I've got it, rhythm, that is, but the problem is that I've only got it in my right foot.

It wasn't always that way. At one time I had rhythm in my entire body. As a six-year-old I was a tap dancer (shuffle, hop, step, slap, step); I took piano lessons all through elementary school; in the fifth and sixth grade I played the mellophone; I played the French horn in junior high. In high school I played around.

But sometime after that I lost it, I lost my rhythm; I lost it everywhere. Everywhere, that is, except in my right foot. There I still have plenty of it.

I can tap my foot in time with the best of them: *Thom Tenny*, church organist extraordinaire; *Carole Cornman*, soprano and choir director (also extraordinary). I love it when she wears sandals; she keeps time with her right big toe. (I don't think I should discuss this fascination any further.) *Deborah Polkinghorn*, the amazing diva-mezzo, can't out-sing my right foot. Jazz pianist *Tom Benjamin* can't out-play my right foot. I've got rhythm.

But try and carry that rhythm out onto the dance floor and it is a total disaster. I've got two right feet. Get me on a dance floor and it's hard to tell if I am dancing a *box trot*, or the *fox step*, or the *Viennese tango*. The last two dance styles that I mastered were the *limbo* and the *twist*. I know I can no longer get under even a high limbo bar and I doubt that I can still *do the twist*. You'd think it would have gotten a little easier for me now that I have gotten a little *"chubby"*, but I feel more comfortable sitting and playing a game of *"checkers"* than I do dancing.

But, while I don't dance myself, I love to watch others dance. Dee and I are major, major fans of *Dancing with the Stars*. Don't invite us to do anything on Monday night unless it is to watch *Dancing* with you.

Our friend *Ann Lewis*, and her late husband, *Jack*, would often do that, and feed us too! Ann and Jack loved to dance and were near-professionals, having taken ballroom lessons and danced competitively. We so enjoyed those nights with them. It was almost like having two additional judges right there in the room with you. Plus they had this really BIG-screen TV and some gizmo that if dinner went a little long Jack could back the show up to the beginning and skip the commercials until we got back live and on track.

Jack died this past year and is he ever missed by his family and friends. Jack had retired but he spent much of his free time at *The Episcopal Church of the Annunciation*, as volunteer treasurer. He had big shoes to fill (size 13, I think); it took a part-time financial secretary, two co-treasurers and an expanded finance committee to replace him.

But, back to *Dancing with the Stars*. It was probably at the end of the third season that I first learned that *Dancing* had a roadshow that performed around the country between seasons and that they were coming to Charlotte. They were to perform in the basketball arena and unfortunately by the time I went to purchase tickets they were almost totally sold out. The only seats left were on the top two rows of the arena. We enjoyed the show, but it was difficult to watch the dancing at the same time I was trying to stop my nose bleed.

A few years later the show was back in North Carolina, in Greensboro, and not only was I able to purchase good seats, I was able to upgrade them using American Express points. We ended up sitting at a table right on the dance floor. It was non-stop action. As soon as one dance ended the next one began. In order to maintain the flow, the dancers for the next set would que-up just off stage (the dance floor). Our table was next to one of the aisles. I happened to glance over to my right and who was there, so close that if I had leaned over I could have brushed against her? *Edyta Sliwinska*! What a thrill. *Who could ask for anything more; who could ask for anything more.* It was like having a pacemaker kick in. And you know what, she looked even better in person than she did on TV.

Enough lustful reminiscing. End of story.

p.s.   Those of you who have absolutely no idea about what I am writing don't know what you have missed. It's too late to see Edyta; she left the show in a snit a few years ago. But it's not too late to enjoy the rest of the dancers. Monday nights – ABC – twice a year for about ten weeks.

*"I grew up with six brothers. That's how I learned to dance – waiting for the bathroom."*

Bob Hope

# Liver Mush

A writer for the *Christian Science Monitor* once wrote *"There are few words you can put in front of 'mush' to make it sound even worse, right? Now add the word 'liver.' Sounds enticing, doesn't it?"* But it's not just the name that has made this only the second recipe in this book that I have not personally cooked and eaten. (The other is *Batter Fried Chitterlings,* see page 301.)

What really turned me off was finding out how liver mush was made, what ingredients go into it. I should like it as it contains grits, and I love grits. And it's not even the liver. I've eaten tons of liver and onions and fried chicken livers over the years. It's the "pig head parts" that got to me.

But folks in North Carolina LOVE liver mush! It is one of the most popular breakfast foods, fried crisp and served with scrambled eggs and grits. Others eat it cold, sliced as a sandwich meat. People go so "hog wild" over liver mush that the town of Shelby, NC holds an annual Fall Liver Mush Expo.

Just to give you the "flavor" of how nuts some people go over this stuff the following comments were taken from a blog attached to the Shelby Fall Festival and Liver Mush Expo web site:

bcatfish posted: *"I was excited to go to the expo because I was raised on the stuff but moved and liver mush is not available around where I live. I attended the expo and love it. I brought a cooler and emptied its contents so I could fill it with liver mush to bring back home for all my friends to enjoy."*

Larry posted: *"I carry a small cooler that holds exactly 11 pounds."* (Eleven pounds! Do you realize how many pig head parts and livers it takes to make eleven pounds of the stuff?)

Marvin posted from Oklahoma City: *"Do you know of any companies that would be willing to ship liver mush?"*

If you can't wait until the fall to go to the Expo, make your own liver mush using this recipe:

### Liver Mush

1 ½ lbs. of fatty pork, preferably from the hog's head
2 cups stiff-cooked grits, cooked in the pork water
1 fresh hog liver
eggs, 2 for every 2 cups of pork mixture
red and black pepper
salt
sage

Place the hog's head parts in a pot of water and cook until tender. Remove the meat and use the broth to make a batch of grits. Fry the hog liver and grind it in a food processor along with some of the pork meat until it is finely ground. Put the grits in a large bowl and add the spices to taste. Begin to slowly add the liver mixture to the grits and use a hand mixer to mix it up well. Put in two eggs for every two cups of liver mush mixture and continue to mix. Check seasonings.

Once the mixture is mixed well, put it into a loaf pan that has been lined with foil or greased to prevent sticking. Cook it in the oven at 350 degrees for 1 hour. Let it cool before turning it out. Keep the loaf in the refrigerator until ready to use.

As bad as pig head parts sounds to me, that is not as bad as the partially defatted cooked pork fatty tissue, the mechanically separated chicken parts and the beef lips and utters (now referred to as meat by-products) that used to be listed on the label of a can of *Armour's Potted Meat*. Don't let a can of that stuff into your house!

Liver Mush's popularity has been increasing, perhaps due to my including this recipe in my earlier North Carolina cookbook and restaurant guide. Over 10,000 people are expected at this year's festival. Since I last wrote about the festival they have added a *Little Miss Liver Mush Pageant.* How would you like to have that on your daughter's resume: *Named Little Miss Liver Mush 2013.*

The festival has become so popular that *CNN* and *The Travel Channel* both ran features on it this past year.

Our long-time friend, *Diane Keowan* of Fort Wayne, Indiana, was so taken with this story that she drew me a picture showing a can of Armour Potted Meat with arms and legs being denied entrance in Dee and Phil's home. It is framed and proudly hung in my kitchen!

# Mytilus Edulis, the Edible Blue Mussel

In the AMI section of the book I wrote about coquina, the tiny bivalve found on the beaches in Florida. I decided not to give you a recipe for Coquina Soup because it so time consuming to collect enough to make a meal.

In its place I am giving you this recipe for a bivalve found on the shores of North Carolina and points northward to the Arctic Ocean, the delicious and versatile blue mussel.

The coquina shell is about the size of the fingernail on your little finger; a mature blue mussel is about the size of your thumb, 2 to 4 inches long and about an inch high.

The mussel is closely related to the clam and oyster and is abundant along both the Atlantic and Pacific coasts. On the Pacific coast the blue mussel can be found from San Francisco to Alaska. There is a closely related California mussel (Mytilus californianus) that can be found as far south as Mexico.

In Europe almost everyone is familiar with this delicious mollusk and it has been a part of their regular diet for centuries. But is has only been in the past thirty or forty years that the mussel has found its way onto more than just a few menus in North America and there is still a very large percentage of the population that has never tasted one.

Stone crabs, oysters, clams, conch and other seafood are getting more and more expensive as the consumption of red meat has declined and seafood has become more popular. But mussels are still very inexpensive, compared to other types of seafood.

And they are very nutritious. In fact, no seafood is more nutritious than mussels and no other shellfish gives such a high yield of meat. The U.S.D.A. reports that 3.5 ounces of raw mussel meat and a 3.5 ounce piece of T-Bone steak each contain about 14.5 grams of protein. But, the mussels only produce 95 calories, compared to 395 for the steak and only 2.2 grams of fat compared to 37 grams of fat in the steak. The mussels are also a good source for carbohydrates, with 3.3 grams compared to zero grams for the steak.

Beachcombers in the Northeast can easily find blue mussels since they often attach themselves to rocks and pilings in tidal areas. But the easiest way to gather mussels is to go to your local fish market. Farm-raised mussels are available at most good fish markets and large grocery stores with a fresh seafood department. Many feel that farm-raised mussels have a richer and sweeter flavor than those harvested in the wild and they are generally larger and cleaner. The suspended culture system in which mussels are grown (clinging to ropes hanging from barges) is one of the most environmentally – sound forms of aquaculture.

Most of the mussels sold in the U.S. are harvested in Canada or Maine, with a large number raised in Rhode Island as well. Mussels from Prince Edwards Island, Canada are especially prized.

When cooking mussels there are two very important things to keep in mind: first, live mussels should respond by closing their shells when rinsed or soaked in cold water, and, shells that have not opened after cooking should not be eaten and thrown away.

When Dee and I were in Chartres, France a few years ago we ate in a Belgium-based restaurant that only served mussels – fourteen different ways. I picked up a little card that contained three of their recipes. We liked this recipe for Blue Mussels with Saffron over Pasta. The recipes were in French but I think I have translated the following one correctly:

24 mussels

½ shallot, thinly sliced

1 clove garlic, finely sliced

¼ cup olive oil

1 cup diced fresh tomato

¾ cup dry white wine

3-4 threads saffron

12 ounces spaghetti or linguini, cooked and set aside

4 T olive oil

1 large leek, thinly sliced, white part only

1 T fresh basil, torn in small pieces

1 T fresh Italian parsley, roughly chopped

Rinse the mussels well under cold water, removing any of the small pieces of black thread-like pieces (beard) with a sharp knife. Dry the mussels, discarding any shells that did not close when rinsed. Over medium-high flame heat the ¼ cup of olive oil in a large sauté pan or Dutch oven and add the mussels and toss for about 30 seconds. Add the shallot, garlic, tomato, saffron and wine. Stir to distribute the vegetables and seasoning and cover. Bring to a boil and steam the mixture for about five minutes or until the mussels have opened. Add the cooked pasta, remaining olive oil, leek, and basil. Season with salt and pepper. Toss well and serve topped with grated cheese and the chopped parsley. Serves two.

A year or so ago, Dee and I tried a new restaurant that had recently opened on Anna Maria Island. I ordered the steamed mussels. The ones that I ate were well-prepared and tasty, but there were four mussels on my plate that were not open. I mentioned this to my server and he responded by asking if I would like for him to ask the chef to open them for me. "Definitely not," I responded. "You should never eat a mussel that has not opened when being cooked." The server began to argue with me saying, "No, you have it backwards. You should not eat a mussel that has not closed." I asked if the cook would come to our table, which he did. Realizing what had happened the cook apologized and explained to the server his error. Both were wrong. The cook should never have let the plate out of the kitchen and the server did not know what he was talking about. An unknowledgeable diner could have become seriously ill. Needless to say that was our one and only visit to the restaurant. You don't have to worry, however. They were out-of-business in less than six months. (Note that the server referred to the chef; I referred to him as the cook. A real chef would never have made such a mistake. And no well-trained server would ever argue with a customer.) As I wrote earlier, some restaurants deserve to fail, others don't. This one definitely did.

# "Official"
# Key Lime Pie

There are several good Key Lime Pie recipes being served in restaurants all around Florida (and more than a few awful ones), but there is only one original, "official" way to make a Key Lime Pie. My mother taught me how to make this pie when I was six years old and I am still making it all these years later. The key lime tree is probably still growing in the backyard of our old home on N.W. 46 Street in Miami.

First of all, let me tell you a little about key limes. They are a specific variety of lime and, despite its name, they do not grow exclusively in the Florida Keys. While rumored to have been brought to the Caribbean by Christopher Columbus, it is actually a native plant of Southeast Asia. No one knows for sure when the first key lime plant actually arrived in Florida, but whoever brought it deserves our thanks. A Key Lime Pie made without real key lime juice is NOT a Key Lime Pie. And the juice makes a difference.

The "regular" lime you see in grocery stores is a Persian lime. It is about twice the size of a key lime. A fully developed key lime is about the size of a Ping-Pong ball. Some Persian limes may get a tinge of yellow to its skin when they are fully ripe, but basically they are dark green-colored. A ripe key lime is yellow.

A Persian lime has virtually no seeds; a key lime is filled with seeds. The Persian lime's skin is thick; key lime skin is thin. Despite the difference in size, you can get about the same amount of juice from each fruit.

You almost have to have your own tree or know someone

that has one to get real key lime juice. Most of the key limes being sold these days are coming out of Mexico and that's fine, except that they are being harvested too soon. You may see small bags of key limes being sold in produce markets and grocery stores but they are usually small, half-grown and hard as rocks. A ripe key lime does not hold its freshness for very long so it is obvious why the growers are picking them too soon. These under-developed limes do not have much juice and the juice that they do produce is somewhat bitter. Key limes should not be "picked"; the way to harvest a key lime is to shake the tree. The ripe limes will fall to the ground.

Beware also of the bottled "key lime juices" being sold in some grocery stores. Read the label carefully: most say "Key *West* Lime Juice". And even if it is a bottle of juice from real key limes, chemicals have been added to prevent spoilage.

But, back to the pie.

6 egg yolks
1 15-oz. can Eagle-Brand sweetened condensed milk
½ cup real, freshly squeezed key lime juice
1 Graham cracker pie shell, baked and cooled

Preheat oven to 325 degrees. Combine egg yolks and sweetened condensed milk in a bowl and mix well with an electric mixer for about 3 minutes. Slowly add the lime juice while continuing to mix until well blended. Total mixing time should be about 4 or 5 minutes. Pour mixture into pie shell and bake for 10 minutes. Remove from oven and refrigerate, uncovered, for 2-3 hours or until set. Purists serve it plain.

**Note:** I just received a catalogue from the King Arthur Flour company and see that they are selling "100% Pure Key Lime Juice." I haven't tried it yet, but most of their products are very high quality. www.kingarthurflour.com.

# Pan Seared Grouper

Grouper is a very forgiving fish that will take well to almost any type of cooking. One of the most simple and successful preparations is pan searing. Many of the island restaurants prepare it this way.

2 6-oz pieces grouper filet
4 T clarified butter
1 T unsalted butter
1 garlic clove, chopped fine
2 sprigs of fresh thyme
Juice of 1 lime

Preheat oven to 400 degrees.

Salt and pepper fish and set aside. Heat an oven-proof sauté pan on the stove until hot; add clarified butter and sear one side of the fish until it begins to brown. Transfer pan to oven for 5 to 9 minutes, depending upon the thickness of the filet. Do not flip or move the fish. Remove from oven and add 1 T butter, garlic, sprig of thyme and the lime juice and mix. Spoon the melted butter/lime sauce over the fish, top each piece with one of the thyme sprigs and serve.

If you do not have an oven-proof frying pan you can transfer the fish to a piece of parchment paper on a cookie sheet and place that in the oven.

# Peaches

Next to North Carolina blueberries and North Carolina apples, my favorite North Carolina fruit is peaches. Not as well-known as Georgia or South Carolina peaches, for my money they are just as flavorful and delicious and are one of the best things about summer in the mountains.

The bulk of the 3,000 or so acres of peach orchards are in the sandhills area of the state, just east of Charlotte, but an ever increasing number of orchards are being planted in western North Carolina. An estimated 11 to 12 million pounds of peaches are grown each year in the state.

Available for just a few months – around the first of June through early August – fresh peaches are sold at farmers markets and roadside stands throughout the area.

Here are some tips from the North Carolina department of Agriculture for selecting, storing, ripening and preparing fresh peaches:

*When Selecting*: look for peaches with a creamy to gold undercolor that best indicates ripeness. The amount of red blush is an indicator of variety and not always a sign of ripeness. Two other indicators of ripeness are a well-defined crease and a good fragrance. Select fruit that has begun to soften for immediate use. Firm ripe fruit can be held for a few days at room temperature to ripen further. Never select a peach with green undercolor since they will not ripen well. They will shrivel, become flabby and never achieve a good flavor.

When Storing: peaches should be held at 32-35 degrees with high humidity. Fully ripened fruit should be refrigerated immediately and kept there until ready for consumption.

Sound and mature, but not overripe, peaches can be expected to hold 1-2 weeks at 32-25 degrees with little adverse effects. Peaches deteriorate rapidly when held for longer periods.

*When Ripening*: a room temperature of 65-70 degrees is best for mature peaches. There is no gain in sugar content once the peach is picked from the tree. Its ripening consists mainly of softening, developing juiciness, and developing flavor. So the riper a peach is at harvest the more sugar it will contain.

Remember, once a mature peach begins to ripen, it never stops; but you can slow down the rate of ripening by storing at low temperatures.

*When Preparing*: wash peaches gently, peel and remove pits. Handle carefully to avoid bruising. To peel a peach, dip it in boiling water for 30 seconds, and then in cold water. The peel should slide off easily. To keep peaches from darkening, dip in lemon juice or ascorbic acid solution.

A medium-size peach is full of vitamins and low in calories (about 40). There is no fat or cholesterol in a peach.

I've selected from the North Carolina Department of Agriculture and some local sources several peach recipes that I think are particularly good.

# Peach Cobbler

Everyone probably has a favorite peach cobbler recipe in their files. This recipe has been passed around western North Carolina for a long while. No one can seem to remember who originated it, but lots of folks are using it. It is the recommended peach cobbler recipe from the *North Carolina Department of Agriculture*. And it's not just for peaches; it works well with almost any kind of fruit. Try blueberries; or mix the blueberries and the peaches together. It's easy and delicious.

½ cup butter (1 stick)
¾ cup sugar
1 cup milk
1 t. vanilla
1 cup self-rising flour
2 cups fresh sliced North Carolina peaches

Preheat the oven to 375 degrees.

Melt the butter in the oven in a shallow 2-quart baking dish. Mix together the flour, sugar, and milk to make a batter. Pour batter over the hot melted butter. Do not stir. Arrange peaches evenly over the top. Bake for 40 to 50 minutes, or until top is nicely browned.

Try this one; you may find you like it better than your "favorite".

# Peach Pound Cake

During peach season we often end up with more peaches than we can eat before they get over-ripe. We freeze some of them, but are always looking for peach recipes that can be frozen. Here is a low-fat recipe that is still moist and very flavorful and yet holds up well to freezing.

vegetable no-stick cooking spray for baking
1/3 cup vegetable oil
½ cup plain Greek-style yogurt (not no-fat)
1 ½ cups sugar, divided
3 eggs, plus
2 egg whites
1 t vanilla
3 cups all-purpose flour, divided
1 ½ t baking powder
½ t salt
2 cups medium-finely chopped fresh peaches

Preheat oven to 350 degrees.

Spray a 10-inch tube pan with cooking spray. Sprinkle with 1 teaspoon of sugar. In a large bowl combine the oil and yogurt, gradually adding the remaining sugar, beating well. Add whole eggs and egg whites, one at a time, beating well after each addition. Add vanilla and mix well. Combine 2 ¾ cups of flour, baking powder and salt. Gradually add to the yogurt mixture; beat until well blended. Dredge the peaches in the remaining ¼ cup of flour and fold them into the batter. Pour batter into the prepared pan and bake for 1 hour and 10 minutes. Remove from the pan and cool completely on a rack.

# Pecan Crisps

*Fran Isbell*, of Rutherfordton, NC is a wonderful cook and a most gracious hostess. It was always a treat whenever we were invited to her home for tea or dinner or to watch a movie, which Fran loves to do. Since we moved to Anna Maria Island we have kept in touch with Fran, but we only get to see her about once a year, and we miss her.

Fortunately we don't miss her *Pecan Crisps* . . . she gave me the recipe. Of all the delightful and delicious things that Fran has served us*, it is the Pecan Crisps that I enjoy the most. It is a simple recipe and relatively easy to prepare, but the result is outstanding. I feel bad that my favorite dish of hers is an easy one when she worked so hard preparing many other things for us. They have all been appreciated and enjoyed, but these goodies are the BEST!

24 Graham crackers
1 cup light brown sugar
1 cup butter (2 sticks)
1 cup chopped pecans

Preheat the oven to 350 degrees.

Place crackers in 10x13 jelly roll pan or cookie sheet that has been lined with non-stick aluminum foil. Cook the brown sugar, butter and pecans over medium heat to just boil. Pour the syrup over the graham crackers and bake for 10 minutes at 350 degrees. Remove the pan and allow the mixture to cool. Cut or break apart. Makes about 48 pieces.

*One thing she never served us was frog legs.

# Pick 'em out!

Last summer we hosted at our Lake Tahoma home eleven of the youth from *The Episcopal Church of the Annunciation* and four parent/grandparent chaperones for a week in the mountains. Fortunately we have enough bedrooms, and with three floors we were able to separate the girls from the boys; or was it the other way around? They had a great time and we enjoyed having them there.

One thing I learned from the experience is that you do not ask a group of eleven teenagers and five adults, "*What would you like for breakfast?*"

If I recall correctly, there were eleven different orders, including an *Egg McMuffin*. It has been at least 25 years since I have been to a McDonald's restaurant and I certainly have never eaten or prepared an Egg McMuffin. The young angel explained to me how to make it and then added, "*And I like extra catsup on it.*"

Ann Lewis, one of the chaperones and more experienced with dealing with groups of young people, handled breakfast the next morning and announced, "*We having blueberry pancakes for breakfast.*"

"*I don't like blueberries,*" said one of the youth.

"*Pick 'em out,*" was Ann's quick response.

Way to go, Ann!

# Pregnant Women:
# Be Careful What You Eat

When Dee was pregnant with our second son, David, her ob/gyn's office was just down the street from a wonderful little bakery that sold the most delicious fried apple fritters. They were actually more like a very large glazed apple donut, but whatever they chose to call them they were great.

OB doctors are usually very careful to monitor their patients' weight gain during pregnancy. My then-nurse wife explained to me that a number of complications could develop if the mother gained too much weight, complications that could affect the baby as well as lead to a more difficult delivery. Dee worked hard to limit her weight gain and would never think about stopping by the bakery on her way to the doctor's office.

But . . . , as a reward for doing so well, she would always stop by the bakery *on her way home* from the doctor's office! Dee ate so many apple fritters while she was pregnant that for a short while we considered naming David "Jonathan." If he had been a girl she might have been named "Delicious" or "Golden Delicious," if she had been a blonde.

Over the years I have unsuccessfully searched for a recipe that would come close to matching that used by the bakery in Macon, Georgia, even though I knew the fritters would have been just as unhealthy to non-pregnant women, and men, as they were to pregnant women.

Some thirty-years after David was born we were back in Macon visiting friends and happened to think about the apple fritters. Dee said, *"Do you think that bakery is still open? Let's drive by and see.*"

Well, it was still there and they still made apple fritters. Dee and I each ate one right there in the store and then each got two more to go! *Big Macs* are what has kept *McDonald's* going all these years; the apple fritters apparently had had the same positive effect on business for *Lary's Bakery.* Unfortunately something finally went wrong; maybe Lary died. The last time we were in Macon Lary's Bakery was an empty store front. Too bad.

As the late *Paul Harvey* would say, "*Now let me tell you the rest of the story*":

David was about five years old and we were back living in Miami. Dee had stopped by a bakery to pick up some bread for dinner. David was with her and was looking hungrily at the glass-enclosed case containing dozens of different pastries and cookies. "*You can pick something out,*" Dee told him. What do you think he selected from all those choices? Yep, an apple fritter! Just a coincidence? I don't thin-n-n-nk so.

So, pregnant women, be careful what you eat. Fortunately Dee also ate lots and lots of my collard greens when she was pregnant. Collard greens are "brain food." Both our sons ended up "smart as whips" (whatever that means) and both are handsome too! The collard green recipe is on page 307.

# President Jimmy Carter's Sweet Tooth

Q: What's better than a chocolate pie?
A: Two chocolate pies.

Elsewhere in this recipe section you will find a classic chocolate pie recipe that has been handed down through several generations of the Hovis/Henson families. Here is one that found its way through the *White House*. Yes, the real White House, not that white house down on the corner that needs a coat of paint.

Part of the time that we lived in Macon, *Jimmy Carter* was governor of Georgia. (When we first arrived Lester Maddox was governor. That old fool once led off a 20-mile *Cancer Walk-A-Thon* in which I participated by sitting on the handlebars of his bicycle and peddling backwards. Too bad that wasn't the only stupid thing he ever did. But that's another story.)

Jimmy Carter's first cousin, Don Carter, was editor of *The Macon Telegraph*. Whenever Governor Carter was in town he would always stop by the paper to say hello to Don and spend some time with the editorial page editors. More than a few times I was invited to sit in on those meetings and once had some one-on-one time with the then-governor. We discussed, among other things, the worm farm in Plains, Georgia, run by the governor's uncle (Don's father) who had raised Jimmy. Jimmy Carter invited me to Plains to meet Mr. Carter and tour the worm farm, which Dee and I did. My only regret was that while we were there we didn't get to meet Billy Carter and share a Billy Beer.

Years later, while once reading an issue of *Guidepost Magazine*, (to which if you do not subscribe you should) I came across an article by *Roland Mesnier*, who for twenty-five years had been head pastry chef at the White House, serving five First Families. Come to find out President Carter's favorite dessert was chocolate pie.

I feel confident that Chef Mesnier will not mind if I share his recipe with you. But, President Carter might object; I think he is still miffed at me. During his last year in office, I was invited to the White House as part of a group for a briefing and to spend a little time with the President. It was only after I arrived there that they discovered that I was the only non-Democrat in the group they had invited. Someone got chewed out, I'm sure. Not surprisingly, I was never invited back and they never did send me a copy of the photograph they took of me shaking hands with the President. All the Democrats in our group received their photos, however. I guess "that's politics." But anyway, I'd rather have the memory and the story than the photo.

Here's Chef Mesnier's recipe that he often used to satisfy President Carter's sweet tooth:

6 T sugar
¼ cup cornstarch
8 large egg yolks
1 qt. whole or 2% milk
8 oz. semisweet chocolate, finely grated
4 T unsalted butter, cut into small pieces
1 prebaked 9-inch pie shell
1 ½ cups heavy cream, chilled
2 T confectioners' sugar
1 t vanilla extract
1 pound chocolate shavings (that's what the recipe calls
for, but no-way could you use that much chocolate.)

Whisk sugar and cornstarch together in a bowl with electric mixer. Add egg yolks; beat on high speed until thick and pale, about 4 minutes. Place milk in a saucepan and bring to a boil over medium-high heat, stirring frequently to make sure the bottom doesn't burn. Whisk about 1/3 of the hot milk into the egg mixture and return egg mixture to the saucepan.

Cook over medium-high heat, whisking constantly, until the mixture reaches a full boil, 3 to 4 minutes. Remove pan from heat; whisk in grated chocolate and butter until melted. Scrape pudding into pie shell and cool.

Cover and refrigerate until chilled, at least 2 hours or up to one day. Two or three hours before serving, place heavy cream, confectioners' sugar and vanilla in a chilled bowl and whip with an electric mixer until the cream holds stiff peaks. Smooth whipped cream over pudding. Scatter chocolate shavings (surely not a pound of) over the whipped cream and serve. Serves eight Republicans or Democrats; this is a bi-partisan dessert.

It is a lot of work to make this pie but I guess there's nothing too good for our Presidents. Even the first one supposedly had a hankering (that's a mountain term) for Cherry Pie.

# Spicy Fruit Salsa

Most everyone knows that lemon and lime are good seasonings for seafood, but other tropical fruits go equally as well with most seafood dishes. I make this salsa often and serve it with almost any grilled or fried seafood dish.

1 cup diced (¼ to ½-inch) fresh pineapple
1 cup diced mango
1 cup diced papaya (optional)
1 cup sectioned and diced orange segments
1/2 cup small-diced red bell pepper
1 cup chopped cilantro leaves (about 1/2 bunch)
1 T jalapeno, finely diced
1 t Scotch Bonnet or Habanero pepper, finely diced
1 T olive oil
1 T lime juice
Salt and pepper

Mix all ingredients in glass bowl; cover with plastic wrap and refrigerate at least ½ hour before serving. Spoon the salsa on top of or alongside grilled or fried fish.

You will note that the recipe calls for two different varieties of hot peppers: the Jalapeno for flavor and the Scotch Bonnet or Habanero for heat. It is best to put on a pair of disposable rubber gloves when handling hot peppers but most cooks think that is being a sissy. Rub your eye just once after handling a Scotch Bonnet and you'll discover that being a sissy is not such a bad idea.

**Hot Stuff:** Back in 1912, a chemist by the name of Wilbur Scoville, working for the Parke-Davis pharmaceutical company developed a way to measure the spicy heat of chili peppers, now referred to as the Scoville Scale. To give you a comparison of various peppers you'll find in most large supermarkets today, the typical green bell pepper rates zero on the scale. The popular Jalapeno pepper will vary from between 2,500 and 8,000 on the scale. The Scotch Bonnet pepper called for in the salsa recipe typically will range between 150,000 and 300,000 units on the scale; the Habanero can range from 200,000 units to 1,000,000. And there are peppers that are even hotter but who would want to eat them. Them's devil's food!

I have always thought that while Habaneros are green when unripe they gradually changed color from green to yellow to orange to red as they matured. "No," says my brother-in-law Chuck, who grows them in his yard. "The different colors are different varieties. All unripe Habaneros are green but the color at maturity varies." The most common varieties are orange and red, but they can also turn white, brown and pink, depending upon the variety. But they are all hot, hot, hot, regardless of the color.

# Strawberry-Romaine Salad

*Anita Smith*, of Macon, Georgia has been our close friend since 1971. We've moved eight times since we left Macon in 1978, but have remained close to Anita and her husband Reg and their daughter Amy and her family ever since.

Anita makes scratch biscuits that melt in your mouth; her German Chocolate Cake is the best I have ever eaten. But it is her Strawberry-Romaine Salad that has them lined up outside her door. I'm sure she will be pleased that I am sharing the recipe with you.

1 cup vegetable oil
¾ cup sugar
½ cup red wine vinegar
2 cloves of garlic, minced
½ t salt
¼ t paprika
¼ t ground black pepper
3-pack of hearts of romaine
1 head Boston lettuce
1 pint strawberries, sliced
1 cup shredded Monterey Jack cheese *
½ cup walnut pieces, toasted

In a large jar combine the first seven ingredients. Cover tightly and shake vigorously. This dressing can be stored for up to one week and makes more than enough for the salad. Tear each head of lettuce into bite-size pieces and pour the dressing over the salad and toss gently. Combine the straw berries, shredded cheese and walnuts and add to the salad, tossing gently again. Serves up to twelve, but six of us have been known to polish off the bowl.

*By mistake I once picked up a wedge of Pepper Jack cheese at the store. The salad wasn't as good as with plain Monterey Jack.

# Sunshine Grouper

This is one of the simplest fish recipes I know but it is one of our favorites. The recipe was in my Florida Keys cookbook. If you cannot find grouper at the fish market this week select another recipe and save this one for later. It really is a "grouper only" dish.

2 lbs. grouper filets
1 T lemon juice
¼ cup melted butter
¼ cup orange juice
1 T grated orange rind
salt and pepper
 1 T freshly ground nutmeg
chopped parsley

Preheat oven to 350 degrees. Salt and pepper the filets and put them in a well-buttered baking dish. Sprinkle fish with the lemon juice and set aside. Mix melted butter, orange juice and orange rind and pour it over the fish. Sprinkle the nutmeg over the fish and bake for 15 to 20 minutes, depending upon the thickness of the filets, or until the fish will flake easily with a fork. Sprinkle with chopped parsley.

Goes with just about any side, but we usually serve it with rice and roasted asparagus. (Put fresh and trimmed asparagus on a baking sheet and place in the oven during the last 5-6 minutes that the fish is cooking. Serve with butter and a little lemon juice and grated rind.)

# Tomatoes

Tomatoes are, of course, available year-round thanks to hot houses . . . is it the curse of the hot houses? And, of course, there are Florida field-grown tomatoes available in the winter. But, with all the genetic engineering or cross pollination or intentional breeding or whatever it is they have done to increase yield, or speed up maturity, slow down ripening, or lessen shipping damage, etc., they have virtually removed all taste from tomatoes. On top of all that they pick them green and then gas them to ripen. The only valid reason to ever pick a green tomato is if you are going to fry it!

They look great in the produce section of the grocery, all bright red and of uniform size and shape, but looks aren't everything. In fact, as far as I am concerned, looks aren't *anything* when it comes to tomatoes. I'd rather have a gnarly, misshapen, slightly bruised purple-colored tomato with full flavor any day instead of a tasteless red "pretty boy" that has been grown in Canada in January.

It used to be that all a tomato needed was a little salt and maybe a splash of vinegar or a drop or two of oil. Now you really need to "doctor a tomato up" to get any taste at all. That is unless you can get your hand on some tomatoes that have ripened on the vine.

Thank goodness for vine-ripened tomatoes that are available at farmer's markets and roadside stands during different times of the year, although the flavor of some varieties being grown and sold locally have had the flavor engineered out of them also. A heirloom tomato is typically a non-hybrid and can be found in a variety of sizes, shapes, flavors and colors. It is difficult to raise heirlooms for a profit as some are prone to cracking or lack disease-resistance, but they are increasingly in demand by shoppers and have become more readily available in recent years.

But farmers in Florida and in western North Carolina are now experimenting with hybrid heirloom tomatoes bred to resist disease. The goal is to produce a tomato that has the full-flavor of a vine-ripened heirloom but one that is also a commercially-viable product. Some of the more popular heirloom varieties include Brandywine, Mr. Stripey, Cherokee Purple, and Lilian's Yellow Heirloom. You won't find them at your regular supermarket, but *Fresh Market* stores usually have a nice selection of heirlooms.

Your best bet to assure yourself of great tasting tomatoes is to plant a few tomato bushes yourself, or be extra nice to that neighbor who has a couple of stakes in his backyard. Dee's brother Chuck, who lives in East Point, Georgia, successfully raises a few bushes each summer in pots, on his back deck.

Scattered throughout this recipe section of the book are several tomato recipes you might enjoy.

*Lewis Grizzard* once said that *"It is difficult to think anything but pleasant thoughts while eating a homegrown tomato."* I couldn't agree more.

It is also difficult to think of anything but pleasant thoughts while rocking in a rocking chair on our screened-in porch looking at the mountains and Lake Tahoma and drinking a glass of wine. Does it get any better? I don't think so. That is, unless it's sitting on an Anna Maria Island beach at sunset. Oh, the best of two worlds! Thank you, Lord.

# Tossed Avocado Salad

Avocados were a precious commodity at one time, as were mangoes. You could only get them at certain times of the year, when they were in season. During the summer we would anxiously await for the green mangoes to finish growing and begin to turn red and yellow, ripe for picking. Likewise for the avocados; they would not be ready until late summer/early fall. Now both fruit (yes, an avocado is a fruit, not a vegetable) are available year-round in supermarkets thanks to imported fruit from Mexico and parts of South America.

Guacamole is the most common use for avocados but that can get boring. Here is a recipe for a tossed salad using avocado and citrus fruits that I think you will enjoy.

> container of baby arugula
> 2 ripe avocados
> 1 ½ cups orange sections, cut in bite-size pieces
> 1 cup grapefruit sections, cut in bite-size pieces
> ½ cup sliced heart of palm
> Balsamic vinaigrette
> salt and pepper

Cut the avocados in half and remove the seed. Make cross-hatch ½-inch cuts through the flesh, but not the skin, then use a soup spoon to scoop out the bite-size pieces of avocado. Lightly toss all the ingredients and sprinkle with salt and freshly ground black pepper. Add enough Balsamic vinaigrette (Balsamic vinegar, extra virgin olive oil, chopped garlic clove) to lightly coat.

# Tropical Coleslaw

If you enjoy coleslaw, but are tired of that same old taste, you might enjoy this change of pace. The flavors blend nicely with grilled fish and grilled or jerk chicken.

8 cups shredded green cabbage*
2 cups fresh orange sections cut in bite size pieces
1 cup thinly sliced celery
½ cup grated carrot
1 cup plain yogurt, not no- or low-fat
½ cup sour cream, same as above
2 T honey
1 T celery seed
Salt and pepper

Toss together the cabbage, celery, carrots and orange pieces. In a separate bowl combine the remaining ingredients and mix well. Pour over the slaw mixture and toss until well-mixed. Add salt and pepper to taste. Cover and refrigerate for an hour or more before serving. Toss and check seasoning again before serving, and adjust if necessary.


*This is one of the few pre-packaged salad items that I will buy. It costs more, but I hate to get out, and then clean, the food processor just to shred some cabbage. I guess I could use a knife.

# Ultimate Flourless Chocolate Cake

This recipe has been around for a long time but does not seem to be made very often. Probably because it takes about $10 worth of ingredients and a lot of work to make and it is very, very rich. But, oh, is it ever good. If you are a fan of bittersweet chocolate I doubt that you have ever tasted anything better.

The cake is a fitting way to end an enjoyable meal and thus a fitting way to end what I hope has been an enjoyable book. The recipe was developed by a Chef Philip (not me) who worked at *The Big Splash* restaurant in Broward County back in the 1980s.

Cake:
20 ounces (2½ 8-ounce packages) semisweet chocolate
10 ounces (2½ sticks) unsalted butter
10 egg yolks
5 egg whites
1 T corn starch
¼ cup strong coffee or espresso (at room temperature)
1 cup whole milk

Coating:
4 ounces (remaining ½ of 8-ounce package) semisweet chocolate
1 T unsalted butter
1 T heavy cream

Cake: Melt chocolate along with the butter in a double boiler, stirring until smooth. Beat egg yolks in bowl and add coffee and milk and stir to combine. Sift the corn starch into the egg mixture and stir. Combine the egg yolk mixture with the chocolate mixture. In a separate bowl beat the egg whites to a stiff peak and then fold gently into the egg yolk/chocolate mixture. Gently pour the mixture into a greased and papered 10-inch cake pan and bake in a water bath (place cake pan in a larger pan with enough water to come halfway up the sides of the cake pan) for 1½ hours in a 300-degree oven. Remove from oven and cool on a rack.

Coating: In a double boiler melt the chocolate, butter and heavy cream stirring until smooth, adding a little more cream in necessary to make the coating spreadable. Spread a light coating over the cooled cake and refrigerate.

Serve thin slices, chilled. It tastes even better with a glass of champagne.

# Indexes:

# Anna Maria Island General Index:

# North Carolina Mountains General Index:

# Essays, Stories and Regional Recipes Index:

# Concluding Thoughts
# and Bits of Wisdom*

*The authors of most of which are unknown. Those that I have been able to identify I have credited.

*Don't forget that people will judge you by your actions, not your intentions. You may have a heart of gold, but so does a hard-boiled egg!*

*The person who does things that count usually does not stop to count them.*

*We should take a tip from nature: our ears are not made to shut, but our mouth is.*

*All our guests bring us happiness – some in coming, some in going.*

*The two best gifts that grandparents can give to their grandchildren are roots and wings.*

*Obstacles are those things you see when you take your eyes off the goal.*

*What we are is God's gift to us; what we make of ourselves is our gift to God.*

*Instead of putting others in their place, we should try putting ourselves in their place.*

*I used to think that God's gifts were on shelves – one above the other and the taller we grew, the more easily we could reach them. I now find that God's gifts are on shelves one beneath the other and that it is not a question of growing taller but of stooping lower.*

F. B. Meyer

*A young applicant for a job as a shipping clerk for a department store was asked if he was married. "No," he replied. "I'm not – but I can take orders, if that is what you mean."*

*My most brilliant achievement has been my ability to be able to persuade my wife to marry me.*

Phil de Montmollin (stolen from Winston Churchill.)

*When you see someone without a smile give him one of yours.*

*When a train goes through a tunnel and it gets dark,*
*you don't throw away the ticket and jump off.*
*You sit still and trust the engineer.*

*Youth is not a time of life, it is a state of mind. You are as young as your faith, as old as your doubt; as young as your self-confidence, as old as your fear; as young as your hope, as old as your despair.*

*To stay youthful, stay useful.*


*Age is a question of mind over matter.*
*If you don't mind, it doesn't matter.*

Satchel Paige